FARMING TECHNIQUES AND CROP PRODUCTION

ENV BOOKS SERIES

FARMING TECHNIQUES AND CROP PRODUCTION

Editors

Dr. Alka Chauhan
Society for Environment, Health, Awareness of Nutrition & Toxicology (SEHAT)
1775, Sohan Ganj, Near Clock Tower
Delhi - 110 007 (INDIA)

Dr. Anubhuti Sharma
Directorate of Rapeseed-Mustard Research (ICAR Institute)
Sewar, Bharatpur
Rajasthan - 321 303 (INDIA)

Jaswant Ray
Society for Environment, Health, Awareness of Nutrition & Toxicology (SEHAT)
H.O. F-119, Pandav Nagar
Meerut (U.P.) (INDIA)

Series Editor

Dr. Pawan Kumar 'Bharti'
Vice President
Society for Environment, Health, Awareness of Nutrition & Toxicology (SEHAT)
1775, Sohan Ganj, Near Clock Tower
Delhi - 110 007
(INDIA)
E-mail: gurupawanbharti@gmail.com

DPH

DISCOVERY PUBLISHING HOUSE PVT. LTD.
INDIA

Published by:

Namit Wasan

DISCOVERY PUBLISHING HOUSE PVT. LTD.

4383/4B, Ansari Road, Darya Ganj
New Delhi-110 002 (India)
Phone : +91-11-23279245, 43596064-65
Fax : +91-11-23253475
E-mail : discoverypublishinghouse@gmail.com
namitwasan9@gmail.com
sales@discoverypublishinggroup.com
website: www.discoverypublishinggroup.com

***First Edition:* 2017**

ISBN: 978-93-5056-855-2

Farming Techniques and Crop Production

Printed at:
Infinity Imaging Systems
Delhi

ENV Books Series, (India)

Calls lengthy and error free chapters for further volumes of books on various environmental issues. (Send your manuscripts to envbooks@gmail.com)

***Founding Editor* (*Editor-in-Chief*)**

Dr. Pawan Kumar 'Bharti'

Society for Environment, Health, Awareness of Nutrition & Toxicology (SEHAT-India)
1775, Sohanganj, Near Clock Tower, Delhi-7, (India)
E-mail:*gurupawanbharti@rediffmail.com*

Other Titles by Editor-in-Chief:

1. **Advances in Biotechnology and Ecological Sciences (2013)**
   Bharti, P.K., Chauhan, A. and Ray, J. (eds.)
   (ISBN: 978-93-5056-358-8).
2. **Advances in Agriculture and Ecology (2013)**
   Bharti, P.K.; Chauhan, A. and Ezeaku Peter Ikemefuna (eds.)
   (ISBN: 978-93-5056-362-5).
3. **Agriculture and Environmental Biotechnology (2014)**
   Bharti, P.K. and Chauhan, A. (eds.)
   (ISBN: 978-93-5056-479-0).
4. **Agriculture Development and Sustainable Environment (2015)**
   Ray, J. and Bharti, P. K. (eds.)
   (ISBN: 978-93-5056-759-3)
5. **Agriculture Ecology and Environment (2014)**
   Bharti, P.K. and Olubukola O. Babalola (eds.)
   (ISBN: 978-93-5056-480-6).
6. **Agriculture Ecology, Sustainable Development and Agribusiness Management (2017)**
   Mehta Piyush; Sharma Pankaj; and 'Bharti' P.K. (eds.)
   (ISBN: 978-93-5056-851-4)
7. **Agriculture, Environment and Nano-science (2015)**
   Bharti, Pawan K. (ed.)
   (ISBN: 978-93-5056-760-5)
8. **Agro-biodiversity:** ***Conservation & Sustainable Development*** **(2016)**
   Sharma, Pankaj; Singh, Narayan; and Bharti, P.K. (eds.)
   (ISBN: 978-93-505-782-1)
9. **Agro-forestry and Climate Change (2014)**
   Bharti, Pawan K. and Singh, Narayan (eds.)
   (ISBN: 978-93-5056-514-8).

10. **Agro-forestry and Sustainable Agriculture (2016)**
Sharma, Pankaj; Bharti, P.K. (eds.)
(ISBN: 978-93-5056-786-9).
11. **Aquaculture and Fisheries Environment (2014)**
Gupta, S.K. and Pawan K. Bharti (eds.)
(ISBN: 978-93-5056-408-0).
12. **Aquatic Biodiversity and Pollution (2013)**
Bharti, P.K.; Chauhan, A. and Kaoud, H.A.H. (eds.)
(ISBN: 978-93-5056-359-5).
13. **Aquatic Ecology and Biotechnology (2014)**
Bharti, P.K. and Zaki, M.S.A. (eds.)
(ISBN: 978-93-5056-451-6).
14. **Aquatic Environment and Toxicology (2013)**
Bharti, Pawan K. (ed.)
(ISBN: 978-93-5056-236-9).
15. **Biodiversity, Biotechnology and Environmental Conservation (2015)**
Bharti, P.K. and Bhandari, G. (eds.)
(ISBN: 978-93-5056-750-0).
16. **Biodiversity of Aquatic Ecosystem: *Significance, Threat and Conservation* (2013)**
Bharti, P.K. and Kaoud, H.A.H. (eds.)
(ISBN: 978-93-5056-297-0).
17. **Biological Diversity and Ecology (2016)**
Arya, M.K.; Bharti, P.K. and Ritesh Joshi (eds.)
(ISBN: 978-93-5056-785-2).
18. **Bioremediation and Microbial Biotechnology (2016)**
Gupta, Sandeep; and Bharti, P.K. (eds.)
(ISBN: 978-93-5056-783-8)
19. **Biotechnological Approaches & Water Ecosystem (2016)**
Zaki, M.S.A.; and Bharti, P.K. (eds.)
(ISBN: 978-93-5056-779-1)
20. **Biotechnology, Agro-ecology and Environment (2015)**
Chauhan, Avnish and Bharti, P.K. (eds.)
(ISBN: 978-93-5056-757-9).
21. **Clean Technologies and Environmental Protection (2015)**
Chauhan, A.; Sharma, S. and Bharti, P.K. (eds.)
(ISBN: 978-93-5056-731-9).
22. **Climate Change and Agriculture (2012)**
Bharti, P.K. and Chauhan, Avnish (eds.)
(ISBN: 978-93-5056-148-5).
23. **Climate Change and Biodiversity (2013)**
Bharti, P.K. and Chauhan, Avnish (eds.)
(ISBN: 978-93-5056-360-1).
24. **Climate Change, Disaster Management and Environment (2016)**
Chauhan, Alka; Bharti, P.K. (eds.)
(ISBN: 978-93-5056-784-5).

25. **Conservation and Cultivation of Medicinal Plants (2015)**
Bharti, P.K. and Singh Narayan (eds.)
(ISBN: 978-93-5056-740-1).

26. **Crop Productivity and Plant Disease Management (2016)**
Chauhan, Alka; Bharti, P.K. and Sadana, Deepti (eds.)
(ISBN: 978-93-5056-791-3)

27. **Eco-toxicology and Eco-technology (2013)**
Bharti, P.K. and Zaki, M. (eds.)
(ISBN: 978-93-5056-313-7).

28. **Environmental Biotechnology and Application (2013)**
Bharti, P.K. and Chauhan, Avnish (eds.)
(ISBN: 978-93-5056-262-8).

29. **Environmental Conservation and Biotechnology (2014)**
Chauhan, A. and P.K. Bharti (eds.)
(ISBN: 978-93-5056-512-4).

30. **Environmental Health and Problems (2013)**
Bharti, P.K. and Gajananda, Kh. (eds.)
(ISBN: 978-93-5056-263-5).

31. **Environmental Pollution and Biodiversity (2012)**
Bharti, P.K.; Chauhan, Avnish and Kumar, P. (eds.)
(ISBN: 978-93-5056-149-2).

32. **Fisheries and Toxicology (2014)**
Zaki, M.S.A.; Bharti, P.K. and Chauhan, A. (eds.)
(ISBN: 978-93-5056-452-3).

33. **Fish Habitat and Aquaculture (2015)**
Bharti, P.K.; Gupta Kr. Sanjay (eds.)
(ISBN: 978-93-5056-744-9).

34. **Food Processing, Management and Nanotechnology (2016)**
Chauhan, Avnish; Bharti, P.K. (eds.)
(ISBN: 978-93-5056-796-8).

35. **Freshwater Ecosystem and Xenobiotics (2013)**
Bharti, P.K.; Zaki, M. and Chauhan, A. (eds.)
(ISBN: 978-93-5056-299-4).

36. **Limnology and Aquatic Science (2015)**
Sharma, S. and Bharti, P.K. (eds.)
(ISBN: 978-93-5056-735-7).

37. **Medicinal Plants:** ***Distribution, Utilization and Significance*** **(2015)**
Sharma, P.; Bharti, P.K. and Narayan Singh (eds.)
(ISBN: 978-93-5056-734-0).

38. **Microbial Applications and Environment (2014)**
Bharti, Pawan K. (ed.)
(ISBN: 978-93-5056-515-5).

39. **Microbial Ecology and Habitat (2014)**
Bharti, Pawan K. (ed.)
(ISBN: 978-93-5056-514-8).
40. **Natural Ecosystem and Climate Change (2015)**
Bharti, P.K., and Kh. Gajananda (ed.)
(ISBN: 978-93-5056-745-6).
41. **Pest Management and Agro-Techniques (2016)**
Biswas, Asim; Bharti, P.K., Chauhan, Avnish (eds.)
(ISBN: 978-93-5056-794-4).
42. **Prakriti me Aushadhi (*in Hindi*) (2012)**
Singh, J.R.; Bharti, P.K. and Bharti, B.
(ISBN: 978-93-5056-200-0).
43. **Seed Technology, Plant Growth and Cropping System (2015)**
Tyagi, P.K. and Bharti, P.K. (eds.)
(ISBN: 978-93-5056-738-8).
44. **Seed Treatment, Plant Heath and Agro-technology (2016)**
Chauhan, A. and Bharti, P.K. (eds.)
(ISBN: 978-93-5056-810-1).
45. **Soil Characteristics and Agro-ecology (2015)**
Avnish Chauhan and Bharti, P.K. (eds.)
(ISBN: 978-93-5056-758-6)
46. **Soil Contamination and Conservation (2015)**
Ezeaku, P.I. and Bharti, P.K. (eds.)
(ISBN: 978-93-5056-737-1).
47. **Soil Quality and Contamination (2013)**
Bharti, P.K. and Chauhan, Avnish (eds.)
(ISBN: 978-93-5056-361-8).
48. **Sustainable Aquaculture Management (2016)**
Gupta, S.K.; Bharti, P.K (eds.)
(ISBN: 978-93-5056-797-5).
49. **Waste Disposal and Management (2015)**
Bharti, P.K.; Tabassum, B. and Bajaj, P. (eds.)
(ISBN: 978-93-5056-729-6).
50. **Waste Generation and Utilization (2016)**
Bajaj Priya; Tabassum, B., and Bharti, P.K. (eds.)
(ISBN: 978-93-5056-792-0).
51. **Waste Management and Environmental Health (2016)**
Tabassum, B., Bajaj Priya, and Bharti, P.K. (eds.)
(ISBN: 978-93-5056-777-7).
52. **Water Resources and Agriculture (2014)**
Bharti, P.K. and Ezeaku Peter Ikemefuna (eds.)
(ISBN: 978-93-5056-481-3).
53. **Waste Resources Management: *Monitoring and Assessment* (2016)**
Gupta, Sandeep and Bharti, P.K. (eds.)
(ISBN: 978-93-5056-799-9).

Preface

Agriculture is the cultivation of plants, animals and fungi for food, fiber, biofuel, medicinal plants and other products used to sustain and enhance human life. Agriculture was the key development in the rise of sedentary human civilization, where by farming of domesticated species created food surpluses that nurtured the development of civilization. The study of agriculture is known as agricultural science. The history of agriculture dates back thousands of years, and its development has been driven and defined by greatly different climates, cultures, and technologies. Industrial agriculture based on large-scale monoculture farming has become the dominant agricultural methodology.

Modern agronomy, plant breeding, agrochemicals such as: pesticides and fertilizers, and technological developments have in many cases sharply increased yields from cultivation, but at the same time have caused widespread ecological damage and negative human health effects. Selective breeding and modern practices in animal husbandry have similarly increased the output of meat, but have raised concerns about animal welfare and the health effects of the antibiotics, growth hormones, and other chemicals commonly used in industrial meat production. Genetically modified organisms are an increasing component of agriculture, although they are banned in several countries. Agricultural food production and water management are increasingly becoming global issues that are fostering debate on a number of fronts. Significant degradation of land and water resources, including the depletion of aquifers, has been observed in recent decades, and the effects of global warming on agriculture and of agriculture on global warming are still not fully understood.

The major agricultural products can be broadly grouped into foods, fibers, fuels, and raw materials. Specific foods include: cereals (grains), vegetables, fruits, oils, meats and spices. Fibers include: cotton, wool, hemp, silk and flax. Raw materials include lumber and bamboo. Other useful materials are also produced by plants, such as: resins, dyes, drugs, perfumes, biofuels and ornamental products such as: cut flowers and nursery plants. Over one third of the world's workers are employed in agriculture, second only to the service sector, although the percentages of agricultural workers in developed countries has decreased significantly over the past several centuries.

Studies relating to crop production and field crops involve plant breeding, genetics and molecular physiology plant physiology and production ecology, soil and water science, and weed science. The studies are showing grain producers how to successfully use no-till and reduced tillage systems. And technologies such as: Geospatial and Precision Technologies are being to utilized to determine input variances – such as: fertilizer – which affects profitability and environmental impact.

Sustainable agriculture provides high yields without undermining the natural systems and resources that productivity depends on. Farmers who take a sustainable approach work efficiently with natural processes rather than ignoring or struggling against them – and use the best of current knowledge and technology to avoid the unintended consequences of industrial, chemical-based agriculture. One important result is that farmers are able to minimize their use of pesticides and fertilizers, thereby saving money and protecting future productivity, as well as the environment.

Below are some of the most common sustainable agriculture techniques employed by farmers today to achieve the key goals of weed control, pest control, disease control, erosion control and high soil quality:

- Soil Enrichment.
- Natural Pest Predators.
- Crop Rotation.
- Cover Crops.
- Integrated Pest Management.

Crop production is a branch of agriculture that deals with growing crops for use as food and fiber.

Crop production includes: grains, cotton, tobacco, fruits, vegetables, nuts and plants. Different crops grow best in different areas of the country. Warmer climates are ideal for growing citrus crops; northern states are best for growing apples and blueberries and the Midwest is ideal for growing grains, including wheat. Crop producers usually work from sunrise to sunset during planting and harvesting seasons. They sell the crops they've produced, plan crops for the next season and repair machinery.

The present book updates the subject content of sustainable agriculture, crop production, farming techniques, crop rotation, grain production and crop cultivation. Thanks are due to contributors and publisher of the book. The book will be helpful for the researchers, academic working in the field of sustainable agriculture, crop production, farming techniques, crop rotation, grain production and crop cultivation.

Editors

(envbooks@gmail.com)

Contents

FARMING TECHNIQUES AND CROP PRODUCTION
Edited by : **Dr. Alka Chauhan; Dr. Anubhuti Sharma & Jaswant Ray**
Edition : **2017**
ISBN : 978-93-5056-855-2
Published by : **Discovery Publishing House Pvt. Ltd., New Delhi (India)**

1 Integrated Farming Systems

Livelihood Security for Marginal and Small Farmers

Alok Kumar Patra[1]; L.M. Garnayak[2]
K.N. Mishra[3] & S.K. Swain[4]

ABSTRACT

Integrated farming system is focused around a few selected, inter-dependent, inter-related and often inter-linking production systems based on crops, livestock and related subsidiary enterprises. The entire philosophy of farming system revolves around better utilization of time, money, resources and family labour. A combination of one or more enterprises with cropping, when carefully chosen, planned and executed, gives higher dividends than a single enterprise, especially for small and marginal farmers. The rationale of integrated farming system is to minimise the wastes from the various subsystems on the farm and thus it improves employment opportunities, nutritional security and income of the rural people. In this chapter, an attempt has been made to enumerate the characteristics, scope, goals and objectives, components, advantages of integrated farming systems.

INTRODUCTION

Integrated farming system is a multidisciplinary whole farm approach, which enables the farmers to identify opportunities and threats and act

1. Professor (Agronomy), All India Co-ordinated Research Project on Integrated Farming Systems, Orissa University of Agriculture and Technology, Bhubaneswar - 751 003, Odisha, India.
2. Dean, College of Agriculture, Orissa University of Agriculture and Technology, Bhubaneswar - 751 003, Odisha, India.
3. Professor (Soil Science), All India Co-ordinated Research Project on Integrated Farming Systems, Orissa University of Agriculture and Technology, Bhubaneswar - 751 003, Odisha, India.
4. Professor (Agronomy), All India Co-ordinated Research Project on Integrated Farming Systems, Orissa University of Agriculture and Technology, Bhubaneswar - 751 003, Odisha, India.

accordingly. It is a dynamic approach which can be applied to any farming system around the world. It is very effective in solving the problems of small and marginal farmers. The approach aims at increasing income and employment from small-holding by integrating various farm enterprises and recycling crop residues and by-products within the farm itself. It involves attention to detail and continuous improvement in all areas of a farming business through informed management processes. Integrated farming combines the best of modern tools and technologies with traditional practices available at a given location and situation. Preserving and enhancing soil fertility, maintaining and improving a diverse environment and the adherence to ethical and social criteria are indispensable basic elements of integrated farming systems.

Concept and Definitions

'Farming' is a process of harnessing solar energy in the form of economic plant and animal products. 'System' implies a set of interrelated practices and processes organized into functional entity, *i.e.*, an arrangement of components or parts that interact according to some process and transforms inputs into outputs (Fresco and Westphal, 1988).

The International Organization of Biological Control describes integrated farming as a farming system where high quality food, feed, fibre and renewable energy are produced by using resources such as: soil, water, air and nature as well as regulating factors to farm sustainably and with as little polluting inputs as possible. Integrated farming system (IFS) is a commonly and broadly used word to explain a more integrated approach to farming as compared to monoculture approaches. In this system an inter-related set of enterprises are maintained and by-products or wastes from one production system becomes an input for another production system, which reduces cost and improves production and/or income. Thus, IFS works as a system of systems (Soni *et al*. 2014). FAO (1977) stated that 'there is no waste', and 'waste is only a misplaced resource which can become a valuable material for another product' in IFS. For example, paddy straw, by-product from rice crop can be used as a valuable input for mushroom cultivation or dry fodder for dairy animals. Similarly spent of mushroom cultivation (used straw) can be used as a raw material in compost or vermicompost pits and by-products from dairy unit like dung can be used as fish feed or raw material for vermicompost unit. The farming system is essentially cyclic, organic resources - livestock - land - crops. Therefore, management decisions related to one component may affect the others. Combining ecological sustainability and economic viability, the integrated livestock-farming system maintains and improves agricultural productivity while also reducing negative environmental impacts.

Fig. 1.1: Integration of several components on the farm - a schematic representation

Source: http://www.agriculturesnetwork.org/magazines/india/family-farming/integrated-farming

Different scientists have defined a farming system differently. However, many definitions, in general, convey the same meaning that it is the strategy to achieve profitable and sustained agricultural production to meet the diversified needs of farming community through efficient use of farm resources without degrading the natural resource base and environmental quality. Farming system is a decision-making unit comprising the farm household, cropping and livestock system that transform land, capital and labour into useful products that can be consumed or sold (Fresco and Westphal, 1988).

Lal and Miller (1990) defined farming system as a resource management strategy to achieve economic and sustained agricultural production to meet diverse requirements of farm livelihood while preserving resource base and maintaining a high level of environment quality. On the other hand, a farming system is the result of complex interactions among a number of inter-dependent components, where an individual farmer allocates certain quantities and qualities of four factors of production, *viz;* land, labour, capital and equipments to which he has access (Mahapatra, 1994).

Farming system represents an appropriate combination of farm enterprises (cropping systems, horticulture, livestock, fishery, forestry, and apiculture) and the means available to the farmer to raise them for profitability. It interacts adequately with environment without dislocating the ecological and socioeconomic balance on one hand and attempts to meet the national goals on the other (Jayanthi *et al.* 2002). Thus, integrated farming is a system which tries to imitate the nature's principle, where not only crops but, varied types of plants, animals, birds, fish and other aquatic flora and fauna are utilized for production. These are combined in such a way and proportion that each element helps the other; the waste of one is recycled as resource for the other through 'low external input and sustainable agriculture' (LEISA) techniques (Das, 2013).

Okigbo (1995) defines IFS as a mixed farming system that consists of at least two separate but logically interdependent parts of a crop and livestock enterprises. Enterprises in the integrated farming system are mutually supportive and depend on each other (Csavas, 1992). Mixed farming system consists of components such as: crops and livestock that coexist independently from each other. In this farming, integrating crops and livestock serves primarily to minimise the risk and not to recycle resources. But in IFS, crops and livestock interact to create a synergy, with recycling allowing the maximum use of available resources (Sasikala *et al.* 2015). Crop residues can be used for animal feed, while livestock and livestock by-product production and processing can enhance agricultural productivity by intensifying nutrients that improve soil fertility, reducing the use of chemical fertilizers. A high integration of crops and livestock is often considered as a step forward, but small farmers need to have sufficient access to knowledge, assets and inputs to manage this system in a way that is economically and environmentally sustainable over the long term (FAO, 2001). Thus, IFS is an integrated set of elements/components and activities that farmers perform in their farms under their resources and circumstances to maximize the productivity and net farm income on a sustainable basis (Singh and Ratan, 2009). The integration is made in such a way that the product *i.e.*, output of one enterprise/component should be the input for the other enterprises with high degree of complementary effects. The rationale of IFS is to minimize the wastes from the various subsystems on the farm and thus it improves employment opportunities, nutritional security and income of the rural people (Panke *et al.* 2010).

Characteristics of Farming Systems

The term 'farming system', in its broadest sense, is any research that views the farm in holistic manner and considers interactions (between the components and of components with the environment) in the system (CGIAR, 1978). This type of research is most appropriately carried out by interdisciplinary teams of scientists who in association with extensionists, continually interact with the farmers in the identification of problems and in devising ways to solve them. It aims at generating and transferring technologies to increase the resource productivity for an identified group of farmers. Major characteristics of farming systems are:

- Farmer-oriented.
- System-oriented.
- Problem-solving approach.
- Interdisciplinary.
- Complements mainstream disciplinary research.
- Tests technology in on-farm trials.
- Provides feedback from farmers.

The farming system research activities are to be farmer oriented, system oriented, problem-solving approach, inter-disciplinary, compliments mainstream disciplinary research, test the technology in on-farm trials and provides feedback from the farmers. The strategy of farming system research should emphasise that the research agenda should be determined by explicitly define farmers' needs through an understanding of the existing farming systems rather than its perception by the researchers. The farming systems research and extension should be dealt in holistic manner on farmers participatory mode with problem solving approach, keeping genders activity, inter disciplinary and interactive approach. Thus farming system represents an appropriate combination of farm enterprises *viz;* cropping systems, horticulture, livestock, fishery, forestry, poultry and the means available to the farmer to raise them for profitability. It interacts adequately with environment without disclosing the ecological and socio-economic balance on one hand and attempts to meet to national goal on others. Hence, there is need to carryout intensive research on farming systems keeping the needs and resource base of the sustainable income along with the maintenance of natural resources. It is designed to understand farmers' priorities, strategies and resource allocation decisions.

Farming system research is thus, an approach to agricultural research and development that view the whole farm as a system and focus on the interdependencies between the components under the control of members of the household and how these components interact with each other in respect of physical, biological and socio-economic factors not under the household's control (Shaner *et al.* 1982).

Many authors define characteristics of farming system research in different ways. The farming system core characteristics may be summarised as below (Behera, 2013; Kumar, 2013).

1. *It is problem-solving:* As an applied problem-solving approach, it emphasizes on developing and transferring appropriate technologies to overcome the production constraints through the diagnosis of biophysical, socio-economic and institutional constraints that influence the technological solutions.

2. *It is holistic*: The whole farm is viewed as a system encompassing interacting subsystems; and no potential enterprise is considered in isolation.
3. *It acknowledges the location specificity of technological solutions:* Recognizing the location specific nature of agricultural production problems, it emphasizes on testing and adaptation of technological solutions based on agro-ecological and socio-economic specificities.
4. *It defines specific client groups*: Emphasis is made on the identification of specific and relatively homogeneous groups of farmers, with similar problems and circumstances for whom the technology is to be developed, as the specific client group. On tile basis of common environmental parameters, production patterns and management practices, relatively homogeneous recommendation domains need to be identified.
5. *It is farmer participatory:* It revolves round the principle that successful agricultural research and development efforts should start and end with the farmers (Rhoades and Booth, 1982). Farmer participation is ensured at different stages of technology generation and transfer processes such as: problem diagnosis, design and implementation of on - farm trials, and providing feedback through monitoring and evaluation.
6. *It gives weightage to ITK system*: The Indigenous Technical Knowledge (ITK) which is time-tested at the farmer's 'level for sustainability through a dynamic process of integrating new innovations into the system as they arise, has to be properly understood by the scientists and utilized in their research activities.
7. *It is concerned with 'bottom-up' research strategy:* It begins with an understanding of the existing farming systems and the identification of key production constraints.
8. *It is interdisciplinary:* It lays greater emphasis on interdisciplinary co-operation among the scientists from different areas of specialization to solve the agricultural problems that are of concern to farmer.
9. *It emphasises extensive on farm activities:* It involves problem analysis through diagnostic surveys, on-farm, testing of the developed technologies, and providing feedback through evaluation to influence the research agenda of the research stations. It provides a structural framework for the farmers to express their preferences and apply their evaluation criteria for selecting technologies suiting to their circumstances.
10. *It is gender sensitive*: while explicitly acknowledging the gender-differentiated roles of farms family in agriculture, emphasizes the critical review of farming systems in terms of activities, analysis, access and control over the resources and benefits, and their implications in developing relevant research agenda.

11. *It is iterative*: Instead of trying to know everything, about a system at a time, it requires step-by-step analysis of only key functional relationships.
12. *It is dynamic*: It involves recurrent analysis of the farming systems, permitting continuous learning and adaptations.
13. *It recognizes interdependencies among multiple clients*: The generation, dissemination and adoption of relevant technologies to improve the productivity and sustainability of agriculture require productive and interactive linkages among the policy planners, scientists, developmental agencies and farmers. The approach attaches more importance for this critical factor.
14. *It focuses on actual adoption*: It is to be judged by the extent to which it influences the production of socially desirable technologies that diffuse quickly amongst specified groups of farmer clients.
15. *It focuses on sustainability*: It seeks to harness the strengths of the existing farming practices, and to ensure that the productivity gains are environmentally acceptable. Towards preserving the natural resource based and strengthening the agricultural production base, it attempts to develop technologies that are environment friendly and economically viable.
16. *It complements experiment station research*: It only complements, but does not substitute, the on-station research. It has to draw upon the scientific knowledge and technologies generated at research station. It has to be kept in mind that approach is not being promoted as panacea for all e maladies of local agricultural production systems.

Scope of IFS

Farming enterprises include: crop, livestock, poultry, fish, tree crops, plantation crops, etc. A combination of one or more enterprises with cropping, when carefully chosen, planned and executed, gives greater dividends than a single enterprise, especially for small and marginal farmers. Farm as a unit is to be considered and planned for effective integration of the enterprises to be combined with crop production activity (CARDI, 2010). Integration of farm enterprises to be combined on many factors such as:

1. Soil and climatic features of the selected area.
2. Availability of resources, land, labour and capital.
3. Present level of utilization of resources.
4. Economics of proposed integrated farming system.
5. Managerial skill of the farmer.

There are a number of situations and conditions that can be alleviated by an integrated farming System. The following situations are ideal for the introduction of IFS (CARDI, 2010).

1. The farmer wishes to improve the soil quality.
2. The farm household is struggling to buy food or below the poverty line.

3. Water is stored on-farm in ponds or river-charged overflow areas.
4. Fertilizers are expensive or the recommended blend is unavailable.
5. Soil salinity has increased as a result of inorganic fertilizer use.
6. The farmer is seeking to maximize profits on existing holding.
7. The farm is being eroded by wind or water.
8. The farmer is looking to reduce chemical control methods.
9. The farmer wants to reduce pollution or waste disposal costs.

In agriculture, crop production is the main activity. The income obtained from crops may hardly be sufficient to sustain the farm family throughout the year. Assured regular cash flow is possible when the crop is combined with other enterprises. Judicious combination of enterprises, keeping in view of the environmental conditions of a locality will pay greater dividends. At the same time, it will also promote effective recycling of residues/wastes. A grower can use IFS to:

1. Improve productivity.
2. Regulate nutrient and material flows.
3. Increase on-farm biodiversity.
4. Limit disease.
5. Reduce the smell of some livestock operations.

Integrated farming system gives insurance against recurrent natural disasters, creates employment opportunity for rural youth and ensures nutritional security particularly for children and women.

Goals of Farming Systems Research

Farming system research aims to meet the following interrelated goals (Plucknett *et al.* 1987).

1. To understand the physical and socio-economic environment within which agricultural production takes place.
2. To gain an understanding of the farmer in terms of his or her skills, constraints, preferences and aspirations.
3. To comprehend and evaluate existing important farming system, in particular the practice and performance of these systems.
4. To improve the identification of problem and opportunities for change in existing farming system and thereby better focus research on specific key aspects.
5. To enhance the capacity of research organizations to conduct research on priority problems.
6. To conduct research on new or improved practices or principles and to evaluate these for possible testing on-farms.
7. To evaluate new or improved systems or system components on-farms in major production areas under normal farm conditions.
8. To assist the extension, monitor the adoption and assess the benefits of improved farming systems.

Objectives of IFS

The overall objective of integrated farming systems is to evolve technically feasible and economically viable farming system models by integrating cropping with allied enterprises for irrigated, rainfed, hilly and coastal areas with a view to generate income and employment from the farm. The major objectives of integrated farming systems can be listed as below (CARDI, 2010; Behera, 2013).

1. Maximisation of yield of all component enterprises to provide steady and stable income at higher levels.
2. Rejuvenation/amelioration of system's productivity and achieve agro-ecological equilibrium.
3. Control the buildup of insect-pests, diseases and weed population through natural cropping system management and keep them at low level of intensity.
4. Reduction in the use of chemical fertilizers and other harmful agro-chemicals and pesticides to provide pollution free, healthy produce and environment to the society at large.
5. Utilization and conservation of available resources and effective recycling of farm residues within system and to maintain sustainable production system without damaging resources/environment.

Factors Governing Choice of IFS Modules

Farmers make decisions about what to grow, what animals to keep, the level and type of inputs and the methods they will use. Their decisions are based upon a range of social, economic and environmental factors. The farmers' attitudes and level of knowledge are also important. However, the selection of enterprises must be based on cardinal principle of minimising the competition and maximising the complementarities between the enterprises (Annadurai *et al.* 1994).

1. Climatic conditions.
2. Soil type.
3. Farmers' preferences.
4. Size of the farm.
5. Knowledge, skill and technology.
6. Storage, transport and marketing.
7. Resource mobilizing power.
8. Credit facilities available.
9. Socioeconomic conditions.
10. Customs, sentiments and believes.

The productivity of farming system depends upon natural resource climate, available science and technology, policies, institutions and public goods, besides latest information of market technology and human resources.

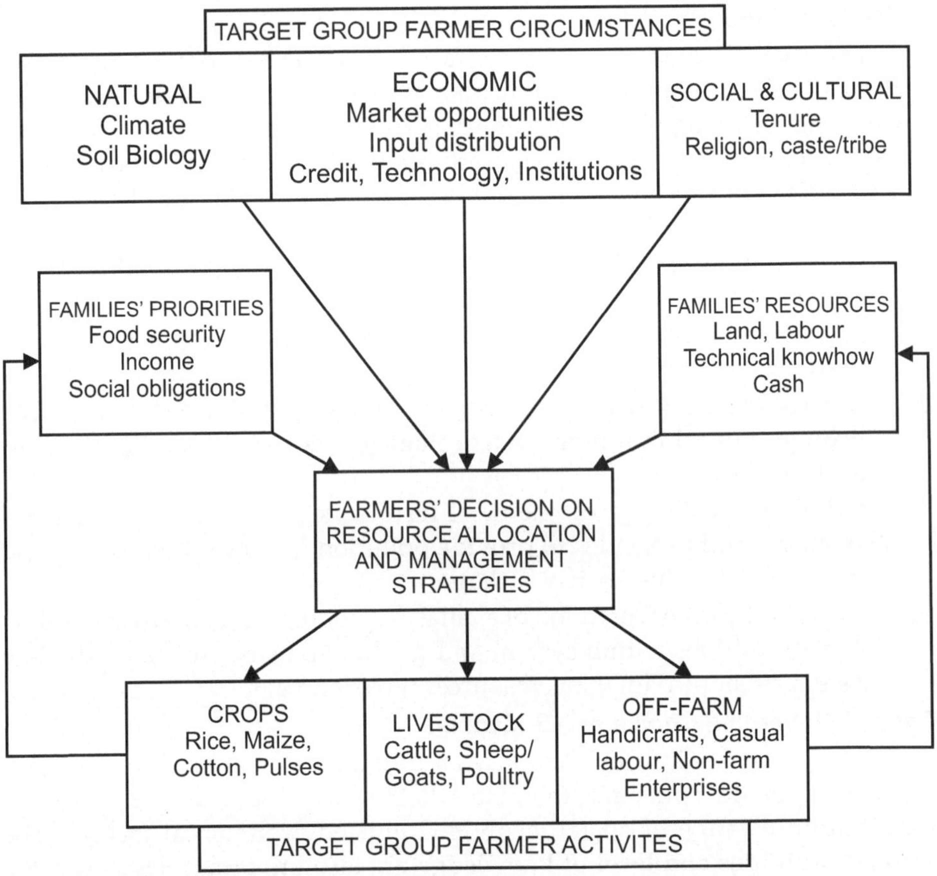

Fig. 1.2: Farming system model showing interrelationships at the farming system level

Source: Collinson, 1987.

Components of IFS

Farming system is an integrated resource management strategy for obtaining economic and sustained crop and livestock production and preserving the resource base with high environmental quality. The entire philosophy of farming system revolves around better utilization of time, money, resources and family labour. Integrated farming system is focused around a few selected, inter-dependent, inter-related and often inter-linking production systems based on few crops, animal and related subsidiary enterprises. It involves the utilization of primary and/or secondary produce of one system as raw material for other system, thus making the entire system mutually interdependent as one whole unit. There is a need for effective linkages and complementarities of various components to develop holistic farming system. Important components of the farming system include:

1. Field crops.
2. Vegetable crops.
3. Fruit crops.
4. Floriculture.
5. Livestock (cow, buffalo, sheep, goat, pig, etc).
6. Pisciculture.
7. Poultry.
8. Duckery.
9. Agroforestry.
10. Bee keeping.
11. Mushroom cultivation.
12. Bio-gas.
13. Vermicompost.

The crop activities in the IFS consist of grain crops (rice, wheat, maize, sorghum, pulses, soybeans), oilseeds (groundnut, sesame, rapeseed and mustard, linseed, niger, sunflower, castor), vegetable crops, plantation crops (coconut, arecanut), short duration fruit crops (papaya, banana, citrus, pineapple), root crops (cassava, sweet potato), sugarcane, tree crops (moringa, mulberry, teak, acacia, sissoo) and fodder crops. The selection of crops is dependent on preferences based on family consumption, market, soil type, and rainfall and type of animals raised.

Integrated farming system comprising crop and livestock has been sustainable over the centuries. In this system animals are raised on agricultural wastes and animal power is used for agricultural operations and animal excreta are used as manure and fuel. In coastal areas, the rice + fish system can stabilise the productivity and profitability in rice production areas. Cereal based crops in combination with livestock (poultry, dairy, sheep and goat) systems can improve the profitability of the farmers along with the sustenance of natural resources.

The livestock activities in IFS consist of cows, goat, sheep, poultry, ducks, pigs and small ruminants. The selection of livestock is also dependent on preference based on family consumption, potential market and availability of resources. Livestock and livelihoods are intimately related and the ownership of livestock is more egalitarian than that of land (Swaminathan, 2010). The livestock component acts as a stabilising factor in the system, thus needs strengthening of the crop and livestock linkage to enhance the economic viability and sustainability of the farming systems (Baishya *et al.* 2007).

Crop livestock integration involved the natural resources (crops, animals, land and water) in which these subsystems and their synergetic interactions have a significant positive and the greater total effect than the sum of their individual efforts. These systems increase crop yields and soil fertility and improve the livelihoods with promotion of stable households and increased economic output. The livestock farming systems can be grouped into small holder livestock production with little and low land and commercial livestock production dominating with poultry and dairy. The livestock production in IFS should conserve the natural resource base and raise the productivity through efficient utilization, optimised allocation and rational management of available of resources.

Agroforestry systems like: agri-silvicultural, silvi-pastoral, horti-silvicultural, horti-silvi-pastoral, agri-horti-silvipastoral, aquaforestry, etc., can be integrated to farming systems. Besides timber and fuel wood agroforestry systems offer lot of other products like: gum, resin, fibre, oils, medicines and other non-forest timber products depending upon the tree/shrub species covered in the system.

The suitable species for hedgerow planting are: *Cassia siamea, Leucaena leucocephala, Glyricidia sepium, Calliandra calothyrsus, Sesbania sesban, Acacia mangium, Gmelina arborea, Albizia* spp., *Cajanus* spp., *Chamaecytisus* spp., *Desmodium* spp., *Erythrina* spp., *Flemingia* spp., *Inga* spp., and *Tephrosia* spp., (Patra, 2013). Tree species commonly used as fuel wood are *Acacia nilotica, Acacia* auriculiformis, *Acacia mangium, Gmelina arborea, Dalbergia sissoo, Albizia lebbeck, Casuarina equisetifolia, Prosopis juliflora, Cassia siamea, Eucalyptus tereticornis,* etc. Multipurpose trees like: *Acacia nilotica, Acacia albida, Casuarina equisetifolia, Azadirachta indica, Acacia senegal, Cocos nucifera, Leucaena leucocephala* and *Acacia mangium* are planted on field bunds and boundaries (Patra, *et al.* 2011).

In the agri-horti-silvicultural system, suitable arable crops are grown in inter-spaces of perennial fruit or multipurpose tree rows. In between two trees one fruit crop like: mango, guava or pomegranate may be planted. When annual crop yield is substantially reduced due to canopy closure the system is converted to a horti-silvicultural system. With appropriate management practices this practice can give a sustainable production system (Patra, 2013).

In silvi-pastoral and horti-pastoral systems, suitable fodder grasses like: guinea (*Panicum maximum*), dinanath grass (*Pennisetum pedicellatum*), napier grass (*Pennisetum purpureum*), thin napier (*Panicum polystachion*), anjan grass (*Cenchrus ciliaris*) and fodder legumes like: stylo (*Stylosanthes hamata* and *Stylosanthes scabra*), cowpea (*Vigna sinensis*) are grown in inter-spaces of perennial fruit or multipurpose tree rows. These systems are very effective to control soil erosion as the grasses give a permanent soil cover.

The aquaforestry system comprises composite fish culture in farm ponds, and various trees and shrubs, leaves of which are preferred by fish (Ex. *Leucaena leucocephala, Morus alba, Gliricidia sepium, Moringa olifera,* etc.,) are planted on the boundary and around fish ponds. Leaves of these trees are used as feed for fish. Inland fish such as: catla, rohu, mrigal, common carp, silver carp and grass carp can be grown in the ponds. In the coastal regions farmers are cultivating fish and prawn in saline water and growing coconut and other trees on bunds of ponds. Now fish culture in the mangroves is also advocated, which form a rich source of nutrition to the aquatic life and breeding ground for juvenile fish, prawn and mussels. Other terms that have been used for this practice are silvi-pisciculture, agri-silvi-aquaculture and aquasilviculture. Some other modified aquaforestry systems are:

1. A well-balanced system of animal husbandry including: goatery, poultry, duck farming, turtles and fishes in the small ponds in home gardens make a balanced system of high moisture, energy and nutrient use efficiency per unit area.
2. In paddy field, fish can easily be reared by planting trees on field bunds or boundary. This system can be practised in high rainfall areas.
3. Coconut plants can also be successfully planted on raised paddy field bunds with an alley space of 5 m width depression which is utilized for pisiculture purpose (Patra, *et al*. 2008).

In apisilviculture, various honey or nectar producing trees frequently visited by honeybees are planted on the boundary of the agricultural field. Bees benefit trees and trees in turn provide series of benefits to bees. The primary purpose of this system is to produce honey. Api-silviculture with *Eucalyptus, Gliricidia, Grevillea, Gmelina, Leuceana* and *Albizia* species were more remunerative and a good source of generating additional farm income. Fruit trees can also be integrated with apisilviculture for more profits.

Mushroom cultivation can also be integrated to farming system to augment the overall household income. Besides some of the homestead vocations like: *khali/patravali* making, bamboo/cane work, chalk/candle making, tailoring, embroidery, food processing, doll making, carpentry, hand paper, packaging, paper packet, spice making, *papad* making, composting, marketing agricultural produce, etc can be considered in the farming system.

Integrated farming systems are often less risky and, if managed efficiently, benefits from synergisms among enterprises, diversity in produce, and environmental soundness (Mahapatra, 2010). On this basis, IFS models have been suggested by several workers for the development of small and marginal farms across the country (Behera and Mahapatra, 1999; Singh *et al.* 2006). Dominant farming systems of the different agroclimatic regions are presented in the following Table 1.1.

Advantages of IFS

Farming systems approach introduces a change in farming techniques for higher production from the farm as a whole with the integration of all the enterprises. The farm products other than the economic products, for which crops are grown, can be better utilized for productive purposes in the farming systems approach. A judicious mix of cropping system with associated enterprises like: dairy, poultry, fishery, apiary, sericulture, piggery, etc., suited to the given agroclimatic conditions and socio-economic status of farmers would bring prosperity to farmer (Panda, 2004).

Table 1.1: Dominant Farming Systems in different Agro-climatic Regions of the Country

Agroclimatic Region	States	Most Dominate Farming Systems in the Region
Western Himalayas	J&K, Himachal Pradesh, Uttarakhand	1. Crops + Dairy 2. Agri-horti system
Eastern Himalayas	Assam, Meghalaya	1. Crops + Fish + Cattle + Piggery 2. Monocropping of rice and maize + Piggery + Backyard poultry + 2-3 cows
Trans Gangetic Plain	Punjab, Haryana	1. Crops + Dairy
Upper Gangetic Plain	Uttar Pradesh	1. Crops + Dairy
Middle Gangetic Plain	Uttar Pradesh, Bihar	1. Crops + Dairy 2. Crops + Fishery
Lower Gangetic Plain	West Bengal	1. Crops + Dairy 2. Crops + Dairy + Poultry + Duckery
Easter Plateau and Hills	Chhattisgarh, Jharkhand	1. Crops + Dairy 2. Crops + Backyard Poultry + Fish
Central Plateau and Hills	Madhya Pradesh	1. Crops + Dairy
Western Plateau and Hills	Maharashtra	1. Crops + Dairy 2. Crops + Goatery 3. Crops + Horticulture
Southern Plateau and Hills	Andhra Pradesh, Telengana, Tamilnadu, Karnataka	1. Crops + Dairy 2. Crops + Horticulture 3. Crops + Horticulture + Dairy
East Coast Plain and Hills	Odisha	1. Crops + Dairy 2. Crops + Dairy + Fish
West Coast Plain and Hills	Maharashtra, Goa, Kerala	1. Crops + Dairy 2. Coconut based homestead farming 3. Rice based farming systems
Western Dry Region	Rajasthan	1. Crops + Dairy
Gujarat Plain and Hills	Gujarat	1. Crops + Dairy
Islands	Andaman and Nicobar	1. Plantation crops + Piggery 2. Crops + Cattle + Fish

Source: Singh, 2010.

Integrated farming system has the advantages of increasing economic yield per unit area per unit time, profitability, sustainability and provides balanced nutritious food for the farmers, pollution free environment and provide opportunity for effective recycling of one product as input to other component, money round the year and solve the energy, fodder, fuel and timber crisis, avoids degradation of forests and enhance the employment generation, increase input use efficiency and finally improve the livelihood of the farming community (Suba Reddy and Ramakrishna, 2005). Thus the IFS is part of the strategy to ensure sustainable use of the natural resources for the benefit of present and future generations. The major benefits of integrated farming system can be summarised as below.

1. *Productivity*: IFS improves space utilization and increase productivity per unit area. Thus it provides an opportunity to increase economic yield per unit area per unit time by virtue of intensification of crop and allied enterprises.
2. *Profitability:* In IFS waste materials of one component are uses as inputs of another component at the least cost. Thus cost of production is reduced and interference of middle man in procuring most of the inputs is eliminated. Therefore, return per rupee invested or benefit to cost ratio in the farming is increased.
3. *Sustainability:* In integrated farming systems, organic supplementation through effective utilisation of by-products of linked components as a measure is possible and this provides opportunity to promote soil health and to sustain the potentiality of the soil for much longer periods.
4. *Balanced food*: In IFS, components of different nature are linked enabling production of different sources of nutrition, namely: protein, carbohydrates, fats, minerals, vitamins, etc., from the same unit. It provides opportunity to mitigate malnutrition problem of the farm family.
5. *Pollution abatement:* In crop based activity, some of the organics are left as waste materials which in turn pollute the environment on decomposition. Application of huge quantities of fertilisers, pesticides, herbicides, insecticides, etc., pollutes soil, water and air. Much of the wastes could be converted/recycled to some other forms of economic/ecological/social value, under the integrated farming system. Integrated farming will also help in environmental protection through effective recycling of waste from animal activities like: piggery, poultry and pigeon rearing.
6. *Recycling:* Effective recycling of waste materials (crop residues and livestock wastes) is possible in IFS. Therefore, there is less reliance to outside inputs like: fertilizers, agrochemicals, feeds, energy, etc.

7. *Income rounds the year:* IFS provides diversified products. It provides flow of money to the farmer round the year due to integration of enterprises like: crops, birds, animals, mushroom, honey, fish, etc. Thus it provides opportunities as crop insurance cover as money round the year is obtained from different farm produces. There is higher net return to land and labour resources of the farming family.
8. *Adoption of new technology:* Resources farmer (big farmer) fully utilise technology. On the other hand money flow in IFS round the year gives an inducement to the small/marginal farmers to go for the adoption technologies. IFS promotes technology infusion through Research and Development (R&D) integrated with indigenous/traditional knowledge.
9. *Saving energy:* IFS provides an opportunity to identify an alternative source to the fossil energy. Effective recycling technique of the organic wastes available in the system can be utilised to generate biogas.
10. *Meeting fodder crisis:* Every piece of land area is effectively utilized. Plantation of perennial legume fodder trees on field borders and farm boundary will greatly relieve the problem of non-availability of quality fodder to the farm animals. This practice also improves soil fertility through atmospheric nitrogen fixation. Cultivation of fodder crops as intercropping and as border cropping will also result in the availability of adequate nutritious fodder for animal components like: milch cow, goat/sheep, pig and rabbit.
11. *Solving fuel and timber crisis:* The production level of fuel and industrial wood can be enhanced by integrating suitable perennial tree species in farming system (agroforestry) without affecting the crop productivity. This will also greatly reduce pressure on forest resource, thus it preserves the natural ecosystem.
12. *Employment generation:* Integrating crop with livestock enterprises would increase the labour requirement significantly and would help in reducing the problems of unemployment to a great extent. IFS provides enough scope to employ family labour round the year.
13. *Agro-industries:* Integrated farming also provides opportunities for agri-oriented industries, tourism and related tourism based activities. When produce of any component of the IFS is increased to commercial level there will be surplus for value addition, leading to development of allied agro-industries.
14. *Increasing input efficiency:* IFS provides good scope to use inputs in different components with greater efficiency and benefit cost ratio.
15. *Improving/maintaining soil health:* IFS improves soil fertility and soil physical structure through practice of appropriate crop rotation, cover crop, green manuring, composting farm organic wastes and recycling

crop residues. Soil erosion can also be checked by agroforestry and proper cultivation of each part of land by integrated farming.

16. *Reduction of pests:* Adoption of appropriate crop rotation in the farming system can reduce the infestation of weeds, insect pests and diseases.

Case Study

A pond based farming system was developed at Bhubaneswar, Odisha under All India Co-ordinated Research Project on Integrated Farming Systems, Orissa University of Agriculture and Technology during 2013-13. The farm size was 1.25 ha. The economics of the system for the year 2014-15 is presented in the following Table 1.2.

Table 1.2: Economics of An IFS Model of 1.25 ha Farmland at OUAT, Bhubaneswar, 2014-15

Component	Net Area (ha)	Total Cost (^{1}/ha)	Gross Return (^{1})	Net Returns (^{1}/ha)	BCR	Relative Contribution (%)		
						Total Cost	Gross Return	Net Returns
Boundary plantation	0.03	724	1620	896	2.24	0.40	0.55	0.78
Cropping systems	0.32	18837	35970	17133	1.91	10.38	12.14	14.94
Dairy animals	0.0086	82861	127280	44419	1.54	45.65	42.97	38.73
Fisheries	0.5839	15456	20915	5459	1.35	8.52	7.06	4.76
Horticulture	0.195	15752	38082	22330	2.42	8.68	12.86	19.47
Kitchen garden	0.03	4618	8212	3594	1.78	2.54	2.77	3.13
Mushroom	0.0102	2820	3240	420	1.15	1.55	1.09	0.37
Poultry	0.0041	39825	59280	19455	1.49	21.94	20.01	16.96
Vemicompost	0.0033	620	1600	980	2.58	0.34	0.54	0.85
Total		1,81,513	296199	1,14,686	1.63	100	100	100

Source: Annual Report, AICRP on IFS, OUAT, Bhubaneswar, 2015.

Since recycling of farm products and by-products, and creation of labour days are the two major objectives of the IFS the relative contribution of outside purchase, recycled within the system and labour cost towards the total production cost of the different components of the system are presented in the following table for the unit of 1.25 ha area at Bhubaneswar during 2014-15.

Conclusion

Integrated farming system is often less risky and, if managed efficiently, benefits from synergisms among enterprises, diversity in produce, and environmental soundness. It has the advantages of increasing economic yield and profitability per unit area per unit time. A judicious mix of cropping system with associated enterprises like: dairy, poultry, fishery, duckery, agroforestry, vermicompost, apiary, sericulture, piggery, etc., suited to the given agroclimatic conditions and socio-economic status of farmers would bring prosperity to farmers, particularly marginal and small farmers.

Table 1.3: Component-wise Cost of Production and their Relative Contribution, 2014-15

Enterprise	Cost of Production (`)				Relative Contribution (%)		
	Outside Purchase	Recycled within the System	Man days	Total	Outside Purchase	Recycled within the System	Man days
Boundary plantations	81	0	643	724	11.19	0	88.81
Cropping Systems	5701	3884	9252	18837	30.26	20.62	49.12
Dairy	37890	21520	23451	82861	45.73	25.97	28.30
Fishery	8961	2640	3855	15456	57.98	17.08	24.94
Horticulture	1101	4758	9895	15752	6.99	30.21	62.82
Kitchen Garden	0	1148	3470	4618	0.00	24.86	75.14
Mushroom	1278	0	1542	2820	45.32	0	54.68
Poultry	33400	0	6425	39825	83.87	0.00	16.13
Vermicompost	0	234	386	620	0.00	37.74	62.26
Total cost	88,412	34,184	58,917	1,81,513	48.71	18.83	32.46

Source: Annual Report, AICRP on IFS, OUAT, Bhubaneswar, 2015.

The overall objective of integrated farming systems is to evolve technically feasible and economically viable farming system models by integrating cropping with allied enterprises for irrigated, rainfed, hilly and coastal areas with a view to generate income and employment from the farm. Integrated farming system involves the utilization of primary and/ or secondary produce of one system as raw material for other system, thus making the entire system mutually interdependent as one whole unit. The productivity of farming system depends upon natural resources climate and soil, available technology, besides latest information of market technology and human resources.

REFERENCES

Annadurai, K., Palaniappan, S.P., Chinnusamy, C. and Jayanthi, C. (1994). Integrated Farming System: Need of the Hour. *Kisan World* 21(9): 39.

Baishya, A., Kalita, M.C., Mazumdar, D.K., Hazarika, J.P. and Ahmed, S. (2007). Characterization of Farming Systems in the Borpeta and Kamrup districts of lower Brahmaputra valley zone of Assam. *Journal of Farming Systems Research and Development* 13(2): 168-175.

Behera, U.K. (2013). A Textbook of Farming Systems. Agrotech Publishing Academy, Udaipur. pp. 280.

Behera, U.K. and Mahapatra, I.C. (1999). Income and Employment Generation of Small and Marginal Farmers through Integrated Farming Systems. *Indian Journal of Agronomy* 44(3): 431-439.

CARDI. (2010). A Manual on Integrated Farming Systems. Caribbean Agricultural Research and Development Institute, Ministry of Economic Development, Belize.

CGIAR. (1978). Farming Systems Research at International Agricultural Research Centres. TAC Secretariat, Rome, Italy.

Collinson, M.P. (1987). Farming System Research: Procedures for Technology Development. Experimental Agriculture 23: 365-386.

Csavas, I. (1992). Regional Review on Livestock-fish Production Systems in Asia. In: Mukherjee, T.K., Moi, P.S., Panandam, J.M., and Yang, Y.S. (eds.). Proceedings of the FAO/IPT Workshop on Integrated Livestock-fish Production Systems, 16-20 December 1991, Institute of Advance Studies, University of Malaya, Kuala Lumpur, Malaysia.

Das, A. (2013). Integrated Farming: An Approach to Boost up Family Farming. *LEISA India* 15(4): 1-5.

FAO. (1977). Recycling of Organic Wastes in Agriculture. FAO Soil Bulletin 40. Food and Agriculture Organization, Rome.

FAO. (2001). Mixed Crop-Livestock Farming: A Review of Traditional Technologies based on Literature and Field Experience. Animal Production and Health Papers, 152. Food and Agriculture Organization of the United Nations. Rome.

Fresco, L.O. and Westphal E. (1988). A Hierarchical Classification of Farm Systems. *Experimental Agriculture* 24: 399-419.

http://sustainable-agriculture.org/integrated-farming

http://www.agriculturesnetwork.org/magazines/india/family-farming/integrated-farming

http://www.agriinfo.in

Jayanthi, C., Rangasamy, A. and Chinnusamy, C. (2000). Water Budgeting for Components in Lowland Integrated Farming Systems. *Agricultural Journal* 87: 411-414.

Kumar, S. (2013). Integrated Farming System Models for Food and Nutritional Security. In: Meena, M.S., Singh, K.M., Bhatt, B.P. and Kumar, U. (eds.). Gender Perspective in Integrated Farming System, pp. 33-46. ICAR Research Complex for Eastern Region, Patna, Bihar.

Lal, R. and Miller, F.P. (1990). Sustainable Farming for Tropics. In: Singh, R.P. (ed.) Sustainable Agriculture: Issues and Prospective Vol. 1, pp. 69-89, Indian Society of Agronomy, IARI, New Delhi.

Mahapatra, I.C. (1994). Farming System Research – A Key to Sustainable Agriculture. *Fertilizer News* 39(1): 13.25.

Mahapatra, I.C. (2010). Policy and Methodological Issues: Road Map and Strategy for Integrated Farming Systems Research in India. pp. 12-19. In: Gangwar, B., Varughese, K., John, J., Rani, B. Vijayan, M. and Mathew, T. (eds.) Manual on Integrated Farming Systems, KAU Cropping Systems, Thiruvananthapuram and Project Directorate of Farming Systems Research, Modipuram, Meerut.

Okigbo, B.N. (1995). Major Farming Systems of the Lowland Savanna of SSA and the Potential for Improvement. In: Proceedings of the IITA/FAO workshop, Ibadan, Nigeria.

Panda, S.C. (2004). Cropping and Farming Systems. Agrobios (India), Jodhpur. 431 pp.

Panke, S.K., Kadam, R.P. and Nakhate, C.S. (2010). Integrated Farming System for Suatainable Rural Livelihood Security. In: 22nd National Seminar on Role of Extension in Integrated Farming Systems for Sustainable Rural Livelihood, 9th-10th December, 2010, Maharashtra, pp. 33-35.

Patra, A.K. (2013). Agroforestry: Theory and Practices. New India Publishing Agency, New Delhi. 242 pp.

Patra, A.K. (2013). Alley Cropping, *Science Horizon* 3(11): 6-10.

Patra, A.K. and Mohapatra, A.K., Gantayat, B.P. and Das, S. (2011). Evaluation of *Acacia nilotica* as bund Plantation in Coastal Odisha, *Journal of Research, OUAT* Special Issue 1(1): 81-85.

Patra, A.K., Mohapatra, A.K., Gantayat, B.P. and Das, S. (2008). Performance of Coconut (*Cocos nucifera*) based Agrihorticultural System in Coastal Orissa, *Journal of Research, OUAT* 26(2): 53-58.

PDFSR. (2013). Farming Systems Scenario: Vision 2050. Project Directorate for Farming Systems Research, Modipuram. pp. 1-23.

Plucknett, D.L., Dillon, J.L. and Vallaeys, G.J. (1987). Review of Concepts of Farming System Research: What, Why, and How. In: Proceedings of Workshop on Farming Systems Research, February 17-21, 1986, ICRISAT, Hyderabad. pp. 2-9.

Rhoades, R.E. and Booth P.H. (1982). Farmer Back to Farmer: A Model for Generating Acceptable Agricultural Technology. *Agricultural Administration Journal* 11(2): 127-137.

Sasikala, V., Tiwari, R. and Saravanan, M. (2015). A Review on Integrated Farming Systems. *Journal of International Academic Research for Multidisciplinary* 3(7): 319-328.

Shaner, W.W., Phillip, P.E. and Schmehl W.R. (1982). Farming System Research and Development: Guidelines for Developing Countries. West View Press, Boulder, and Colorado, USA.

Singh, J.P. (2010). Scenario of Farming Systems in different Agroclimatic Zones. pp. 20-41. In: Gangwar, B., Varughese, K., John, J., Rani, B. Vijayan, M. and Mathew, T. (eds.) Manual on Integrated Farming Systems, KAU Cropping Systems, Thiruvananthapuram and Project Directorate of Farming Systems Research, Modipuram, Meerut.

Singh, K., Bohra, J.S., Singh, Y. and Singh, J.P. (2006). Development of Farming System Models for the North-eastern Plain zone of Uttar Pradesh. *Indian Farming* 56(2): 5-11.

Singh, R.P. and Ratan. (2009). Farming System Approach for Growth in Indian Agriculture. In: National Seminar on Enhancing Efficiency of Extension for Sustainable Agriculture and Livestock Production, December 29-30, 2009, Indian Veterinary Research Institute, Izatnagar.

Soni, R.P., Katoch, M. and Ladohia, R. (2014). Integrated Farming Systems - A Review. *Journal of Agriculture and Veterinary Science* 7(10): 36-42.

Suba Reddy, G. and Ramakrishna, Y.S. (2005). Farming System Modules in Rainfed Agriculture. In: Singh, A.K., Gangwar, B. and Sharma, S.K. (eds.). Proceedings of Symposium on Alternative Farming Systems: Enhanced Income and Employment Generation Options for Small and Marginal Farmers, September 16-18, 2004, Project Directorate for Cropping Systems Research, Modipuram. pp. 65-71.

Swaminathan, M.S. (2010). Enhancing the Disaster Resilience of Agriculture. *The Hindu Survey of Indian Agriculture*: 7-10.

Page 21-45

FARMING TECHNIQUES AND CROP PRODUCTION
Edited by : **Dr. Alka Chauhan; Dr. Anubhuti Sharma & Jaswant Ray**
Edition : **2017**
ISBN : 978-93-5056-855-2
Published by : **Discovery Publishing House Pvt. Ltd., New Delhi (India)**

2 Seed Priming and Germination

Techniques, its Physiological, Biochemical and Molecular Events

***Sridevi R. & G. Gopalakrishnan**

ABSTRACT

Insufficient seedling emergence and inappropriate stand establishment are the main constraints in areas receiving less rainfall. Management of soil texture and soil structure is a big challenge in semi-arid regions. Poor farmers do not have sufficient resources to meet the requirements of fine seedbed preparation for sowing and they are at more risk as compared to progressive farmers. On the other hand, good establishment increases competitiveness against weeds, increases tolerance to drought periods, increases yields and avoids the time-consuming need for re-sowing that is costly too. It is well accepted fact that priming improves germination, reduces seedling emergence time and improves stand establishment. It is a simple, low-cost, easily performable; on-farm seed priming can, if refined and developed by ensuring the farmer participation, make a good impression on farmers livelihoods enhancing the crop emergence rate, thus increasing rates of crop development, decreasing the total crop duration and getting higher productivity. A lot of work has been done on seed priming and results of these studies indicate well the importance of priming to get a good crop stand and final emergence. It is well accepted fact that priming improves germination, reduces seedling emergence time and improves stand establishment. A method to improve the rate and uniformity of germination is the priming or physiological advancement of the seed lot. The general purpose of seed priming is to partially hydrate the seed to a point where germination processes are begun, but they would exhibit rapid germination when re-imbibed under normal or stress conditions.

Ph.D Research Scholar, Department of Seed Science and Technology, Tamil Nadu Agricultural University, Coimbatore - 641 003, Tamil Nadu, India.

INTRODUCTION

Priming allows some of the metabolic processes necessary for germination to occur without germination take place. In priming, seeds are soaked in different solutions with high osmotic potential. This prevents the seeds from absorbing in enough water for radicle protrusion, thus suspending the seeds in the lag phase (Taylor *et al.* 1998). Seed priming has been commonly used to reduce the time between seed sowing and seedling emergence and to synchronize emergence (Parera and Cantliffe, 1994). In seed priming, the osmotic pressure and the period for which the seeds are maintained in contact with the membrane are sufficient to allow pre-germinative metabolic processes to take place within the seeds up to a level limited to that immediately preceding radicle emergence. Methods for germinating seed and inducing desiccation tolerance in seed are also provided. Preferably the semipermeable membrane is provided in the form of a tube of circular or polygonal cross-section which is rotated with the seeds on its inner surface and the solution retained between its outer surface and a further body to which the membrane is sealed in a watertight manner.

What is Seed Priming?

Seed priming is a controlled hydration process followed by re-drying that allows seeds to imbibe water and begin internal biological processes necessary for germination, but which does not allow the seed to actually germinate. The priming process gives the seed a 'head-start' at germination and emergence when planted in the soil (Glen *et al.* 1988). Accelerating and homogenizing the germination process is a prerequisite for a good crop establishment, the efficient use of resources, and eventually to increase yields (Harris, 1996). Seed priming is reported as an efficient method for increasing of seed vigour and improvement of germination and seedling growth (Ascherman-Koch *et al.* 1992; Jumsoon *et al.* 1996). A robust seedling establishment enhances competitiveness against weeds, improves tolerance to environmental stresses and maximizes biological and grain yields (Hosseein *et al.* 2011). There are several reports that under diverse environmental stresses such as: salinity, water deficiency and high and low temperatures osmo-priming leads to cellular, sub-cellular and molecular changes in seeds and subsequently promotes seed vigour during germination and emergence in different plant species (Godfery *et al.* 2004; McDonald, 2000; Numjun *et al.* 1997).

Priming is usually followed by re-drying of seeds to allow storage and handling. It involves exposing seeds to an external water potential which is low enough to restrict germination and yet permit pre-germinative physiological and biochemical activities (Bradford, 1986). Priming may help seed production in the tropics by ensuring that seed plants grow uniformly and vigorously (Harris *et al.* 2001). The principle of priming is based on the fact that it is possible to hydrate seed in some ways at a moisture level sufficient to initiate the early events of germination but not sufficient to permit radical protrusion (Moradi and Younesi, 2009).

In a seed, the natural stages of germination occur up to the point of radicle emergence. Radicles are the first parts of the seedlings that sprout from the seeds. Radicle emergence requires a high seed water content. So when we prime seeds, we limit their water content, and the metabolic steps necessary for germination can occur without the irreversible act of radicle emergence. With primed seeds, plant stands emerge more rapidly and uniformly.

Seed priming is a method of improving seed performance by preparing (usually with water) the seeds with a specific moisture for a predetermined time and temperature. The preparation starts the germination process but the process is stopped before the seed actually sprouts (no root or shoot). After preparation, the seeds are dried back to normal moisture until needed. The resulting seed will germinate faster and more uniformly than non-primed (raw) seed. The seed will also germinate well over a wider range of temperatures since many of the most temperature sensitive pathways have been completed during priming. Primed seed has been used for many years in protected culture crops like bedding flowers and specialty vegetables and is increasingly used in field grown crops.

Within the wider seed industry, broad adaptation of priming was led by the protected culture flower and vegetable seed industry. Acceptance of priming was relatively quick due to several factors positively impacting the bottom line of the customers. One, priming allowed the growers to germinate primed seeds at lower temperatures in the winter compared to raw seed. This helped to significantly reduce their heating cost in the winter months when greenhouse production is at its peak for spring sales. Two, as the case with many plant species, the completion of germination process can take upwards of 35 days. Priming these slow germinators significantly cuts the germination time down to a few days in many instances. Growers found that the accelerated growth given by priming would result in the ability to get an extra crop out of the greenhouse during a single growing season. Additionally, priming increases usable transplants allowing greater production against a relatively constant overhead meant greater profit per unit greenhouse area. Priming brings tremendous value to the grower and has been the main driver for its wide adaption in the protected culture greenhouse industry.

Over the past two decades seed enhancement through seed priming has led to great improvements in a grower's ability to routinely achieve this goal in both the field and greenhouse. Numerous vegetable and ornamental crop species have been primed successfully. In order to maintain a superior product, seed companies have to maintain seed quality and longevity in the primed seed. Rapid and uniform field emergence are two essential prerequisites to increase yield, quality, and ultimately profits in crops. Uniformity and percentage of seedling emergence of direct-seeded crops have a major impact on final yield and quality. Rate and uniformity of emergence are inherent to seed quality and environmental conditions during seedling emergence. Slow emergence results in smaller plants and seedlings, which are more vulnerable to soil-borne diseases.

Heydecker acknowledged the use of the term priming of seeds to describe a presowing seed treatment to enhance germination and increase seedling emergence uniformity under adverse environmental conditions. Terms such as: halopriming (soaking in salt solutions) or osmopriming (soaking in other osmotic solutions) were proposed as alternatives to priming. The use of a salt as an osmoticum can lead to an increase in fresh weight of a seed. In this case, germination is delayed through increased solute potential of the embryo. Osmoconditioning or osmotic conditioning is also used to describe the same treatment when materials such as: polyethylene glycol (PEG) are used as the osmoticum. Solid matrix priming (SMP) is a term used for a presowing seed treatment in which a solid-matrix instead of an osmotic solution is used to enhance germination. It is a process that uses solid matrix materials, water, and seed in combinations to control water, oxygen, and temperature effects on germination. The process controls the hydration of seed to a level that allows a pre-germination activity but that prevents radicle emergence. Matriconditioning was proposed as an alternative term to SMP, to distinguish seed conditioning by matric and osmotic forces. It is generally agreed that priming reduces time to germination and also reduces the natural spread in germination from seed to seed, resulting in an increase in uniformity of the final product. However, a potential disadvantage of primed seeds is their reduced shelf life. The reduction in shelf life complicates the logistics of treating seeds. One solution is to require more accurate control of temperature and moisture than for untreated seeds. In general, storage of primed seeds for more than one year is not advisable, though this conclusion is species and temperature dependent.

Benefits of Seed Priming

The benefits of seed priming have been well documented in previous review articles (Bradford, 1986; Khan, 1992; Taylor *et al.* 1998).

Priming has also alleviated secondary dormancy mechanisms that can be imposed if exposure to supra-optimal temperatures lasts too long or in photo-sensitive lettuce varieties. The other benefit of priming has been to increase the rate of germination at any particular temperature. On a practical level, primed seeds emerge from the soil faster and often more uniformly than non-primed seeds because of limited adverse environmental exposure. Priming accomplishes this important development by shortening the lag or metabolic phase (or phase II in the triphasic water uptake pattern, in the germination process. The metabolic phase occurs just after seeds are fully imbibed and just prior to radicle emergence. Since seeds have already gone through this phase during priming, germination times in the field can be reduced by approximately 50 per cent upon subsequent rehydration.

For practical purposes, seeds are primed for the following reasons:

- To overcome or alleviate phytochrome-induced dormancy in lettuce and celery.
- To decrease the time necessary for germination and for subsequent emergence to occur.
- To improve the stand uniformity in order to facilitate production management and enhance uniformity at harvest.
- Emergence occurs before soil crusting becomes fully detrimental.
- Crops can compete more effectively with weeds.
- Increased control can be exercised over water usage and scheduling.
- Enhances the germination percentage.
- Enhances the speed and uniformity of germination.
- Improves the resistance towards water and temperature stress.
- Increases the shelf life of seed.
- Highly suitable for small seeds.
- Enhances the yield.
- Emergence can occur before soil crusting becomes fully detrimental.
- Crops can compete more effectively with weeds.
- Priming allows growers to better control their water usage and scheduling.
- Priming can eliminate or greatly reduce the amount of seed-borne fungi and bacteria.
- To extend the temperature range at which a seed can germinate.
- To increase the rate of germination at any particular temperature.
- It decreases the time to germination for subsequent germination.
- Increase the rate of germination at a given temperature.
- Primed seeds emerges from the soil most faster and uniformly.
- To improve the stand uniformity and crop establishment.
- It extends the temperature range for germination of seed.
- Also allows the seeds to germinate at supra-optimal temperature.
- It alleviates the secondary dormancy mechanism in the seeds.
- Priming shortens the lag and metabolic phase of the seeds.
- Reduces the time to germination about 50 per cent.
- Crops can compete bitterly with the weeds.
- Proper utilization of water takes place.

- Reduces the seed born bacteria and fungi.
- Organisms such as: *Xanthomonas campestris* in *Brassica* seeds and *Septoria* in celery have been shown to be eliminated within seed lots as a by-product of priming.

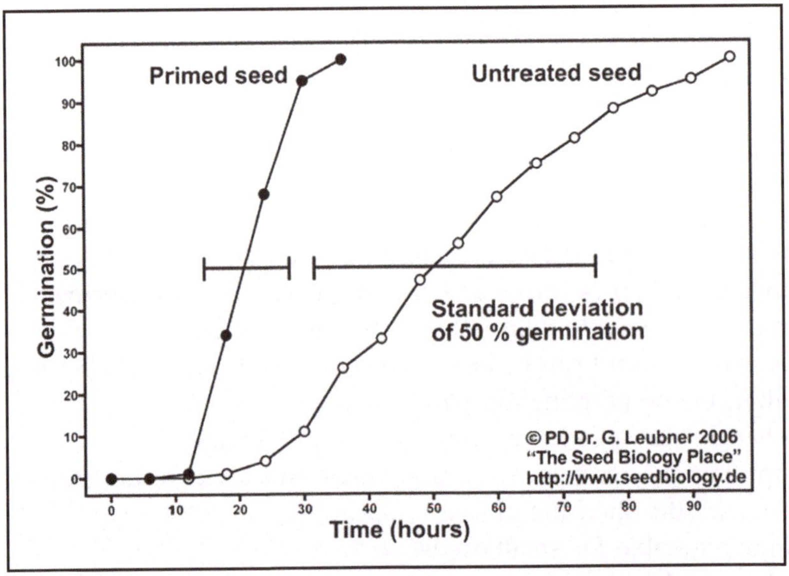

Fig. 2.1: Priming can reduce germination times in the field by approximately 50 per cent upon subsequent rehydration

Understanding of Seed Priming

The term 'priming' is used to describe a seed pre-sowing treatment. During priming seeds are partially hydrated and then they are dried in the next step. In general, water uptake by dry seed under optimal conditions during germination can be divided into three phases. Phase I, where imbibition is rapid that is largely as a consequence of the matric forces exerted by the seed. This phase occurs in dormant or non-dormant, viable or non-viable seeds. During first phase, DNA and mitochondria are repaired and proteins are synthesized using existing messenger ribonucleic acid (mRNA) (McDonald, 2000). Phase II is the lag phase, where there is very little net gain of water but considerable metabolic activities that prepare viable non-dormant seeds for radicle emergence. In this phase, the syntheses of mitochondria and proteins by new mRNA occur. Phase II is also called activation phase (Bradford, 1995). In phase III (final phase) water uptake increases and coupled with radicle elongation (Bewley, and Black, 1994). In primed seeds phases I and II of water uptake are passed, but seeds do not enter the third phase of water uptake. This hydration is sufficient to permit pre-germinative metabolic events but insufficient to allow radicle protrusion (Bradford, 1986).

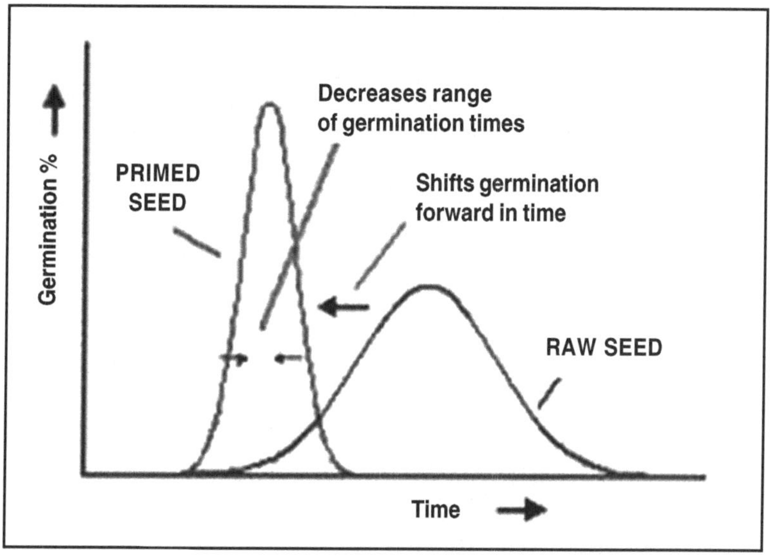

Fig. 2.2: Advancement in germination of primed seed over non primed seed

Seed priming is a controlled hydration process that involves exposing seeds to low water potentials that restrict germination, but permits pregerminative physiological and biochemical changes to occur (Heydecker and Coolbear, 1977; Bradford, 1986 and Khan, 1992). Upon rehydration, primed seeds may exhibit faster rates of germination, more uniform emergence, greater tolerance to environmental stress, and reduced dormancy in many species (Khan, 1992). Heydecker (1973) used different terms depending upon the method adopted for priming, namely: *(i)* hydropriming - soaking the seeds in water; *(ii)* osmopriming - soaking the seeds in osmotic solution; *(iii)* halopriming - soaking the seeds in salt solutions, (iv) biopriming - coating the seeds with biological agents like: bacteria and *(v)* solid matric priming - mixing the seeds with an organic or inorganic carrier and water for a specific period of time.

Seed Priming and Germination

Earlier germination of primed seeds may be due to increase in activity of enzymes such as: amylase, protease and lipase which have great role in breakdown of macromolecules for growth and development of embryo (Dell-Aquila and Tritto, 1990). It has been reported that resultant effect of priming depends on duration of seed soaking (Ghassemi-Golezani *et al.* 2008b) and priming methods (Ghassemi-Golezani *et al.* 2008a). Germination is an important stage of seedling establishment and therefore it plays a key role in crop production. Crop establishment however depends on the interaction between seedbed environment and seed quality (Perry, 1984) where salinity has been identified as one of the major seedbed factors influencing establishment (Barbour, 1970). Priming is one of the most important physiological method which improves the seed performance and provides faster and synchronized germination. The primed seeds give earlier, more uniform and sometime greater germination and seedling establishment and growth (Bradford, 1986).

Seed Priming Techniques

The purpose of priming is to reduce the germination time, make germination occur over a short period and improve stand and percentage germination. Priming materials include substances for both matric and osmotic priming, although some seed priming carriers include both osmotic and matric processes. Some are available commercially while others are held for private competitive business use. Osmotic priming is accomplished using chemicals that lower osmotic potential in the seed environment. Polyethylene glycol is a commonly used osmotic priming material because it is readily available and has no physiological reaction with seed. Very large molecules of this substance do not pass through seed cell membranes. Other osmotic priming agents include: glycerol; mannitol, and Agro Lig. Matric seed priming substances or materials control ψ by reducing the matric potential of the water in them through adsorption on particle surfaces. Seeds are mixed with materials of high surface area, with variable particle size (including colloidal) and a non-soluble solid state with low chemical reactivity. Specialized vermiculite compounds (Zonolite), Celite and Micro Cel are used. These have High matric potential and low osmotic potential.

Types of Priming

There are different methods of seed priming: *(i)* hydro-priming or soaking seeds in water; *(ii)* halo priming or hydration in inorganic salt solutions; *(iii)* osmo-priming or soaking seeds in solutions such as: polyethylene glycol (PEG); *(iv)* thermo-priming or treatment of seeds with low or high temperatures (Ashraf, and Foolad, 2005); *(v)* matri-priming or treatment of seeds with solid matrices, such as: hydrated sand (Hu *et al.* 2005), peat and vermiculite (Taylor *et al.* 1998); *(vi)* bio-priming or coating seeds with bacteria, *e.g., Trichoderma* spp. (Pill *et al.* 2009) and *Pseudomonas aureofaciens* (Warren and Bennett, 1999). In addition, seeds may be primed with plant growth regulators (Subedi and Ma, 2005).

Hydro-priming

Hydro-priming involves soaking the seeds in water before sowing (Pill and Necker, 2001) and may or may not be followed by air-drying of the seeds. In many agricultural areas, a major cause of poor stand establishment and low crop yield is unfavorable environmental conditions for seed germination and seedling emergence. However, rapidly germinating seedlings could emerge and produce deep roots before the upper layers of the soil are dried out and crusted, which may result in good crop establishment and higher crop yield. Rafiq *et al.* (2006) reported that seed priming reduces the effect of salinity on the morphological parameter of the plants. Any factor that facilitates rapid germination may contribute to establishment of a successful crop. A low cost approach, designated as on farm seed priming was proposed by Harris, (1992) and involve soaking of seed in water before sowing. This pre sowing seed treatment, known as hydro-priming, allows the seed to imbibe water and go through the first phase of germination in which pre-germination metabolic activities are started while the latter two phases of germination are inhibited (Pill and Necker, 2001). Although soaking seed in water and drying before sowing is the easiest way to achieve hydration, a major disadvantage is that it may result in uneven hydration and non-uniform germination. Soaking is not suitable for some plant species, as rapid hydration may cause leakage of essential nutrients out of the seed, resulting in seed damage. To overcome these potential problems, various methods have been devised to deliver appropriate hydration to the seed. One method is seed humidification a pre sowing treatment in which seed are treated under conditions of high humidity (Suzuki and Khan, 2001).

The primed seeds also exhibited a faster rate of germination and seedling emergence. The improvements in seed germination and seedling emergence were due to enhanced supply of soluble carbohydrates to the growing embryo, which was caused by an increase in α-amylase activity. Re-drying of seed following hydro-priming did maintain activity of other enzymes at the levels required for occurance of germination.

Halo Priming

Halo priming refers to soaking of seeds in solution of inorganic salts *i.e.* NaCl, KNO3 CaCl2, CaSO4, etc., number of studies have shown a significant improvement in seed germination, seedling emergence and establishment, and final crop yield in salt affected soils in response to halopriming. Seed germination is promoted by halopriming but also stimulate subsequent growth, thereby enhancing final crop yield (Eleiwa, 1989; Sallam, 1999). Seedling establishment is an important for the better growth and development of the plant either treated with priming agent or not. Halopriming have very important role in germination, seedling emergence, and plant growth at all developmental stage of the plants.

Solid Matrix Priming

Matrix priming (matri conditioning) is the incubation of seeds in a solid, insoluble matrix (vermiculite, diatomaceous earth, cross-linked highly water-absorbent polymers) with a limited amount of water. This method confers a slow imbibition. Matric priming (also called matric conditioning, solid matric priming or solid matric conditioning) accomplishes the same type of controlled, limited hydration as hydro-priming and osmo-priming. However, unlike hydro - and osmo-priming, matric priming utilizes a solid medium (the matrix) to deliver water and nutrients to the seed prior to emergence of the radicle (Taylor and Harman, 1990). Khan (1992) recommended the use of vermiculite or calcinated clay as the solid medium due to their good water holding capacity and ease of removal from the seed after the priming process is complete. A clear advantage of matric priming is the ability to provide ample oxygen to the seed during the hydration process. However, as with osmo-priming, waste disposal after priming may become an issue (Warren and Bennett, 1997).

This kind of treatment includes mixing the seeds with solid substances of high capacity for keeping water (like: soft coal, Ground Leonardite Shale, and dried moss) in water. In this method the seeds potential for absorbing water is controlled by physical and chemical characteristics (Yamamoto *et al.* 1997; Hartz and Gaprile, 1995). Seed priming treatments such as: osmo-priming, hydro-priming, matrico-priming, hormonal-priming have been employed to accelerate germination, seedling growth and yield in most of the crops under normal and stress conditions (Basra *et al.* 2003). It has been declared that priming had resulted in more germination speed especially in drought stress and low temperatures in sorghum, sunflower and melon (Sivritepe *et al.* 2003). Osmo-priming is the most common type of seed priming which involves controlled hydration of seeds by exposure to water (Nyarko *et al.* 2006), either alone or in combination with solid media or osmotic agent, allowing seeds to imbibe, but removing the water and drying seeds to original moisture content prior to radicle emergence (Smith, 2006). Commonly used osmotic priming agents include inorganic salts such as: CaCl2, KNO3, Na2 SO4 and organic agents such as: polyethylene glycol (PEG), mannitol and sorbitol.

Osmopriming

Osmopriming (osmoconditioning) is the standard priming technique. Seeds are incubated in well aerated solutions with a low water potential, and afterwards washes and dried. The low water potential of the solutions can be achieved by adding osmotica like mannitol, polyethyleneglycol (PEG) or salts like KCl. Osmo-priming is the most common type of seed priming in which seeds are soaked in aerated low water potential solution (Farooq *et al.* 2005). Although, the mechanism of seed priming treatments is not fully understood, it has been observed that physiological and biochemical changes take place during the seed treatments (Basra *et al.* 2005; Ghiyasi *et al.* 2008), which could allow seeds to begin the germination sequences before sowing. Osmotic priming consists of the incubation of seeds for a specific period of time at a specific temperature in an osmoticum of -1.0 to -1.5 M Pa, usually salt or polyethylene glycol (PEG, molecular weight 6000) dissolved in water (Karssen *et al.* 1989). Osmo-priming, sometimes referred to as osmo-conditioning, is similar to hydro-priming. As with hydro-priming, seeds are allowed to imbibe water, begin the germination process up to the second phase of the tri-phasic water uptake, and then dried to storage moisture before radicle emergence occurs (Bennett *et al.* 1992). However, various osmotica are added to the water during the imbibitions period to prevent full hydration of the seeds. These osmotical include: sugars, salts, PEG, and mannitol. The solutions created provide osmotic potentials low enough to prevent germination and radicle emergence during priming (Smith, 2006). The concentration of the hydrating solution is an important factor in osmo-priming. High levels of some osmotica may negatively affect seed water potential, may be toxic to the seed, or may be economically unsustainable (Taylor and Harman, 1990). Salim and Todd (1968) applied large numbers of inorganic chemicals at different concentrations to seeds of diverse crop species and concluded that the seed, the chemical and the concentration had all to be right for success. Other limitations with osmo-priming include difficulty in handling of polyethylene-glycol for priming large seed lots (Heydecker and Coolbear, 1977) and chemical waste disposal after priming. Rapid germination and emergence is an important determinant of successful establishment (Ehsan *et al.* 2009).

Drum Priming

A specific method and device for hydro-priming using water and a rotating cylinder has been developed (Rowse, 1991; Rowse, 1992). Seeds are placed into the rotating cylinder and water is added via mist in small amounts over time until the seed within the cylinder reaches a pre-determined target moisture concentration. This process eliminates the concern for the disposal of spent hydrating solution (as in osmotic priming) or spent solid carrier disposal (as in solid matric priming). A device that can be assembled and utilized for drum priming of seed is described in detail by Warren and Bennett (1997). Both maize (Warren and Bennett, 1997) and onion (Caseiro *et al.* 2004) have been primed using a similar device. However, drum priming onion seeds was detrimental, as it resulted in lower final germination percentages and slower germination rates (Caseiro *et al.* 2004).

Biopriming

Use of biological agents integrates biological and physiological aspects of disease control and seed quality enhancement. Kalaivani (2010) reported that maize seeds primed with 20 per cent *Azospirillum* for 12 h had higher germination and also reported that the seeds primed with phosphobacteria at 20 per cent concentration for 12 h recorded higher germination. Seed biopriming with liquid *Azospirillum* 20 per cent for 12 h or liquid phosphobacteria 15 per cent biopriming for 12 h was found to be the best seed biopriming treatment for rice seed to enhance the germination rate, total germination percentage, seedling growth and vigour (Kavitha, 2011). Bhendi seeds bioprimed with liquid phosphobacteria 20 per cent for 12 h or *Azospirillum* 15 per cent for 12 h also resulted in higher germination percentage and seedling vigour (Mariselvam, 2012). *Azospirillum and* Phosphobacteria 20 per cent concentration for 12 h expressed high values for all the parameters studied namely: speed of germination, germination, root length, shoot length, dry matter production, total dry matter production and vigour index in COH(M) 5 maize hybrid (Karthika and Vanangamudi, 2013). Rice hybrid CORH 4 seeds bioprimed with 4 per cent pseudomonas flourescens for 12 h or 20 per cent liquid Azospirillum for 12 h or 15 per cent liquid phosphobacteria for 12 h or 20 per cent Azophos for 12 h had registered earlier germination, higher germination percentage, root length, shoot length, dry matter production, total dry matter production and vigour index (Kokila, 2014).

Fig. 2.3: Primed seeds in comparison with control seeds

Events during Germination

Seed Imbibition

Fundamental to the success of seed priming in the uptake of water that occurs in three phases in a germination seed.

Phase I

Rapid initial water uptake into seed due to the seed's low water potential (water moves from high to low water potential). During this phase, DNA and mitochondria are repaired and proteins synthesized using existing messenger ribonucleic acids (mRNA's).

Phase II

It is represented only in a gradual increase in seed water content, but new physiological activities associated with germination are initiated including the synthesis of mitochondria and proteins relying on the translation of mRNAs. Phase I and II represent the process of germination and are foundation for successful seed priming, where the seed is brought to a seed moisture content that is just short of radicle production.

Phase III

This signify the completion of germination and the start of seedling growth by resumption of radicle growth and is identified by another rapid intake of water. This cereals the turgor necessary for radicle cell elongation.

The Cell Cycle

The cell cycle is the series of molecular events that allows cells to duplicate and segregate their chromosomes to for m new cells. The important phases are G1, G1/S checkpoint, S, G_2, G2/M check point and finally the M phase.

G_1 - Cell doubles in size, new organells and materials formed.
G_1/S - Check point; Cell cycle can stop here or proceed to Sphase.
S - DNA and associated nuclear protein replicated; cells contain 2 full copies of its genetic information.
G_2 - Chromosomes being to condense, band of microlubels forms.
G_2/M - Checkpoint.
M - if conditions are suitable (Mitosis) cell divides.

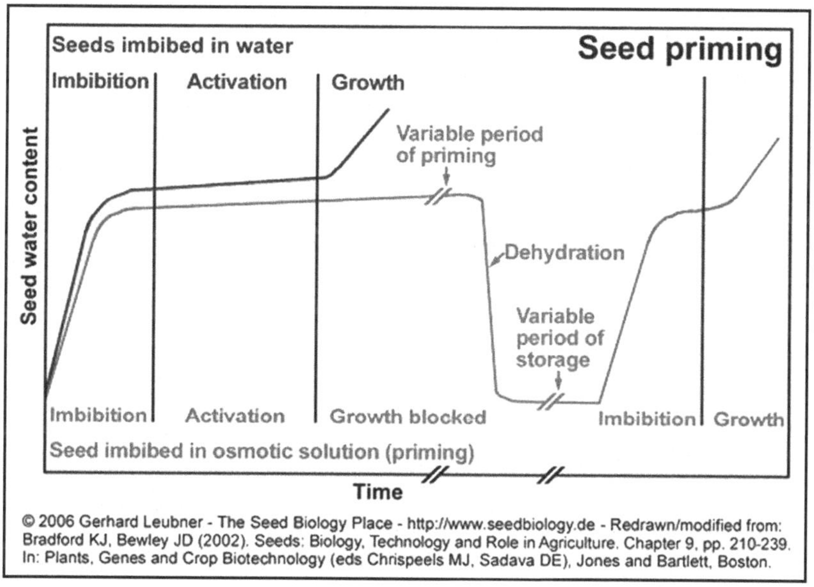

Fig. 2.4, Seed priming can enhance seed germination. Seed priming involves allowing seeds to absorb sufficient water to initiate metabolic processes, but insufficient water to allow completion of germination. After the priming period, the seeds can be dried, stored, and transported to the farmer. When seeds are imbibed again, the lag period before radicle emergence occurs is considerably reduced, impoving the rate and uniformity of germination.

Events that Happens during Priming Process

According to Rashid *et al.* (2004) the germination process accomplishes in three phases: *(i)* Water absorption by seed; *(ii)* Delaying phase; *(iii)* Radicle growing through emergence of testa. During the first two phases, seeds are tolerant of drought but once the third phase started they become highly intolerant of drought. Normally, the seeds sprout when the seed water potential reaches to the critical physiological level (0-2 Mega Pascal). Seeds with a penetrable seed coat usually pass three phases for being sprouted. During the first phase, they absorb water. When the water penetrates into the seed and reaches to embryo, the second phase begins during which the stored hormones and enzymes will be activated and stimulate in turn the physiological growing. Ultimately, growing of the radicle begins in third phase. Through priming operations, replication of DNA, increasing of protein and RNA synthesis, accessibility to more ATP, quick growing of embryo, repair of damaged sections of the seeds, and reducing of metabolites leaking into the seeds are all provided during the delaying phase. Performing seed priming, during G2 and S stages of mitosis the replication accomplishes and nucleus content becomes double but there is not any cell division yet and this condition will advance budding by one stage in later soaking operations. On the other hand, quick absorption of water leads to rupture of cell membrane, celluloid death of cotyledons and embryo axis of cells, and reaction of oxygen. The efficiency of seed priming can be attributed to augmentation of four-string DNA nucleus in radicle meristem (Lanteri *et al.* 1996).

Physiological, Biochemical and Molecular aspects of Priming

Priming also has been shown to induce nuclear DNA synthesis in the radical tip cells in tomato (Liu *et al.* 1997) and several other plant species, including maize (Zea mays L.) (Garcia *et al.* 1995). Osmopriming has been shown to activate processes related to cell cycle. In wild rye (Leymuschinensis) seeds, for example, priming with 30 per cent PEG for 24 h resulted in increase in the activity of superoxide dismutase (SOD) and peroxidase (POD) and a rapid increase in the respiratory intensity, which were associated with an increase in germination vigor (Jie *et al.* 2002). Osmopriming may also contribute to rapid seed germination by reducing the mechanical restraint of endosperm on developing embryo (Mayer and Mayber, 1989). It was determined that osmotic priming of tomato seed increased the endo-beta mannanase activity in the endosperm cap and decreased its mechanical restraint on the germinating embryo (Tooropet *et al.* 1998). A strong correlation was observed between lowering of the mechanical restraint and the activity of endo-beta-mannanase. Primed seeds significantly showed the increased emergence percentage, rate of emergence, root length and seed vigor in all amaranth cultivars. Trigin cultivar showed the best performance among cultivars. Total seed protein, POD and PPO were also increased significantly by seed priming.

Almont and Plainsman cultivars exhibited high protein content and POD activity. PPO activity increased by seed priming comparing to controls for Amont, Plainsman and Mercado cultivars, but for Trigin cultivar, no increase was detected. The highest increase in PPO activity was observed in Mercado cultivar (Moosavi *et al.* 2009).

Enzyme Activation

Enzymes such as: amylases, proteases, and in some cases, lipases, play vital roles in the early growth and development of embryo. Any increase in the activity of these enzymes may result in early vigorous growth and good crop establishment. It has been demonstrated that osmopriming affects the activity of these enzymes in the germinating seed of different plant species. For example, in muskmelon (Cucumis melo), seed osmoconditioned with PEG-6000 showed enhanced activity of dehydrogenase and amylase and improved germination under non-saline conditions. In oilseed crops, the glyoxylate pathway, which converts lipids into sugars, plays an important role in the early development of embryo (Taiz and Zeiger, 2002). Osmoconditioning also enhanced the activity of ATPase in the germinating seed of peanut primed with PEG. Furthermore, acid phosphatase and RNA syntheses were significantly higher in embryonic axes and cotyledons of osmo-conditioned seed compared to control seed. Thus, osmopriming may contribute to improved germination rate in part by increasing various enzyme activities. Osmopriming has been shown to activate processes related to cell cycle. In wild rye (Leymuschinensis) seed, priming with 30 per cent PEG for 24 h resulted in increase in the activity of superoxide dismutase (SOD) and peroxidase (POD) and a rapid increase in the respiratory intensity, which were associated with an increase in germination vigor (Jie *et al.* 2002).

Protein Synthesis

Protein synthesis occur during priming and are increased upon subsequent germination compared with the levels seen in untreated controls, while the activities of several germination associated enzymes have been reported to be increased upon germination after priming (Khan *et al.* 1978; Coolbear and Grierson, 1979; Mayor *et al.* 1984; Fu *et al.* 1988, Bray *et al.* 1989).

Capron *et al.* (2000) observed that conditions of priming closely parallel to that of germination allowed the solulrilization of 11-S globulin storage protein, reinforcing the finding that the beneficial effect of priming correspond to the advancement of germination *i.e.,* into phase II of germination process. The 11-S globulin was proposed as protein marker for optimization of sugar beet priming.

Davison and Bray (1991) showed that the rate of protein synthesis in 4-day germinated unprimed lack seeds in equivalent to that in 2-days germinated primed leek seeds. They observed that a set of five pollypeptides (P_1 - P_5) synthesis during priming were not involved in germination process however, two poly peptides synthesized at the end of priming were still being synthesized upto 2 days of germination after priming, indicating that they may have some role in germination and growth.

However Dell'Aquila and bewley (1989) disputed claims that priming increases protein synthesis.

Patrick Achard *et al.* (2002) reported that in the first hours of imbibition transcription activation occurs at P_1 promoter and it coincides with appearance of transacting factor AUBE 1 a new protein. AUBE 1 bids with P_1 promoter of RPL 21 gene (a short DNA fragment) encoding plastid localized ribosomal proteins *RPL 21* AUBE 1 in stable even after dessication of primed seed). AUBE1 was proposed as marker in spinach seed priming.

Many workers have reported increased hydroylic enzyme activity induced by priming. Berrice and Dearman (1971) in oats and wilson (1971) and Hanson (1973) in wheat grass where an increase in q-amylase activity was noted.

Increase in β-tublin in the radicle tip has been observed during priming by De Castro *et al.* (1995) and Bino *et al.* (1992). Tublin is the main functional protein of microtubules which is necessary for mitotic spindle formation.

Nucleic Acids

Nuclear acid accumulation has been reported in many seeds after priming. Coolbear *et al.* (1980) reported that there is very large accumulation of RNA in ungerminated seeds and there is close correlation between this net synthesis and subsequent germination performance. Bray *et al.* (1989) detected DNA synthesis in leek embryos during priming, which may reflect DNA repair, thus contributing to rapid germination and embryo growth upon priming.

Bino *et al.* (1992) observed nuclear replication in embryo root tips of tomato seeds during priming. Strong correlation existed between the increase in replicated nuclei, 12 h before radicle emergence and the germination speed, indicating the importance of nuclear replication.

rRNA level increase during priming to near theoretical levels. In low vigour leek embryos, damaged and RNA is replaced by intact of rRNA during priming (Davison *et al.* 1991).

Priming also causes a more rapid resumption of cell division and DNA synthesis upon germination. (Dell Aquila and Toranto, 1986). Coolbear *et al.* (1980) opined that increased DNA content can be a result of activation or synthesis of nucleic acid or both Expression of certain protein related to water stress and heat shock has been reported by czarneeka *et al.* (1984) and Davison and Bray (1991).

Advancement of radicle meristerm cells into Sand G_2 phase of the cell cycle, increasing the percentage of nuclei having a 4C DNA content, has been reoprted to occur during priming. It has been suggested that the efficiency of priming is related to the accumulation of 4C nuclei in the radicle meristerm.

An increase in nuclear DNA contents or radicle meriterms from 2C to 4C during priming indicating progression from G_1 to S or G_2 phase of the cell cycle has been reported by Bino *et al* (1992), Lanteri *et al.* (1993, 1994, 1996) Redfearn and Ostrome, (1997). Lanteri *et al.* (1993, 1994) found that mean times to radicle emergence following priming were highly correlated with the 4C/2C ratio of nuclei, 12 h before radicle emergence of chilli and tomato seeds, sugar beet seeds also increased their nuclear DNA content during priming without cell division, indicating that they were arrested after the S phase of the cell cycle. Radicle tip cells of some tomato seed lots advanced through the cell cycle during priming, resulting in an increase in the percentage of nuclei having 4C DNA contents (Guru singhe *et al* 1999) He belived that the increase in 4C nuclei in radicle – cells during priming is almost invariably associated with an accelerated rate of radicle emergence.

Saracco *et al.* (1995) reported the priming treatment at the lower osmotie potential induced a high percentage of nuclei in 4C and was highly effective in decreasing mean germination time. The same treatment performed for shorter period (2d) did not induce DNA synthesis or reduce the mean germination time. At higher osmotie potential, even after 6d, no DNA replication was induced though mean germination time was reduced.

At maturation majority of the tomato and chilli seed cell reveal 2C signals and indicated that cell has been arrested at presynthesic G_1 phase of nuclear division. In seeds of both species, a positive correlation was found between the induction of DNA synthesis, measured as the increase in 4C cells and the efficiency of the osmotic treatments to reduce the mean germination time for all seed lots of chilli and tomato the lowest concentration of PEG (-1, 1 Mpa) induced 4C signals and reduced mean germination time more efficiently. He maintained that induction of 4C signals after priming indicated that during priming the cells of the embryonic root tip had replicated their DNA and arrested at the G_2 phase of the cell cycle. Gurusinh *et al.* (1999) insisted that the apparent absence of DNA replication during priming does not preclude an accelerated germination rate.

Mitochondria

Germination is a energy demanding process that requires the operation of mitochondria, which must survive desiccation in the quiescent seed and become rapidly functional after imbibition to meet the ATP demand.

Benamar *et al.* (2003) reported that mitochondria isolated after 12 h of imbibition readily oxidized exogenous NAD and Krebs cycle substrates at higher states. However, their phosphorylation efficiency was restricted by poor membrane integrity. After 22 h, purified seed mitochondria had intact outer membranes and oxidized the substrate at slightly lower rates but with higher phosphorylation efficiency. Priming treatment appeared to slightly increase the performance of mitochondria. The outer membrane integrity of seeds primed for 16 h was higher than control Mayor *et al.* (1984) also reported that seed priming increases respiration and ATP production.

Seed Repair

The positive effect of priming is also related to reversal of some of the detrimental events occurring during seed deterioration.

Mc Donald (2000) in his revise on seed priming observed that considerable evidence exist that repair of DNA, RNA, protein, membrane and enzymes occurs during imbibition. The knowledge that repair occurs during imbibition has been practically adopted by the seed industry for many crops through seed priming. Generally, it is accepted that repair of seeds deteriorated by lipid peroxidation occurs during hydration (priming). The repaired seed is then dried for normal handling, and the benefits for repair are retained as the primed seed completes germination. It should be noted that the physiological improvements gained by priming are not solely attributable to repair, since newly harvested musk-melon seeds showed great improvement in seed performance following osmopriming (Welbaum and Bradtord, 1991).

Seed Priming on Yield Parameters

Chavan *et al.* (2014) determined the importance seed priming on field performance and seed yield of Soybean. There were two varieties *viz;* Phule Kalyani and JS-335 while six priming treatments *viz;* Control (unprimed seeds), Hydro-priming, KCl @10 ppm, CaC12.2H2O @ 0.5 per cent, KH2PO4 @ 50 ppm and GA3 @ 20 ppm. It may be concluded that soybean seeds positively responded to treatments of priming. Nevertheless, priming generally improves the most parameters of soybean varieties through improving plant height, number of branches, number of pods per plant, number of seeds per pod, seed yield. The highest benefit of priming can be obtained from seeds primed with $CaCl_2.2H_2O$ (0.5%) treatment. Gupta and Singh (2012) in SKUAST-Jammu in *Inceptisols* found out the effects of seed priming on chickpea. The treatments consisted of seed priming (seed soaking in water for 8 h). The observations on plant height, nodule dry weight, seed index, dry matter accumulation, yield and yield attributes of chickpea were recorded. The results revealed that the growth parameters of chickpea were significantly affected by seed priming. Soaking chickpea seeds in water for about 8 h significantly influenced plant height and nodule dry weight in comparison to unsoaked seeds. Seed priming significantly affected dry matter accumulation at various time intervals and at harvest. Seed priming, on an average, yielded 22.1 per cent higher dry matter accumulation at different time intervals after sowing. At harvest, seed priming registered statistically higher pods/plant, seeds/pod, grain and biological yield which were 27.0, 11.9, 23.1 and 22.0 per cent higher over no seed priming. Harris (2006) has reported improvement in seed yield in various crops at farmer's field by seed priming with water. The higher values obtained for growth parameters, periodic dry matter accumulation, yield and yield attributes with seed priming may be due to the fact that primed seeds usually exhibit an increased germination rate and greater germination uniformity (Basra *et al.* 2005). The results are in conformity with Bray *et al.* (1989) and Lin and Sung (2001).

A field experiment was conducted by Afzal *et al.* (2006) to evaluate the role of seed priming with Zn in improving the performance of maize hybrids in Faisalabad. The two maize hybrids namely SIPRA 4444 and SP13 were tested with hydro-priming, priming with 0.5 per cent ZnSO4, priming with 1.5 per cent ZnSO4, priming with 0.5 per cent Zn EDTA and priming with 1.5 per cent Zn EDTA. Observations on seed emergence, physiological parameters, grain yield and yield components were recorded in maize. The results of the study revealed that priming techniques of zinc gave higher values in almost all the physiological and yield parameters. The maximum grain yield (5.35 t/ha), biological yield (16.69 t/ha) were found in priming with ZnSO @1.5 per cent in 4 maize hybrid. Alam *et al.* (2013) conducted an experiment to study the effect of priming on spinach with various sources and soaking durations in Peshawar. Four priming sources (Distilled water, DAP, SSP, SSP+Na2CO3) and soaking durations of 4 hour interval (4 hour to 24 hour) along with control were studied. Number of days to emergence, germination percentage, survival percentage, leaf area (cm2), leaf yield (tons/ha) and 100 number seeds weight (g) were significantly affected by priming sources and durations. Mean values showed that early emergence (5.952 days), maximum germination percentage (88.14), survival percentage (89.96), plant height (31.24 cm), leaf area (63.12 cm2), leaf yield (14.667 tonnes/ha) and 100 seed weight (1.00 g) were observed in plots in which seeds were soaked in SSP+Na2CO3 solution. In case of soaking durations, early emergence (5.917 days), maximum germination percentage (89.42), survival percentage (90.40), plant height (31.16 cm), leaf area (60.72 cm^2), leaf yield (14.340 tonnes/ha) and 100 seed weight (0.966 g) were recorded in the plots in which seeds were soaked for 24 h. Mean values of interactions results showed that early emergence (5.0 days), maximum germination percentage (95.33), survival percentage (95.38), plant height (33.70 cm), leaf area (70.78 cm^2), leaf yield (16.257 tons ha^{-1}) were observed in plots where seed were soaked in SSP+Na2CO3 solution for 24h. Overall SSP+Na2CO3 solution proved the best in most of the parameters while distilled water (control) showed comparatively poor performance.

Factors Affecting Seed Priming

Methods of Priming

Different approaches of priming must be evaluated for each species and seed lot to determine the suitable method of priming to the specific species.

Oxygen

In Osmopriming, highly aerated conditions are narrated for successful priming. In hydropriming, muskmelon priming as low oxygen condition was inferior to high oxygen condition.

Light

Avoidity light will ensure prolongation of imbibition phase providity more time for activation phase during priming without allowing radical protrusion.

Temperature

Lower temperature of 15°C during priming can result in enhanced seed performance (Bradford, 1986). This may be because the physiological process of germination is delayed even as the seeds absorb the increase quantities of water. The optimum temperature of 27-28°C for Osmopriming with PEG at -1.0 Mpa was the same as the optimum temperature for germination of tomato seeds. Further studies are necessary to establish whether lower temperatures or those optimum for germination enhance the seed priming response.

Seed Quality

Initial seed quality or vigour has a bearing on the success of priming. Generally, priming is conducted on highest quality seed lots so as to obtain optimum response. Even in poor quality seed lots, priming can reverse the effects of seed ageing.

Crop Species

Individual crop species behave differently to same of priming. Hence, the method of priming, osmotic potential of osmoticant, duration of priming and priming conditions should be standardized specifically for each crop species.

Addition of Promotive Substance

The addition of promotive substance to seeds during priming can further enhance seed performance. GA_3 is the most successfully incorporated in seed priming treatments. Absicic acid, Kinitin, ethephon have also produced good results. Matripriming of sweet corn seeds with sodium hypochloride, reduced fungal invasion. Biological control organisms can also be added in combination with an Osmopriming treatment. Warren and Bennett (1999) termed it as trio-Osmopriming.

Storage of Primed Seeds

The popular idea is that priming treatments hydrate seeds, therefore the initial physiological, biochemical events of germination are activated. Even though the seed subsequent redried, it is at a more advance physiological point than before priming and more prove to deterioration. The benefits of priming are lost relatively rapidly during seed storage and this is dependent on the crop and the differing temperatures are relative humidities imposed during storage. The decrease in storability may be a feature of extending the pre hydration period too long. Successful storage of primed seed depends on both careful drying and well regulated storage condition. Venkatasubramaniam and Umarani (2004) reported in tomato, brinjal and chilli, the well standardized methods of priming has resulted in improved storability.

Conclusion

Seed priming has been used to improve germination, reduce seedling emergence time, improve stand establishment and yield. The beneficial effects of priming have been demonstrated for many field crops. It is the best solution of germination related problems especially when crops are grown under unfavorable conditions. Many priming techniques have been evolved which are being utilized in many crops now days. It can enhance rates and percentage of germination and seedling emergence which ensure proper stand establishment under a wide range of environmental conditions. Seed priming is a popular and commercially used technique developed mainly to accelerate the process of germination so the effects of low and high temperatures can be minimized. It is the best solution of germination related problems especially when crops are grown under unfavorable conditions. Many priming techniques have been evolved which are being utilized in many crops now-a-days.

REFERENCES

Afzal, Sher. Nadeem, A., Zahoor, A. and Qaiser, M. (2006). Role of Seed Priming with zinc in Improving the Hybrid Maize (*Zea mays*) Yield. *American-Eurasian J. Agric Environ Sci.* 13: 301-06.

Alam, A., Amin, N. U., Ara, N., Ali, M. and Ali, I. (2013). Effect of Various Sources and Durations of Priming on Spinach Seeds. *Pak J. Bot.* 45: 773-77.

Ascherman-Koch, C., Hofmann, P., and A. M. Steiner (1992). Presowing Treatment for Improving Quality in Cereals. I. Germination and vigour. *Seed Science and Technology,* 20: 435-440.

Ashraf, M. and M.R. Foolad, (2005): Pre-sowing Seed Treatment: A Shotgun Approach to Improve Germination, Plant Growth and Crop Yield under Saline and non-saline Conditions. *Advances in Agronomy,* 88: 223-271.

Barbour, M.G. (1970). Germination and Early Growth of the Stand Plant. *Cakile Masitima Bulletin Torrey Botanical Club,* 97: 13-22.

Basra, S. M. A., Farooq, M. and Tabassum, R. (2005). Physiological and Biochemical Aspects of Seed vigour Enhancement Treatments in Fine Rice (*Oryza sativa* L.). *Seed Sci Tech.* 33: 25-29.

Basra, S.M.A., Ehsanullah, E.A.W., Cheema, M.A. and I. Afzal, (2003): Effect of Storage on Growth and Yield of Primed Canola Seeds (Brassica napus). *International Journal of Agriculture and Biology,* 5: 117-120.

Bennett, M., Fritz, V.A. and N.W. Callan, (1992). Impact of Seed Treatments on Crop Stand Establishment. *Horticultural Technology,* 2(3): 345-349.

Bewley, J.D., and M. Black, (1994). Cellular Events During Germination and Seedling Growth. In: Seeds: Physiology of Development and Germination (Eds. Bewley, J.D., Black, M.). *Plenum Press,* New York, USA, pp. 147-197.

Bradford, K.J. (1986). Manipulation of Seed Water Relations via osmotic Priming to Improve Germination under Stress Conditions. *Hortscience,* 21: 1105-1112.

Bradford, K.J. (1995). Water Relations in Seed Germination. In: Seed Development and Germination (Eds. Kigel, J., Galili, G.). *Marcel Dekker, Inc.,* New York, USA, pp. 351-396.

Bray, C. M., Davison, P. A., Ashraf, M. and Taylor, R. M. (1989). Biochemical Changes during osmo-priming of Leek Seeds. *Annals Bot*. 63: 185-93.

Caseiro, R., Bennett, M.A. and J. Marcos-Filho, (2004). Comparison of three Priming Techniques for Onion Seed lots differing in Initial Seed Quality. *Seed Science and Technology*, 32: 365-375.

Chavan, N.G., Bhujbal, G.B. and Manjare, M.R. (2014). Effect of Seed Priming on Field Performance and Seed Yield of Soybean [*Glycine max* (L.) Merill] varieties. *Bioscan* 9: 111-114.

Dell-Aquila, A. and V. Tritto, (1990): Ageing and osmotic Priming in Wheat Seeds: Effects upon Certain Components of Seed Quality. *Annales Botanici*, 65: 21-26.

Ehsan, N., Mohammad, B., Ali, G.M.H. and A. Ali, (2009). Does Hydro and Osmo-Priming Improve Fennel (Foeniculum vulgare) Seeds Germination and Seedlings Growth? Notulae Botanicae. *Horti Agrobotanici Cluj-Nopaca*, 37(2): 190-194.

Eleiwa, M.E. (1989). Effect of Prolonged Seed Soaking on the Organic and Mineral Components of Immature Pods of Soybeans. *Egypt. J. Bot*, 32: 149-160.

Farooq, M., Basra, S.M.A., Hafeez, K. and N. Ahmad, (2005). Thermal Hardening: A New Seed vigour Enhancement Tool in Rice. *Acta Botanica Sinica*, 47: 187-193.

Garcia, F.C., Jimenez, L.F. and R.J.M. Vezquez, (1995). Biochemical and cytological Studies on osmoprimed Maize Seeds. *Seed Sci. Res*, 5: 15-23.

Ghassemi-Golezani, K., Aliloo, A.A., Valizadeh, M. and M. Moghaddam, (2008a). Effects of hydro and osmo-priming on Seed Germination and Field Emergence of lentil (*Lens culinaris* Medik.). *Notulae Botanicae Horti Agrobotanici Cluj-Napoca*, 36: 29-33.

Ghassemi-Golezani, K., Sheikhzadeh-Mosaddegh, P., and M. Valizadeh, (2008b). Effects of Hydro-priming duration and Limited Irrigation on Field Performance of chickpea. *Research Journal of Seed Science*, 1: 34-40.

Ghiyasi, M., Abbasi, A.S., Tajbakhsh, M., Amirnia, R. and H. Salehzade, (2008). Effect of osmo-priming with poly ethylene glycol 8000 (PEG 8000) on Germination and Seedling Growth of wheat (Triticum aestivum L.) Seeds under Salt Stress. *Research Journal of Agriculture and Biological Sciences*, 3(10): 1249-1251.

Glen, D.M. and C.W. Wiltshire (1988). Distribution of slug Species. *In IACR Long Ashton Research Station Annual Report*, 1987, pp. 28.

Godfery, W.N., Onyango, J.C. and E. Beck (2004). Sorghum and Salinity: II. Gas Exchange and chlorophyll fluorescence of sorghum under Salt Stress. *Crop Science*, 44: 806-811.

Gupta, V. and Singh, M. (2012). Effect of Seed Priming and fungicide Treatment on chickpea (*Cicer arietinum*) sown at different Sowing Depths in *kandi* belt of low altitude sub-tropical zone of Jammu. *Applied Bio Res*. 14: 187-92.

Harris, D. (1992). Staying in Control of Rainfed Crops. In 'Proceedings of the First Annual Scientific Conference of the SADCC/ODA Land and Water Management Programme': 257-262. Gaborone, Botswana.

Harris, D. (1996). The Effects of Manure, Variety, Seedlings, Seed Priming, Depth and Date of Sowing on the Emergence and Early Growth of *Sorghum bicolor* (L.) Moench in semi arid Botswana. *Soil and Tillage Research*, 40: 73-88.

Harris, D. (2006). 'On-farm' Seed Priming. A Key Technology to Improve the Livelihoods of Resource-Poor Farmers in Marginal Environments (extended version). DFID/PSP Information Booklet, CAZS Natural Resources, University of Wales, Bangor, UK.

Harris, D., Pathan, A.K., Gothkar, P., Joshi, A., Chivasa, W. and P. Nyamudeza (2001). On-farm Seed Priming using Participatory Methods to Revive and Refine A Key Technology. *Agricultural Systems*, 69: 151-164.

Hartz, T.K. and J. Caprile. (1995). Germination of *sh2* sweet corn following Seed Disinfestations, Solid-matrix Priming and Microbial Seed Treatment. *Hort Science Journal,* 30(7): 1400-1402.

Heydecker, W. and P. Coolbear (1977). Seed Treatments for Improved Performance – Survey and Attempted Prognosis. *Seed Science and Technology,* 5: 353-424.

Heydecker, W., (1973). Accelerated Germination by osmotic Seed Treatment. *Nature.* 246: 42-44.

Hosseein, A., Farahani and M. Karsa (2011). Effect of Hydro-priming on Seedling vigour in Basil (Ocimum basilicum L.) under salinity Conditions. *Advances in Environmental Biology,* 5(5): 828-833.

Hu, J., Zhu, Z.Y., Song, W.J., Wang, J.C. and W.M. Hu, (2005). Effects of Sand Priming on Germination and Field Performance in Direct-sown rice (*Oryza sativa* L.). *Seed Science and Technology,* 33: 243-248.

Jie, L., Gong She, L., Dong Mei, O., Fang Fang, L. And W. En Hua, (2002). Effect of PEG on Germination and Active Oxygen Metabolism in wildrye (Leymu. 7 chinensis) Seeds. *Acta Prataculturae Sinica,* 11: 59-64.

Jumsoon, K., Jeuonlai, C. and J. Ywonok (1996). Effect of Seed Priming on the germinability of Tomato (Lycopercicon esculentum Mill.) Seeds under Water and Saline Stress. *Journal of the Korean Society for Horticultural Science,* 37: 516-521.

Kalaivani, S., (2010). Seed Biopriming Studies with Biocontrol Agents and Liquid Biofertilizers in COH(M)5 maize hybrid. *M.Sc. (Ag.) Thesis,* Tamil Nadu Agricultural University, Coimbatore.

Karssen, C.M., Haigh, A., Van Der Toorn, P. and R. Wages, (1989). Physiological Mechanisms Involved in Seed Priming. In: Recent Advances in t he Development and Germination of Seeds (Taylorson, R.B. Ed.). Proceedings of Third International Workshop on Seeds, Williamsburg, VA, USA. pp. 269-288.

Karthika, C. and K. Vanangamudi, (2013). Biopriming of Maize Hybrid COH(M) 5 Seed with Liquid Biofertilizers for Enhanced Germination and vigour. *African Journal of Agricultural Research,* 8(25): 3310-3317.

Kavitha, S., (2011): Biopriming with Biocontrol Agents and Liquid Biofertilizers for Rice Seed cv. ADT 43. *M.Sc. (Ag.) Thesis,* Tamil Nadu Agricultural University, Coimbatore.

Khan, A.A., (1992). Preplant Physiological Seed Conditioning. *Hortic. Rev,* 13: 131-181.

Kokila, M., (2014). Physiological, Biochemical, Molecular and Histological Basis of Seed Biopriming with Biocontrol Agent and Liquid Biofertilizers in Rice Hybrid CORH 4 and its Parental lines. *Ph.D. (Ag.) Thesis,* Tamil Nadu Agricultural University, Coimbatore.

Lanteri, S., Nada, E., Belletti, P., Quagliotti, L. and R.J. Bino, (1996). Effects of Controlled Deterioration and Osmoconditioning on Germination and Nuclear Replication in Seeds of Pepper. *Annals of Botany,* 77(6): 591-597. http://dx.doi.org/10.1093/aob/77.6.591

Lin, J. M. and Sung, J. M. (2001). Pre-sowing Treatment for Improving Emergence of Bitter Gourd Seedling under Optimal Temperatures. *Seed Sci Tech.* 29: 39-50.

Liu, Q., Hilhorst, H.W.M., Groot, S.P.C. and R.J. Bino, (1997). Amounts of Nuclear DNA and Internal Morphology of gibberellin - and Abscisic Acid-deficient Tomato (*Lycopersicon esculentum* Mill.) Seeds during Maturation, Imbibition and Germination. *Ann. Bot,* 79: 161-168.

Mariselvam, D., (2012). Performance of Bioprimed bhendi (cv. arka anamika) Seeds with Biocontrol Agents and Liquid Biofertilizers under Laboratory and Field Conditions. *M.Sc. (Ag.) Thesis,* Tamil Nadu Agricultural University, Coimbatore.

Mayer, A.M., and A. Poljakoff-Mayber, (1989). The Germination of Seeds, 4 edn. *Pergamon Press, Oxford.*

McDonald, M.B., (2000). Seed Priming. In: Seed Technology and its Biological Basis (Eds. Black, M., Bewley, J.D.). *Sheffield Academic Press, Sheffield, UK,* pp. 287-325.

Moosavi, A., Tavakkol Afshari R., Sharif-Zadeh F., and A. Aynehband, (2009). Effect of Seed Priming on Germination Characteristics, Polyphenoloxidase and Peroxidase Activities of Four Amaranth Cultivars. *J. Food Agri. Environ,* 7: 353-358.

Moradi, A. and O. Younesi (2009). Effects of Osmo- and Hydro-priming on Seed Parameters of Grain Sorghum (Sorghum bicolor L.). *Australian Journal of Basic and Applied Sciences,* 3(3): 1696-1700.

Numjun, K., Yeonok, J., Jeoung, L.C. and M.K. Song (1997). Changes of Seed Proteins Related to Low Temperature and Germinability of Primed Seed of Pepper (Capsicum annuum L.). *Journal of the Korean Society for Horticultural Science,* 38: 342-346.

Nyarko, G., Alderson, P.G. and J. Craigon, (2006): Towards Cabbage Seed Production in the Tropics. *Ghana Journal of Horticulture,* 5, in Press.

Parera, A.C., and D.J. Cantliffe, (1994). Pre-sowing Seed Priming. *Hortic. Rev,* 16: 109-148.

Perry, D.A. (1984). Factors Influencing the Establishment of Cereal Crops. *Aspects Applied Biol,* 7: 65-83.

Pill, W.G, and A.D. Necker, (2001). The Effects of Seed Treatments on Germination and Establishment of Kentucky bluegrass (Poapratense L.). *Seed Sci. Technol.* 29: 65-72.

Pill, W.G., Collins, C.M., Goldberger, B. and N. Gregory, (2009). Responses of Non-primed or Primed Seeds of Cucumber (*Cucumis sativus* L.) Slurry Coated with Trichoderma Species to Planting in Growth Media Infested with Pythium aphanidermatum. *Scientia Horticulturae,* 121: 54-62.

Rafiq, S., Iqbal, T., Hameed A, Rafiqi, Z.A. and N. Rafiq, (2006). Morphobiochemical Analysis of Salinity Stress Response of Wheat. *Pak. J. Bot.* 38: 1759-1767.

Rashid, A., Harris, D., Hollington, P. and A. Shamsher, (2004). On-farm Seed Priming Reduces Yield Losses of Mungbean (Vigna radiate) Associated with Mungbean Yellow Mosaic Virus in the Niorth West Frontier Province of Pakistan. *Crop Protection,* 23(11): 1119-1124.

Rowse, H.R. (1991). Methods of Priming Seeds. U.K. Patent No. 2192781.

Rowse, H.R. (1992). Methods of Priming Seeds. U.S. Patent No. 5,119,589.

Salim, M.H. and G.W. Todd, (1968). Seed Soaking as a Pre-sowing drought Hardening Treatment in Wheat and Barley Seedling. *Agro Food,* 60: 179-82.

Sallam, H.A. (1999). Effect of some Seed-soaking Treatments on Growth and Chemical Components on Faba Bean Plants under Saline Conditions. *Ann. Agric. Sci,* 44: 159-171.

Sivritepe, N., Sivritepe, H.O. and A. Eris, (2003). The Effects of NaCL Priming on Salt Tolerance in Melon Seedling Grown under Saline Conditions. *Scientia Horticulturae,* 97: 229-237.

Smith, T. M. (2006). Seed Priming and Smoke Water Effects on Germination and Seed Vigour of Selected Low-Vigour Forage Legumes.

Subedi, K.D. and B.L. Ma, (2005). Seed Priming does not Improve Corn Yield in a Humid Temperate Environment. *Agronomy Journal,* 97: 211-218.

Suzuki, H. and A.A. Khan. (2001). Effective Temperatures and Duration for Seed Humidification in Snapbean (Phaseolus vulgaris L.). *Seed Sci. Technol,* 28: 381-389.

Taiz, L. And E. Zeiger, (2002). Plant Physiology, 3 edn. *Sinauer Associates, Inc. Publishers, Sunderland, Massachusetts.*

Taylor, A.G. and G.E. Harman, (1990). Concepts and Technologies of Selected Seed Treatments. *Annual Review of Phytopathology*, 28: 321-329.

Taylor, A.G., Allen, P.S., Bennet, M.A., Bradford, K.J., Burris, J.S. and M.K. Misra (1998). Seed Enhancements. *Seed Science and Research, 8,* pp. 245-256.

Toorop, P.E., Van, A.C. and H.W.M. Hilhorst, (1998). Endosperm cap Weakening and endo-beta-mannanase Activity during Priming of tomato (Lycopersicon esculentum cv. Moneymaker) Seeds are Initiated upon Crossing a threshold Water Potential. *Seed Sci. Res,* 8: 483-491.

Venkatasubramaniam, A. and R. Umarani. (2004). Promising Priming Techniques for High Quality Vegetable Seeds. Asian Seed and Planting Material, 11(6): 11-12.

Warren, J.E. and M.A. Bennett, (1997). Seed Hydration using the Drum Priming System. *Hort Science,* 32(7): 1220-1221.

Warren, J.M. and M.A. Bennett, (1999). Bio-osmopriming Tomato (*Lycopersicon esculentum* Mill.) Seeds for Improved Stand Establishment. *Seed Science and Technology,* 27: 489-499.

Yamamoto, I., Turgeon, A.J., and J.M. Duich. (1997). Field Emergence of Solid Matrix Seed Primed Turfgrasses. Crop Science 37(1): 220-225. http://dx.doi.org/10.2135/cropsci1997.0011183X003700010038x.

FARMING TECHNIQUES AND CROP PRODUCTION
Edited by : Dr. Alka Chauhan; Dr. Anubhuti Sharma & Jaswant Ray
Edition : 2017
ISBN : 978-93-5056-855-2
Published by : Discovery Publishing House Pvt. Ltd., New Delhi (India)

3 Modern Concept of Water Management in Vegetable Crops

Chandan Singh Ahirwar[1] Ankit Kumar[2]
Dr. D.K. Singh[3]

INTRODUCTION

Vegetable production occupies prime position in horticultural sector in India. Owing to the increasing demand both in domestic and foreign markets, vegetable production has got commercial importance in recent years. Thus, it would be necessary to introduce measures for increasing the productivity of vegetable crops. Since water is a crucial input for enhancing production, asssured irrigation for fruit crops would be necessary. Therefore, efforts have been made for employing more efficient methods of irrigation. Since most of the vegetable crops are planted on rows, they are ideally suited for drip irrigation.

Micro irrigation technology is rapidly expanding all over the world, especially in the water scarce areas of developed countries. It is very popular in the United States, Israel and some parts of Europe. North America and Europe has the highest record of MIS utilization while Asia is in the development stage. Irrigation plays a vital role in Australian agriculture; here irrigated agriculture uses 75 per cent of consumed water. This technology has also established a stronghold in the Asian regions, where it is best utilized in India and China but still there is ample market potential with a continuously rising population. Drip irrigation is becoming the most demanded technology.

1 Ph.D. Scholar, Department of Vegetable Science, College of Agriculture, Govind Ballabh Pant University of Agriculture and Technology, Pantnagar, Uttarakhand - 263 145, India.

2. M.Sc. Scholar, Department of Horticulture, College of Agriculture, Govind Ballabh Pant University of Agriculture and Technology, Pantnagar, Uttarakhand - 263 145, India.

3. Professor, Department of Vegetable Science, College of Agriculture, Govind Ballabh Pant University of Agriculture and Technology, Pantnagar, Uttarakhand - 263 145, India.

Micro irrigation system market in India has grown at the stupendous CAGR of 27.3 per cent during the period from FY'2008-FY'2013 and is further expected to reach INR ~ million in FY' 2018. Although, adoption of micro irrigation techniques by farmers is growing at a fast pace, the market penetration is still very low. Micro irrigation system sales in India is driven by strong demand in states such as: Gujarat, Rajasthan, Madhya Pradesh Maharashtra, Karnataka, Andhra Pradesh, Tamil Nadu, Rajasthan and Haryana. The state governments of Gujarat, Andhra Pradesh, Tamil Nadu, Chhattisgarh, Himachal Pradesh and Bihar have also conceived micro irrigation projects as part of the Micro irrigation Scheme.

As the major consumer of this global asset, irrigation accounts for about four fifths of the total freshwater consumed and about two thirds of the total diverted for human uses. Irrigation has shaped the economies of many semiarid and arid areas, permanently coloring the social fabric of numerous regions around the world. It has stabilized rural communities, increasing income and providing many new opportunities for economic advancement. Irrigation permits human habitation, at times quite dense populations, where it other-wise could not exist. The supply of freshwater that supports human health and enterprise is basically constant, representing only about 1 per cent of the water available worldwide. Good quality, non-saline water is the global asset most important in satisfying the increasing demand for basic food, fiber, feed and fuels.

Micro irrigation is a system that provides high frequency application of water in and around the root zone of the plant with the help of emitters/ drippers and making the irrigation of even large and complex plantings simple and cost-effective. Micro irrigation works because plants don't need blanket water fall in order to grow. The water that a plant uses, when naturally watered, is a fraction of the actual volume of liquid that falls in a rain shower. Growing plants use only the water they can channel to their roots: everything else is lost as run-off into barren soil. A micro irrigation system recognises this principle and, instead of simulating rainfall targets the root area using tiny dripper nozzles. The amount of water fed into the roots is the same as the quantity actually harvested by plants during rainfall; the amount saved is equal to the amount of useless rain lost into rootless ground.

In India around 88 per cent water is being used in agriculture sector. Due to liberalization of industrial policies and other developmental activities, the demand of water in industrial and domestic sectors is on an increase day-by-day, which forces to reduce the percentage area under irrigation. Micro irrigation, by discarding the useless water plants never see, raises watering efficiency by almost three quarters and allows the farmers to make a saving of roughly 75 per cent in any watering volume. What this means is that micro irrigation lets farmers water even irrigation-intensive spaces year round, without having to worry about water usage or hosepipe controls.

Term Related with Water Management

- *Water-use efficiency (WUE):* Refers to the efficient use of water in plant metabolism. There are two types of water use efficiency in plants:
  - ❖ photosynthetic water-use efficiency (also called intrinsic or instantaneous water-use efficiency);
  - ❖ water-use efficiency of productivity (also called integrated water-use efficiency).
- *Consumptive use:* Total amount of water lost due totranspiration by a crop and evaporation from the surface of soil and vegetation during a specified time from a particular area. It is also called – Evapotranspiration (ET).
- *Water holding capacity:* The weight of water held by a given quantity of absolutely dry soil when saturated.
- *Water potential:* Difference between the activity of water molecules in pure distilled water at atmospheric pressure and 30°C (standard condition) and the activity of water molecule in any other system.
- *Water application efficiency:* It is the percentage of water stored in the root zone for use of crops to the amount of water applied to the field.
- *Effective rainfall:* The fraction of the total precipitation that forms the soil water reserve for consumptive use of crop or that becomes available for crop production.
- *Effective irrigation:* Controlled and uniform application of water to crop field at required time, with minimum cost to produce optimum yield without waste of water and adverse effect on soil and crop.
- *Effective rooting depth:* soil depth from which a full grown crop extracts most of its water need for evapotranspiration.
- *Water requirement:* Includes water lost through evapotranspiration and water used by the crop for plant metabolic activities including that retained in plant body.
- *Water table:* Upper surface of the free water accumulating at a depth bellow the soil surface when a hole is bored into the soil column.

Or

- Upper surface of the saturated water bearing layer bellow the ground.

Soil Water and its Classification

Soil water can be classified according to its available to the plant and to the tenacity with which it is held in soil:

(i) *Gravitational water:* It is the soil water held with a water potential greater than -0.3 bar. In sandy soil this water is held with -0.1 to -0.2 bar water potential. This kind of water drains out of the soil freely by gravitational force, and is not available to the plant.

(ii) *Field capacity:* It is the percentage of soil water that is held with the water potential 0.3 bar and is the measure of the maximum amount of water that a soil can hold or store under condition of complete wilting followed by free drainage or It is the amount of water that a soil can retain against the gravitational pull.

(iii) *Permanent wilting point:* It is the percentage of soil water that is held with water potential at or below 15 bars. This water is held so strongly that plants are not able to absorb it fast enough for their need. So, the plants suffer from water starvation and thereby wilt permanently.

(iv) *Plant-available water:* It is the capillary water of the soil held with a water potential between 0.1 to 15 bar. It is equal to the difference in water percentage at field capacity and permanent wilting point.

(v) *Hygroscopic water:* Soil moisture percentage at or below 31 bar.

(vi) *Soil water at air dry state:* Soil moisture held by water potentials that vary from 300 to 1000 bar

Options for Improving the Productivity of Water

There are several approaches for improving the crop productivity (yields) of water including replacing high water consuming crops with lower-consuming ones and adopting management and systems improvements to increase productivity per unit of water consumed. Reallocation of water from low-value crops to higher-value crops can increase the economic productivity of water; however this conserves water only if the high-value crop has a shorter growing season, and the land is not recropped the same year. Thus, the most significant sources of 'new' water will be through improvements in productivity per unit of water with the adoption of appropriate management and water application systems. Each basin and watershed may have different solutions depending on specific socio-economic, soils, water supply and climatic characteristics. Efficiencies must be considered in terms of both the diverted water that is consumed and the proportion that is not consumptively used that is available for reuse or becomes degraded or otherwise unusable. Efficiencies are increased when the total amount of water consumed by crops, evaporation and other users can be reduced. The available water resource within a basin or subbasin can also be effectively conserved for other uses by improving efficiencies to reduce the unusable water losses.

Method of Soil Moisture Determination

(A) Direct method

(i) *Graviometric method:* Percentage of water calculated by the formula:

$$\text{Percentage water} = \frac{(\text{Wet soil weight}) - (\text{Oven dry soil weight})}{\text{Oven dry soil weight}} \times 100$$

(B) Indirect method

(i) Tensiometer: It measures the metric potential of soil moisture with the use of a porous ceramic attached to a tube filled with water.
It works satisfactorily only upto 0.85 bar

(ii) Resistance blocks: This method based on the principles that electric conductivity decreases with the decrease in soil moisture.

Sources of Irrigation Water

The global water resource availability in the sea as salty water, south and north poles as solid ice form and fresh water on the land, rivers or lakes etc., is depicted separately. In India, monsoon winds are mostly responsible for precipitation, termed as monsoon rains. Out of fresh water available on the earth, India contributes to the extent of 4.5 per cent with 2.4 per cent geographical area and about 16 per cent of world population. The per capita available water of 6000 m3/year has declined to 2300 in the year 2000 and will be declined to 1600 m3/year in the year 2010. Out of the total fresh water available, about 82 per cent of water is used for agriculture sector. Recently it is estimated that 38 per cent of cultivable area has been brought under irrigation in the country. The annual precipitation was estimated to the tune of 400 million ha m out of which 115 million ha m classified as surface flow or runoff losses. Water storage in reservoirs and tanks is about 15 million ha m. The scope of boring tubewells, canals and even lift irrigation is limited, such facilities are confined to the low laying areas. Therefore, the most common source of irrigation remains the small water channels locally called Kuhls which intact accounts for 85.83 per cent of the total area under irrigation in hills. In cold deserts, some villages get water for irrigating their lands from some perennial torrents. In Spiti valley, the source of irrigation water is generally local nallas. Glacial water in cold deserts of Himachal Pradesh which forms the prime source of sustaining life in the region is brought to the field by making Kuhls (Water Channels). In Kinnaur and other regions, the source of irrigation as well as drinking water is melting snow on the high peaks which runs downward in the shape of small and big nallahas (streams) and also spring out at certain points.

Soil-Water-Plant-Relationship

Soil water plant relationship includes the components of physico-chemical properties of effective root zone, plant response and the climatic fluctuations in terms of temperature, relative humidity and wind velocity etc. In brief, this complex phenomenon refers to simple terminology as ('SPAC') Soil Plant Atmosphere Continuum.

Where:

S = Pertinent physico-chemical and hydraulic properties of soil.

P = Plant response in terms of water and nutrients absorption translocation and transpiration mechanism.

A = Atmospheric fluctuation related to temperature (T) relative humidity (RH) and wind velocity etc.

C = Continuity or continual processes.

Criteria for Scheduling of Irrigations

Irrigation need of the crops is decided by the evaporative demand of the ambient atmosphere, soil water status and plant characterizations. The criteria for scheduling of irrigations are mainly grouped into three categories.

(i) Plant criteria *(a)* Critical crop growth stages approach; *(b)* Indicator plant.

(ii) Soil water status criteria soil moisture depletion approach.

(iii) Climate criteria climatological approach.

(i) *Plant criteria:* The plant physiologists have identified the critical growth stages of plantation crops and vegetable crops. This approach is used in cereals, pulses, oil seeds and vegetable crops on large scale as these crops are seasonal short duration crops. The limitation for adoption of this approach is the type of soil and its soil water retentivity and its release. The coarse textured and shallow soils are not suitable to adopt this approach. Plant appearance at temporary wilting stage, stunted plant growth, plant water potential, indicator plant, leaf diffusion resistance, stomatal aperture, plant temperature and critical growth stages are also ways and means available to schedule irrigations under 'Plant Criteria Approach'. The plant shows certain characteristic changes in their constitution, appearance and growth behaviour with changes in available water. The plant physiologists have decided the critical growth stages for all crops when optimum soil moisture availability is necessary. Hence indicator plant and critical growth stages approaches are common for scheduling purpose.

(ii) *Soil moisture status criteria:* Some plants are very sensitive to soil moisture stress. Moreover, early soil moisture stress condition is created in observation plot be one square meter area by modifying soil profile, changing its water holding capacity by sand application. The pre-indication of temporary wilting is reported in that plot for scheduling of irrigation. Moreover moisture stress sensitive crop like sunflower is planted in the observation plot. Soil water status criteria are dependent on soil moisture measurement and soil moisture tension measurement in the effective root zone. It is very precise and depth of water to be applied could be adjusted economically. The soil moisture is monitored by either direct or indirect methods. In general, irrigations are scheduled when 50 per cent available soil moisture is depleted in the effective root zone. This is also termed as management allowable deficit (MAD). It differs from crop to crop depending upon their moisture stress tolerance or moisture availability index. The vegetable crops have hardly 30 per cent available moisture deficit or 30 per cent MAD value to avoid the

stress and maximization of water use efficiency. It requires huge periodical soil moisture sampling for estimation of ASM levels. It is cumbersome and time consuming. Moreover soil moisture status could be measured by the nucleonic neutron probe, which is accurate, but the initial cost is very high. The irrigations are scheduled after reaching specific values (0.5 to 0.6) of IW/CPE ratio. This cumulative Pan evaporation can be converted into number of days or interval in days between two irrigations.

(*iii*) *Climatological approach:* The climatological approach is categorised under empirical formulae. Penman (1968), Thornthwaite (1948), Blaney - Cirddle (1950), and Christiansen (1968) developed the formula for estimating potential evapotranspiration. These ETO values were subsequently used for determination of consumptive use (CU) and deciding schedule for water application. The USWB - class A pan evaporimeter was used on large scale. The pan factor was another parameter. The values of crop coefficient were tested with the help of lysimeter technique. Simple empirical quotient IW/CPE was used for scheduling purpose, where IW is the depth of irrigation, mm and CPE is the cumulative pan evaporation, mm. The reference ETO is defined as evapotranspiration rate of uniform 15 cm tall green alfa-alfa grass cover, actively growing, completely shading the ground when soil moisture existed at field capacity (not short of available water). Similarly, Kc refers to the ratio of ETc/ETo where ETc and ETo are actual evapotranspiration rate at a particular critical growth stage and reference evapotranspiration rate respectively. Some universal methods estimating evapotranspiration on the basis of meteorological parameters are given below:

Irrigation Method

The methods used for water application to crops or plantation crops have an important bearing on water management. These methods include the flooding (ridges and furrows, check basin and border irrigation) applying it beneath the soil surface or spraying it under pressure as well as by applying it on the surface or subsurface drop by drop. The conventional system of irrigation revolves around the concept of replenishing the moisture level to the field capacity (FC) after 50-60 per cent depletion. The system does not permit the restricting of water to meet the requirement at the root zone. It results into deep percolation losses or sometimes run off. The problems of water logging and soil salinity are reported in command areas. The crops have suffered serious moisture due to uneven distribution of water. This necessitates the use of modern irrigation methods which will irrigate the plant or the crops rather than whole field. The effective root zone is brought to field capacity by subsequent shallow ponding and advancement of water front in border or furrow basin. This is possible by adjusting the duration and the rate of stream size, the gradient, the soil structure, infiltration rate, and soil texture. The application efficiency of irrigation water is the relationship between the quantity of water that has wetted the effective root zone of the crop and the quantity of water released from the source. Water management refers to efficient use of water for best possible crop production. The term efficient use includes the optimization of water use and maximization of crop yields. The water losses either through deep percolation beyond the root zone and run off is to be minimized or avoided to the maximum extent. It is important to know the irrigable area, stream size, irrigation depth and opportunity time for uniform water application. Irrigation methods are classified under surface, subsurface and pressurized irrigation.

Micro Irrigation

The micro irrigation system consists of a network of pipes along with water filtration provisions and suitable emitting devices, which could maintain high frequency application of water in and around the root zone of plants as per daily net irrigation requirement (NIR) with very high irrigation efficiency (> 95%). The system is based on the fundamental concept of irrigating only the root zone of the crop, which would maintain excellent soil-water-plant relationship. The root zone is always kept at field capacity (FC) due to which the microbial activities are enhanced to the maximum extent with best aeration properties. The system is known to be able to achieve high water use efficiency (WUE), water saving to the extent of 70-80 per cent and increase in the quality and yield to the extent of 60 per cent. The conveyance and deep percolation loss beyond root zone are totally avoided. In conventional irrigation system, the crop/plant is subjected to moisture stress before irrigation and oxygen stress after irrigation.

Micro-irrigation refers to low-pressure irrigation systems that spray, mist, sprinkle or drip. The water discharge patterns differ because emission devices are designed for specific applications due to agronomic or horticultural requirements. Micro-irrigation components include: pipes, tubes, water emitting devices, flow control equipment, installation tools, fittings and accessories. For first time users, it can be a confusing array of components and gadgets. It can be a challenge to select the right type of system and assemble the components suitable for irrigation needs. A description of various micro irrigation systems, its many uses and limitations will help. The term 'micro irrigation' describes a family of irrigation systems that apply water through small devices.

These devices deliver water onto the soil surface very near the plant or below the soil surface directly into the plant root zone. Growers, producers and landscapers have adapted micro-irrigation systems to suit their needs for precision water application. Micro irrigation systems are immensely popular not only in arid regions and urban settings but also in sub humid and humid zones where water supplies are limited or water is expensive. In irrigated agriculture, micro irrigation is used extensively for row crops, mulched crops, orchards, gardens, greenhouses and nurseries. Micro irrigation works on a very simple efficiency principle: most water used in traditional irrigation (*i.e.,* hosing) methods is wasted. Micro irrigation sends water through tiny pipes to nozzles placed beneath the leaves, at the base of plants where the soil and roots are present.

Micro Irrigation Achievements

It is needless to say that our country was at crawling stage in 1980 when Israel, USA and Australia had achieved rapid progress in micro irrigation. The research on micro-irrigation was mostly initiated by: TNAU, Coimbatore, MPKV., Rahuri and WTC, IARI, New Delhi, Haryana State was leading for sprinkler irrigation on large scale due to sandy soils in Bhiwani district. A major boost to the drip irrigation technology came in India when a private corporation, Jain Irrigation System Ltd. (JISL) entered into this profession. Micro irrigation has received the government support when the Government of Maharashtra had declared the significant subsidy in 1988. The financial support was rendered subsequently by NCPA, NCPAH and Agriculture Ministry, Government of India. Few hundred hectares of micro irrigation mostly experimental areas has grown to few million hectares due to joint efforts of policy makers, scientists, technologists, NGOs and mostly over-whelming response from farmers. The famine and droughts have also taught us the lessons in spreading micro irrigation technology.

Emission Devices used in Micro Irrigation System

The actual application of water in a micro irrigation system is through an emitter. The emitter is a metering device made from plastic that delivers a small but precise discharge. The quantity of water delivered from these emitters is usually expressed in gallons per hour (gph). These emitters dissipate water pressure through the use of long-paths, small orifices or diaphragms. Some emitters are pressure compensating meaning they discharge water at a constant rate over a range of pressures. Emission devices deliver water in three different modes: drip, bubbler and micro-sprinkler. In drip mode, water is applied as droplets or trickles. In bubbler mode, water 'bubbles out' from the emitters. Water is sprinkled, sprayed, or misted in the micro-sprinkler mode. Emitters for each of these modes are available in several discharge increments. Some emitters are adapted to apply water to closely spaced crops planted in rows. Other emitters are used to irrigate several plants at once. There are emitters that apply water to a single plant.

Micro irrigation Systems Components

Irrigation pipeline systems are generally described as branching systems. Various branches are given names such as: main, sub-main, and lateral. Choosing the right size main, sub-main, and lateral pipe to match the flow rates from the water source is important. Basic components can include a pump and power unit, a backflow prevention device if chemicals are used with water, a filter, a water distribution system, and some devices for controlling the volume of water and pressure in the system. If the water source is from a city/municipal/rural water supply, a direct connection is possible.

(A) *Pumps and power unit*: Micro irrigation systems are typically designed to make the best use of the amount of water available. The type and size of pump selected will depend on the amount of water required, the desired pressure and the location of the pump relative to the distribution network. Electric power units or internal combustion engine driven pumps are equally adaptable. However, the electric power unit is preferred because it is easier to automate.

Electric/Diesel Pump

Solar Water Pump

(B) *Filters:* Filters remove sand and larger suspended particles before they enter the distribution network. However, the filters cannot remove dissolved minerals, bacteria and some algae. The three types generally used are screen, disk and sand filters.

(C) *Distribution lines*: The water distribution system is a network of pipes and tubes that can range in size from 1/2 inch to 6 inches in diameter. Water from the pump may be carried to the edge of the field by a single large main. Smaller sub-mains may then carry the water to laterals and ultimately to the emitters.

(D) *Control components*: The control portion may include a combination of the following devices: pressure regulator, valve, vacuum relief valve and timing clock or controller. A flow meter should be used to measure the amount of water. Pressure gauges monitor the water pressure at the pump and other locations. Equipment to inject fertilizers into the water line is also frequently used. Backflow prevention devices are used to prevent contamination of the water source.

1. *Drip Irrigation*: Depending on how the emitters are placed in the plastic polyethylene distribution line, the drip mode can be further delineated as a line source or a point source. The line source type emitters are placed internally in equally spaced holes or slits made along the line. Water applied from the close and equally spaced holes usually runs along the line and forms a continuous wetting pattern. This wetting pattern is suited for close row crops. The point source type emitters are attached external to the lateral pipe. The installer can select the desired location to suit the planting configuration or place them at equally spaced intervals. Water applied from the point source emitter usually forms a round deep wetting spot. The point source wetting pattern is suited for widely spaced plants in orchards, vineyards and for landscape trees or shrubs.

   (a) Line source emitter: Line source emitters are suitable for closely spaced row crops in fields and gardens. Line source emitters are available in two variations:

   - thin wall drip line;
   - thick wall drip hose.

A thin walled drip line has internal emitters molded or glued together at set distances within a thin plastic distribution line. The drip line is available in a wide range of diameters, wall thickness, and emitter spacing and flow rates. The emitter spacing is selected to closely fit plant spacing for most row crops. The flow rate is typically expressed in gallons per minute (gpm) along a 100-foot section. Drip lines are either buried below the ground or laid on the surface. Burial of the drip line is preferable to avoid degradation from heat and ultraviolet rays and displacement from strong winds. However, some specialized equipment to install and extract the thin drip distribution line is required.

(*b*) *Point source emitters*: Point source emitters are typically installed on the outside of the distribution line. Point source emitters dissipate water pressure through a long narrow path and a vortex chamber or a small orifice before discharging into the air. The emitters can take a predetermined water pressure at its inlet and reduce it to almost zero as the water exits. Some can be taken apart and manually cleaned. The typical flow rates range from 0.5 to 2.0 gph.

Advantages of Drip Irrigation

Today it is more important than ever to use water resources wisely and to irrigate intelligently. Consequently, many farmers have turned to drip irrigation and have enjoyed improved profitability by increasing crop yield and quality while at the same time reducing costs from water, energy, labor, chemical inputs and water runoff. Many landscapers have also enjoyed significant water and capital investment savings using drip irrigation, while simultaneously improving plant vigor by delivering water and nutrients directly to the plant roots and avoiding unnecessary wetting of plant leaves.

Drip irrigation System has Certain Specific Advantages

Water saving to the extent of 60 per cent as compared to traditional surface irrigation method. High water application efficiency. Increase in the yield to the extent of 25-30 per cent over traditional irrigation methods. Use of water soluble fertilizer, very high FUE with fertilizer saving to the extent of 25 to 30 per cent. Use of saline water is possible. Reducing inter-culturing and weeding cost.. Excellent soil health and maximum soil microbiological activities. Saving in labour cost, due to atomization. Excellent and cost effective for horticultural crops - widely spaced, low cost and long duration crop. Adoptable for undulating topography, variable soil types and all crops. Drip irrigation is the targeted, intelligent application of water, fertilizer, and chemicals that when used properly can provide great benefits such as:

- Increased Revenue from Increased Yields.
- Increased Revenue from Increased Quality.
- Decreased Water Costs.
- Decreased Labor Costs.
- Decreased Energy Costs.
- Decreased Fertilizer Costs.
- Decreased Pesticide Costs.
- Improved Environmental Quality.

Drip Irrigation System

Impact of drip irrigation on WUE and yield of okra:

Treatment	WUE(q/ha-cm)	Yield (q/ha)
T1(Drip irri. with V vol. of water)	4.24	120.21
T2(Drip irri. with 0.8V vol. of water)	5.52	120.51
T3(Drip irri. with 0.6V vol. of water)	7.37	120.32
T4(Surface irrigation)	1.61	90.21
T5(Drip irri. with V vol. of water + Plastic mulch)	4.78	130.53
T6(Drip irri. with 0.8V vol. of water+ Plastic mulch)	5.99	130.80
T7(Drip irri. with 0.6V vol. of water+ Plastic mulch)	8.30	140.16
T8(Surface irrigation + plastic mulch)	1.79	100.21

2. *Sprinkler Irrigation*: In sprinkler or overhead irrigation, water is piped to one or more central locations within the field and distributed by overhead

high-pressure sprinklers or guns. A system utilizing sprinklers, sprays, or guns mounted overhead on permanently installed risers is often referred to as a *solid-set* irrigation system. Higher pressure sprinklers that rotate are called *rotors* and are driven by a ball drive, gear drive, or impact mechanism. Rotors can be designed to rotate in a full or partial circle. Guns are similar to rotors, except that they generally operate at very high pressures of 40 to 130 lbf/in^2 (275 to 900 kPa) and flows of 50 to 1200 US gal/min (3 to 76 L/s), usually with nozzle diameters in the range of 0.5 to 1.9 inches (10 to 50 mm). Guns are used not only for irrigation, but also for industrial applications such as: dust suppression and logging.

Sprinklers can also be mounted on moving platforms connected to the water source by a hose. Automatically moving wheeled systems known as *traveling sprinklers* may irrigate areas such as: small farms, sports fields, parks, pastures, and cemeteries unattended. Most of these utilize a length of polyethylene tubing wound on a steel drum. As the tubing is wound on the drum powered by the irrigation water or a small gas engine, the sprinkler is pulled across the field. When the sprinkler arrives back at the reel the system shuts off. This type of system is known to most people as a 'water reel' traveling irrigation sprinkler and they are used extensively for dust suppression, irrigation, and land application of waste water. Other travelers use a flat rubber hose that is dragged along behind while the sprinkler platform is pulled by a cable. These cable-type travelers are definitely old technology and their use is limited in today's modern irrigation projects.

Micro-sprinkler Irrigation

Micro-sprinklers are emitters commonly known as sprinkler or spray heads. There are several types of emitters operate by throwing water through the air, usually in predetermined patterns. Depending on the water throw patterns, the micro-sprinklers are referred to as mini-sprays, micro-sprays, jets, or spinners. The sprinkler heads are external emitters individually connected to the lateral pipe typically using 'spaghetti tubing,' which is very small (1/8 inch to 1/4 inch) diameter tubing. The sprinkler heads can be mounted on a support stake or connected to the supply pipe. Micro-sprinklers are desirable because fewer sprinkler heads are necessary to cover larger areas. The flow rates of micro-sprinkler emitters vary from 3 gph to 30 gph depending on the orifice size and line pressure.

The cultivation of horticultural crops is more remunerative on the small terraces of upland areas, due to favourable climatic conditions. However, due to the non-availability of irrigation water, farmers grow rainfed cereals with very low yields. A check basin irrigation method involving high water losses is commonly used in the valley areas. Plant-to-plant hand watering, as used on a small scale in water-scarce upland areas, is commonly used water application method, but it requires a huge amount of labour. Drip irrigation can replace the hand watering system with minimum water losses and labour. Due to topographical advantages, the gravitational head may be used to operate the system, thus eliminating the initial and operational cost of pumping.

Establishing plants in arid lands is a challenging task even with supplemental irrigation. The low relative humidity, extreme temperatures, lack of consistent rainfall, tremendous rate of evaporation, and high wind speeds common in desert environments all play important and interrelated roles in water loss from soil and plants. Deterioration of water quality, drying up of groundwater and salt accumulation in the soil due to inadequate irrigation with saline water problems are often caused by irrigated agriculture in arid lands. Two methods seem to be effective to avoid those problems. One is to irrigate crop with drip irrigation with limited water and the other is to drain the excess water away. These factors make it critical that use of drip irrigation system to deliver water at the root zone of plants in order to maximize survival and growth.

Sprinkler Irrigation System

3. *Bubbler Irrigation*: Bubblers typically apply water on a 'per plant' basis. Bubblers are very similar to the point source external emitters in shape but differ in performance. Water from the bubbler head either runs down from the emission device or spreads a few inches in an umbrella pattern. The bubbler emitters dissipate water pressure through a variety of diaphragm materials and deflect water through small orifices. Most

bubbler emitters are marketed as pressure compensating. The bubbler emission devices are equipped with single or multiple port outlets. Most bubbler heads are used in planter boxes, tree wells, or specialized landscape applications where deep localized watering is preferable. The typical flow rate from bubbler emitters is between 2 and 20 gph.

Ultra-Low Rate Irrigation

Ultra-low rate irrigation, also known as irrigation, supplies water to the soil surface at an extremely low rate, lower than infiltration rate resulting in zero run-off. The rate may be 8-201/h for spitters/mini sprinklers (compared to 35-250 l/h in common for these types) and for dippers 0.15-0.41 l/h (compared to 2-10 l/h in common dippers). Water infiltrates in the soil at a low rates continuously through small pores around the soil particles. The plants under minute irrigation develop more vigorous and larger root system compared to plant irrigated by the regular micro irrigation method. The results in tomatoes and melons irrigated by minute irrigation exhibited much faster growth immediately after transplanting. Plants are healthier, high yields and significant water savings.

Fertigation System

Definition

It implies the application of fertilizers through pressurized systems; thus forming nutrient containing irrigation water desired concentration as per the crop need. Standard practice of fertilizer application in GH.

Advantages

- Fertilizer completely dissolved – no clogging of drippers and emitting pipes.
- Improving growth and productivity due to correct fertigation schedule.
- Nutrients applied as and when required to meet specific requirement of crop.
- No loss of nutrients (applied at root at rhizospere) through volatilization.
- Water soluble 3 major and micro nutrients can be supplied.
- Safer method of application of fertilizer; no leaf burning chance.
- Save water, labor, time, fertilizer (25-50%), energy and cost involvement.
- Incorporation of fungicides, pesticides and nematicides also possible.

Constraints

- Non-availability of water soluble fertilizer at reasonable rates.
- Lack of R&D efforts for developing fertilizers for fertigation.
- Inadequate policy of Government for promoting this technology.

Forms of Fertilizer Application

(A) *Liquid fertilizer*: Solutions which contain one or more plant nutrients in liquid or suspension form.

(B) *Water soluble fertilizer*: Present in a form which is completely soluble to water caring two or more major as well minor nutrients.

Suitable Conditions for Fertigation

Most suitable method drip irrigation system with rain water. Water having pH 5.5 to 6.5, EC less than 0.1, low level of carbonate, bicarbonate, sodium, chlorine is ideal.

Advantages of Micro-irrigation

- *Water savings:* Conveyance loss is minimal. Evaporation, runoff and deep percolation are reduced as compared to other traditional irrigation systems. A water supply source with limited flow rates such as: small water wells or city/rural water can be used.
- *Energy savings*: A smaller power unit is required compared to sprinkler irrigation systems.
- *Weed and disease reduction:* Because of limited wetted area from non-spray type of micro-irrigation, weed growth is inhibited and disease incidences reduced.
- *Can be automated:* Fertilizers and chemicals can be applied with water through the irrigation system. Micro-irrigation systems can be automated which reduces labor requirements.
- *Improved production on marginal land:* On hilly terrain, micro- irrigation systems can operate with no runoff and without interference from the wind. The fields need not be leveled.

Potential Problems

- *Management*: Micro irrigation systems normally have greater maintenance requirements. Soil particles, algae, or mineral precipitates can clog the emission devices.
- *Potential for damage*: Animals, rodents and insects may cause damage to some components. The drip and bubbler irrigation systems need additional equipment for frost protection.
- *High initial cost:* Micro-irrigation systems are ideal for high value installations such as: orchards, vineyards, greenhouses, and nurseries where traditional irrigation methods may not be practical. However, the investment cost can be high.

Future Strategies

- The system should be designed to suit the agro-climatic conditions of the area.
- Adequate extension activities and awareness programme should be taken regarding its utility, knowledge of application and method of operation and maintenance.
- Adequate infrastructure is required to augment the need of after sale service of the system, spares of the system and training to the farmers. The distribution networks needs to be strengthened particularly at rural areas.

- The fertilizer control order need to ensure be reviewed to the availability of liquid fertilizers.
- Extending financial support through NABARD/Government department.
- Ensuring product price.

Conclusion

Micro irrigation lets a person to have total control over what is watered in the garden; when; for how long; and with how much water. In our age of persistent resource concern, that's a reassuring promise. It means person can get more out of their plants for less water use - year round, with complete efficiency. The study shows that micro irrigation increases water saving and productivity of crops and that too with reduced cost of cultivation. While water saving due to adoption of drip irrigation is found in the range of 12-84 percent in different crops, the same is found to be in the range of 8-60 per cent in sprinkler irrigation method. Water saving is found to be relatively higher among the water-intensive crops like sugarcane, banana and vegetable crops Technology helps in conserving water and aid in good growth of plants. It also increases GDP. Micro irrigation removes excess water from agricultural land that can be used in other municipal or social purposes. Micro irrigation technology has been recognized as an answer to meet the increasing demands of water for irrigation efficiently. It ensures increase crop yield of higher quality by utilizing less water and energy.

Therefore, there is a need to find out the ways and means to convince the farmers about the economic and social feasibility of micro irrigation. Since it involves relatively higher amount of fixed investment, farmers often ask the questions such as: what will be the payback period? Whether investment will be viable? How much will be the water saving?. It appears that these questions arise mainly because of poor exposure about the social and economic advantages of drip technology. Thus, efforts are needed to convince the farmers through quality extension network, as India's highly successful green revolution was also the result of extension innovations as much as technology. Considering the fast decline of irrigation potential and competing demand for water from different sectors, all possible efforts are needed to increase the adoption of water saving technologies so as to avoid water scarcity in the future.

REFERENCES

Acharyna, M.S.; Singh, J; Gupta, A.P and Singh, A.K. (1993). "Economic Analysis of Sprinkler Irrigation in Southern Rajasthan", in CBIP (1993), Sprinkler and Drip Irrigation Systems, Central Board of Irrigation and Power, New Delhi, pp. 74-76. 31.

AERT and DSI (1988). Techno-Economic Feasibility Study of Drip Irrigation with Special Reference to Sugarcane, Agri-Energy Round Table (AERT), India and Deccan Sugar Institute (DSI), Pune.

AFC (1998). Evaluation of Drip Irrigation System, Agricultural Finance Corporation (AFC) Limited, Mumbai, October.

Bresler E, McNeal, B L, Carter, D L. (1982). Saline and Sodic Soils: Principles-Dynamics-Modeling. Springer-Verlag, Berlin Heidelberg.

Chadda, K.L., Choudhury, M.L. and Prasad, K.V. (2002). Hi-Tech. Horticulture. ICAR Publication, New Delhi. pp. 105-125.

CWC (2005). Water and Related Statistics. Ministry of Water Resources, Central Water Commission (CWC), Government of India, New Delhi.

INCID. (1994). Drip Irrigation in India. Indian National Committee on Irrigation and Drainage, New Delhi.

Iyer, Ramasamy, R. (2003). Water: Perspectives, Issues, Concerns, Sage Publications, New Delhi.

Keller, J and Bliesner R.D. (1990). Sprinkler and Trickle Irrigation. AVI, Van Nostrand Reinhold, New York.

Kulkarni, S.A. (2005). Looking Beyond Eight Sprinklers. Paper presented at the National Conference on Micro-Irrigation. G.B. Pant University of Agriculture and Technology, Patnagar, India, June 3-5, 2005.

Kundu, D.K; H.U. Neue and R. Singh (1998). Comparative Effects of Flooding and Sprinkler Irrigation on Growth and Mineral Composition of Rice in an Alfisol. Proceedings of the National Seminar on Micro Irrigation Research in India: Status and Perspective for the 21st Century, Bhubaneswar, July 27-28, 1998.)

Majumder, H.D. (2005). Orchard Irrigation and Soil Management Practices. Kalyani Publishers, Kolkata. pp. 1-64.

Postal, S., Polak, P., Gonzales, F., and Keller, J. (2001). Drip Irrigation for Small Farmers: A New Initiative to Alleviate Hunger and Poverty. Water International. Vol. 26, No. 1.

Rosegrant, W. Mark (1997). Water Resources in the Twenty-First Century: Challenges and Implications for Action, Food and Agriculture, and the Environment Discussion Paper 20, International Food Policy Research Institute, Washington D.C., U.S.A.

Saleth, R. Maria. (1996). Water Institutions in India: Economics, Law and Policy, Commonwealth Publishers, New Delhi.

Samuel, J.C. (2001). Micro Irrigation in Fruit Crops in India. Proceedings International Conference on Micro and Sprinkler Irrigation Systems, 8-9 February, 2000. Jalgaon, Maharashtra, India. pp. 281-293.

Seckler, D; R. Barker and U. A. Amarasinghe (1999). Water Scarcity in Twenty-First Century. *International Journal of Water Resources Development*. 15(1-2): 29-42.

Seckler, D; U. Amarasinghe; D. Molden; R. de Silva and R. Barker (1998). World Water Demand and Supply, 1990 to 2025: Scenarios and Issues, Research Report 19, International Water Management Institute, Colombo, Sri Lanka.

Singh, H.P. (2001). Emerging Scenario of Micro Irrigation in India. Proceedings International Conference on Micro and Sprinkler Irrigation Systems, 8-9 February, 2000. Jalgaon, Maharashtra, India. pp. 18-30.

Singh S.D. and Singh P. (1978). Value of Drip Irrigation Compared with Conventional Irrigation for Vegetable Production in a Hot arid Climate. *Agron J* 70: 945-947.

Spehia, R.S., Sharma, I.P. and Bharadwas, R.K. (2010). Cost Economies and Effect of Drip Irrigation on Yield and Water-use Efficiency of okra under mulch and non-mulch Conditions in Mid-Hills of Himachal Pradesh. *Haryana J. Horti. Sci.* 39(1&2): 161-164 (2010).

Suryawanshi, P. (1995). Pre-liminary Studies on Drip vs basin Method of Irrigation in Maharashtra. *Journal of Maharashtra Agrilculture University.*, 16,39-48.

Vaidyanathan, A.; A. Krishnakumar; A. Rajagopal and D. Varatharajan (1994). "Impact of Irrigation on Productivity of Land", *Journal of Indian School of Political Economy*, Vol. 6, No. 4, October-December, pp. 601-645.

Vaidyanathan, A. (1998). Water Resource Management: Institutions and Irrigation Development in India, Oxford University Press, New Delhi.

Vasantdada Sugar Institute (VSI) (1998). Proceedings of the National Seminar on Irrigation Water Management for Sugarcane, VSI, Pune, 5-6 June.

Venugopal, R. and M. Rajkumar (1998). 'Drip Irrigation System – New Concept in Sugarcane Culture at Baramba of Orissa State", in VSI, pp. III 7-III 12.

Varma, C.V.J., and Rao, A.R.G. (Eds.) (1998). Micro Irrigation and Sprinkler Irrigation Systems, Central Board of Irrigation and Power, New Delhi.

Varma, C.V.J. and A.R.G. Rao (Eds.) (1998) Proceedings: Workshop on Micro Irrigation and Sprinkler Irrigation Systems, Central Board of Irrigation and Power, New Delhi. World.

Bank (1991). Irrigation Sector Review, Vol. I and II, Report No. 9518-IN, The World Bank, Washington D.C., December.

Page 66-86

FARMING TECHNIQUES AND CROP PRODUCTION
Edited by : Dr. Alka Chauhan; Dr. Anubhuti Sharma & Jaswant Ray
Edition : 2017
ISBN : 978-93-5056-855-2
Published by : Discovery Publishing House Pvt. Ltd., New Delhi (India)

4 Cultivation Scenario of Freshwater Fish Exotic *Anabas Testudineus* and Combined Farming of Giant Prawn and Tiger Shrimp

Subrato Ghosh & Himadri Chandra*

Abstract

Normal/native Anabas testudineus takes more time to attain marketable size and its small size is less fit for sustainable production per unit area in pond culture system. Thai strain of A. testudineus is accepted to be genetically superior to the native/ normal strain; growth rate of Thai strain is much higher, attaining 80-100gm size within 3-4 months. Fish farmers in Bangladesh are very much interested for its culture. Since 2009, huge availability of Thai A. testudineus (Thai koi) in fish markets of Tripura have been noticed, and some farmers in North 24 Parganas in West Bengal have started its farming. Since 2011, fish farmers in WB particularly in Hili Block of Dakshin Dinajpur district have started farming of the 'Vietnam koi' or the Vietnam strain of A. testudineus. Farming of freshwater fishes Thai koi and Vietnam koi are not yet permitted by State Fisheries Department in West Bengal, nor has been recommended by any technical officer. Morphological differences between the native koi, Thai koi and Vietnam koi and the pond culture practices of exotic koi in Bangladesh and West Bengal have been described in this communication. Interestingly, a farmer in East Midnapore district of WB has succeeded in farming of Scampi and tiger shrimp together in the same environment. An account of it is also presented here.

INTRODUCTION: Biology of Native *Anabas testudineus*

Climbing perch *Anabas testudineus* (Order: Perciformes, Family: Anabantidae) is one of the most popular aquaculture species among Small Indigenous Fishes, also significant in terms of heritage and culture of both

122/1V, Monohar Pukur Road, P.O. Kalighat, Kolkata - 700 026.

rural and urban West Bengal, other parts of Eastern India like: Assam, Bihar, Orissa, Tripura, Manipur, also in Andhra Pradesh, Kerala and Bangladesh. This fish is considered as a valuable component of diet for sick/weak health persons and patients recovering from fever and diseases. It contains high values of physiologically available iron and copper essentially needed for haemoglobin synthesis (Saha, 1971). *A. testudineus* fetches high market price; it is becoming a highly demandable fish in international and domestic markets day-by-day due to its high nutrition, good taste and flavour, good growth and having ability to withstand considerable unfavourable environmental condition in their habitat; both natural waters and culture ponds (Alam *et al.* 2006). *A. testudineus* is encountered only occasionally in Hooghly estuarine system in West Bengal and its contribution in the Hooghly freshwater zone fishery are negligible. Main supply of the fish comes from beels and wetlands. It is highly esteemed for high nourishing quality and prolonged longevity and freshness out of water. *A. testudineus* is popular for its soft meat, which contain easily digestible protein, fat of very low melting point and many essential amino acids making them an ideal nutritious food. Its muscle protein content is 19.50 per cent. It is known to effectively control larvae of *Aedes* sp. mosquitoes. Males and females attain their first sexual maturity when they grow to 11.3gm and 12.2gm in weight and 8.0cm and 8.2cm in body length respectively (Khan and Mukhopadhyay, 1972).

Fecundity has been estimated to be: 10,002 for a 9.8cm sized specimen, 14,560 for a 13cm and 36,477 for a 16.9cm sized specimen. Fertilized eggs are 0.55-0.80mm in diameter. Maturity occurs at the age of one year when the fishes reach a size of 10-12cm in total length (Bhuiyan *et al.* 2000). Females have light brown colour on body and pelvic fins, which turn deep brown during breeding season. Matured male acquires a reddish shade/tinge on the body, particularly on the pectoral and ventral fins. A distinct diamond-shaped black spot appears in the caudal peduncle of males and they acquire glazy black colour during breeding season (from pre- to post-monsoon months). The relative length of the gut of *A. testudineus* (gut length divided by total length of the body) has been estimated to be 0.63 (Dasgupta, 2004). *A. testudineus* ('koi' in Bengali vernacular) was found to suffer from the disease Lymphocystis in sewage-fed culture ponds, detected from proliferous growth of binding tissues on the fins as well as on body proper. Lymphocystis can be cured by the application of terramycin or sulphadiazine with supplementary feed (Dehadrai *et al.* 1985). This fish has a tendency to walk away from the pond during rains; it migrates from one pond to another with the help of their sharp gill plates during rainy season for spawning and return to the permanent water bodies at the onset of dry season. It attains a maximum of 9 inches in length, and can gain upto 52gm body weight in one year.

Pond Culture

Aquaculture production of native *A. testudineus* is increasing very rapidly in Eastern India and some parts of Bangladesh (Belton *et al.* 2011). Cultivation of this fish is possible in small seasonal ponds, reservoirs and rice fields. It can be grown in combination with carp fingerlings of over 10cm size. In polyculture system of *Clarias batrachus*, *Heteropneustes fossilis* and *A. testudineus* (maintained at 2:2:1) in small shallow ponds at a stocking density of 40,000-70,000 fingerlings/ha (10-14gm size), *A. testudineus* has been found to attain body weight of 75-100gm in 9-10 months of culture, and 915-2250kg/ha production of this fish was obtained in 10-12 months with supplementary feed comprising of flat rice/rice bran, mustard oil cake and silkworm pupae. Fish meal and rice bran (2:1) mixture may alternatively be used @ 3-5 per cent of body weight daily. In India, there is a report of *A. testudineus* production of 1,800kg/ha in 170 days of culture by applying mixture of rice bran, mustard oil cake and fish meal as supplementary feed, with a stocking density of 60,000nos./ha (Thakur and Das, 1986). Presently in North 24 Pgs., West Bengal, *A. testudineus* seeds of size 22-24mm stocked @ 8nos./sq.mt attain marketable size of 50-60gm within 4.5-5 months of culture. The fish accepts artificial feeds compounded with protein-rich items such as: fish meal, defatted silkworm pupae, chicken feed, soyabean meal, groundnut oil cake and rice bran, wheat flour or sodium alginate may be used as binder.

Breeding and Larval Rearing

In India, climbing perch has been successfully induced-bred by hormonal treatment at CIFRI (ICAR), Barrackpore. Fifteen sets of *A. testudineus* could be bred, yielding about 46,500 hatchlings. Because of their cannibalistic nature, it is said that only 500 fingerlings survived and attained an average length of 65mm and an average weight of 5.54gm in nurseries during seven months of rearing. Depending on the length (100-164mm) and weight (24-77gm) of the fish, the fecundity was found to vary from 10,710 to 36,477 ova (Devaraj, 1975). Captive breeding of normal/native *A. testudineus* has been conducted with Wova-FH (Sarkar *et al.* 2005); it has been suggested that Wova-FH at the dose of 0.3ml/kg body weight of fish to both sexes is effective which might be considered for raising captive population of *A. testudineus*. Scientists at CIFA (ICAR), Bhubaneswar have succeeded in inducing early and extended breeding of normal *A. testudineus* from February to August using Ovaprim @ 1.5ml/kg body weight to both males and females (Kumar *et al.* 2010).

Exotic Variety *A. testudineus*: Thai koi

Thai climbing perch (*Anabas testudineus*, Thai variety) is an indigenous, delicious, high quality fish species of Thailand being cultured by the farmers in commercial scale also. This species with accessory respiratory organs can be farmed at high stocking density and in relatively poor water quality. Recently, there were some studies conducted with this species with successful technical production (Yakupitiyage *et al.* 1998; Doolgindachabaporn, 1994; Trieu and Long, 2001; Tuan *et al.* 2002) and enough stockable-sized seeds could be produced for fish farmers.

Growth rate of the normal/native *A. testudineus* is slow, taking more time to attain marketable size and its small size does not favour sustainable production per unit area in a culture system (Kohinoor *et al.* 2009). It is much slow in growth in comparison to the other climbing perch 'Thai variety *A. testudineus*'. Thai variety *A. testudineus* was first brought in Bangladesh in 2000 by Talukdar Farm at Rupganj. For commercial aquaculture, it was first introduced in Bangladesh from Thailand in 2002 (BFRI, 2006; Kohinoor *et al.* 2012), which is recognized as a distinct strain of *A. testudineus*. In that year, private entrepreneurs first imported seeds of growing exotic *A. testudineus* strain from Thailand. Effective result was obtained in induced breeding of this Thai strain at Brahmaputra Fish Seed Complex in Shambhuganj, Mymensingh district in 2004. The name *A. testudineus* is widely used for both the native/normal and Thai strains of climbing perch. Morphologically, spots on body surface are present in the Thai variety *A. testudineus* but those are 100 per cent absent in normal/native *A. testudineus*. In the native species, colour at the pelvic fin region has been observed to be yellowish (63.3%) or whitish to yellowish (36.7%), but in Thai variety it is only whitish (46.2%) or whitish to yellowish (53.8%). Thai variety *A. testudineus* do not show yellowish colour at pelvic fin region even in mature stage. Numbers of spines in anal fin in the native species and Thai variety are 10 and 9 respectively (Biswas and Shah, 2011).

Importance of Thai koi

- Thai strain of *A. testudineus* is accepted to be genetically superior to the native/normal strain; it attains a larger size than native *A. testudineus* in culture ponds.
- It is nutritive, regarded as a good food to curing patients. The fish flesh has easily digestible essential amino acids and lipid. It contains higher level of Vitamin-A, iron, copper; regarded as the precursor for haemoglobin formation.
- It can be marketed in live condition and can be cultivated in higher density.

In Bangladesh, mainly two morphological forms of *A. testudineus* are present: the wild *A. testudineus* (native) and the Thai variety (introduced from Thailand). Hybrid strains have also been developed in Bangladesh (Biswas and Shah, 2009). In Bangladesh, hatchery seed production technology of this native/normal strain has been developed at Bangladesh Fisheries Research Institute, but more importance and preference is given to seed production of the Thai variety. The Freshwater Station of Bangladesh Fisheries Research Institute has developed the induced breeding technique of the exotic climbing perch, *i.e.* Thai variety *A. testudineus* (Kohinoor and Zaher, 2006).

Morphological differences between local/native *A. testudineus* and Thai variety *A. testudineus* are presented below:

Native *A. testudineus*	Thai Variety *A. testudineus*
1. Comparatively smaller in size, less fleshy, body elongated and laterally compressed.	Comparatively larger, more fleshy and body is flat.
2. In younger condition, body colour is dark to pale greenish, on maturity it attains light green on dorsal side and pale yellow on belly.	Body colouration is pale grey compared to local variety. Many small black spots present on lateral sides of body and the fins are light yellow.
3. Black spots present on back side of the gill cover and no black spots on the base of pelvic fins.	Black spots present on both sides of the gill cover and on the base of pelvic fins.
4. Mouth anterior, small and 'V' shaped.	Mouth large, spread and 'U' shaped, operculum is soft in comparison to that of native *A. testudineus.*
5. Fin rays are very strong, irregular and sharp. engraved.	Fin rays are comparatively soft, regular and
6. Design of scale is 'V' shaped in caudal portion.	Design of scale is 'U' shaped in caudal portion.

During breeding season, the highest GnSI value of male Thai variety *A. testudineus* was found to be 7.54±9.10 in May and the lowest was 0.64±0.07 in April. For females, GnSI was highest in June (9.71±5.07) and lowest in April (2.54±0.18). GnSI values indicate that native/normal male *A. testudineus* gets highest maturity of testis in June and male Thai *A. testudineus* in May. Female native species gets highest maturity of ovary in May and the Thai variety in June. In ovaries of Thai variety *A. testudineus*, maximum numbers of oocytes occurring in mature stage are observed in June, indicating its peak breeding season (Biswas Ulka *et al.* 2012). In northern region of Bangladesh, there are many ditches and small ponds which retain water only for 4-6 months and are used for various household works. These seasonal water bodies have potentialities for intensive culture of species like: Thai variety *A. testudineus.* Out of thirty commercial hatcheries in three upazilas Gouripur, Trisal and Sadar in Mymensingh district, eight hatcheries produce seeds of major carps and Thai variety *A. testudineus*, rest produce seeds of monosex tilapia *Oreochromis niloticus*, Indian major carps and Thai pangas *Pangasianodon hypophthalmus* (Faruq *et al.* 2012).

The rapid increase in aquaculture output in Bangladesh since 2003 has been partly based on species diversification, one of which is the introduction of this Thai strain of climbing perch. It has high market price compared to other species and can be cultured with other catfishes like: *Clarias batrachus*, *Heteropneustes fossilis* and *Mystus cavasius*. As the intensive culture of Thai variety *A. testudineus* is gaining popularity in Bangladesh, fish farmers are facing problems due to the high price of commercial pelleted feeds. Fish farmers can use a mixture of protein concentrate, and meat and bone meal (1:1) to substitute fish meal upto 75 per cent level in the diet of *A. testudineus* to reduce the cost of production without compromising fish growth (Hossain *et al.* 2013).

Improved Growth Rate

The high growth rate and bigger size of Thai variety *A. testudineus* instigate the fish farmers to become enthusiastic for its artificial breeding and culture in Bangladesh (Hasan *et al.* 2010). Presently, the Thai variety is getting more popularity than the native/normal strain as the growth rate of Thai strain is much higher, which attains 80-100gm size within 3-4 months. Culture of this Thai variety has started to meet the demand of consumers. In Bangladesh, culture of native/normal *A. testudineus* has not yet been flourished. Fry collection of native *A. testudineus* strain from natural sources is difficult; therefore fish farmers in Bangladesh stock Thai climbing perch strain in their aquaculture ponds. Farmers prefer to stock Thai variety because it enjoys a higher consumer preference and market value. The Thai variety *A. testudineus* is presently used for production purposes by large number of farmers in that country (Kohinoor *et al.* 2012). As mentioned earlier, this exotic strain has some exceptional characteristics such as: faster growth rate, larger size at harvest, shorter culture period and higher survival rate (Mahmood *et al.* 2004).

Marginal fish farmers in Bangladesh are very much interested for its culture due to its high growth rate and better return in comparison to other species. Considering the culture potentials very recently, a sharp increasing trend has been observed on culture of this Thai variety *A. testudineus* in some selected areas of Bangladesh, particularly it is predominant in Mymensingh and Gazipur districts. Newly hatched larvae are normally fed formulated nursery feed, comprising egg yolk, maize powder and rice polish powder. When they attain average body weight of 1.5gm, they are stocked in culture ponds. From an initial body weight of 1.50±0.46gm at stocking and stocking density of 1,50,000nos/ha, the fishes were found to attain mean body weight and length of 59.73±4.22gm and 12.75±1.50cm respectively on 105th day of culture in 33 decimal pond (Adhikary *et al.* 2009). Commercially available pelleted feed with 35.5 per cent protein on wet weight basis was provided to them. A study carried out in Thailand in nursery practices exhibited that survival rate of climbing perch nursed in the hapa enclosures was high (89.3-91.4%). Using supplementary feed with high protein level (40%), it proved to have low FCR (1.28) and improved the growth rate of climbing perch (Van and Hoan, 2009).

Culture of Thai *A. testudineus* and Production Rate in Bangladesh

Generally a two-pond culture system is recommended. First 1 inch-sized fry are stocked in a small pond of 0.24-0.32ha @ 500000 fry/ha and reared for

20 days. Water depth is maintained about 4-5 feet. Subsequently the fry are transferred to a second pond and stocked @ 125000-250000nos./ha. Before stocking, 25000gm flour/ha area is added to the pond water to facilitate growth of zooplankton. Commercially available grower feed (floating type, with 30% protein) is effective for culture of Thai variety *A. testudineus*, which is applied thrice a day. The feeding schedule is maintained accordingly: crumble-type feed for 1st 10 days and 2nd 10 days @ 50 per cent and 30 per cent of body weights respectively; starter-type feed for 3rd 10 days, 4th 10 days and 5th 10 days @ 20 per cent, 15 per cent and 10 per cent of body weights respectively; grower-type feed for 6th 10 days and 7th 10 days and onwards till harvest @ 5 per cent and 3 per cent of body weights respectively. Normally, they attain 90-100gm at the end of 120 days of culture. Harvested fishes weighing more than 85gm fetch high market price (Waheduzzaman, 2006).

Production performance of Thai variety *A. testudineus* in culture ponds of 50-60 decimal under different stocking densities have been studied in a 90-day period. Fry of size 4.8-5.2gm have been stocked @ 350, 400 and 550 individuals per decimal water body. Supplementary diet containing 34 per cent protein was applied initially @ 20 per cent of total fish weight per day; feeding rate was gradually reduced to 15, 12, 10, 8 and 5 per cent of total fish weight per day. At time of harvest, body weights attained by fishes individually were found to be 90.03±0.04gm, 87.73±0.95gm and 84.15±0.49gm in ponds stocked @ 87500, 100000 and 137500 individuals per hectare area respectively. Body lengths attained by fishes individually were found to be 14.95±0.07cm, 14.30±0.28cm and 13.55±0.07cm respectively. Growth of fish at the end of three months was observed to be higher in ponds with lower stocking density than in ponds with higher stocking density. But the average total production was higher in highly stocked ponds than in ponds with lower stocking density. Those were 4,037kg/acre, 2,872kg/acre and 3,132kg/acre in ponds stocked @ 87500, 100000 and 137500 individuals per hectare area respectively. The ponds with a stocking density of 137500 fry per hectare were recognized to be the most profitable culture system. If 137500 fry of Thai variety *A. testudineus* are stocked per hectare water area in grow-out ponds, it will yield a good production to fish farmers in Asian countries (Jannat-Most *et al.* 2012). This exotic fish attain body length and weight of 14.66cm and 57.22gm in 50 days from fry stage when reared in ponds and fed hand-made supplementary feed (Noor, 2005).

In ponds of average area 0.006ha with depth of 1-1.3mt, fingerlings of Thai *A. testudineus* (6.15-6.67gm weight) were stocked @ 50,000, 75,000 and 1,00,000nos./ha as three culture conditions. A floating pelleted type feed containing 35 per cent protein was applied twice daily; the fingerlings were fed @ 14 per cent of their body weight for the first three weeks and it was reduced to 4 per cent from the subsequent weeks. In a culture period of five months, the mean body weights (individual) attained by the fishes were

102.63±9.03gm (93% survivability), 85.35±11.99gm (81% survivability) and 74.57±15.44gm (74% survivability) in ponds with stocking densities of 50,000, 75,000 and 1,00,000nos./ha respectively. Production rate of harvested fishes had been 4800.40±348.09kg/ha, 5279.61±914.39kg/ha and 5582.23kg/ha in the three successive culture conditions respectively (Rahman *et al.* 2013). Production rate of native/normal *A. testudineus* is generally much lower than this amount. In monoculture condition, the production of native *A. testudineus* has been observed to be 1916±125kg/ha in 5 months, when the stocking density was 50,000 individuals/ha (Kohinoor *et al.* 2009).

In another study, Thai variety *A. testudineus* collected from Thailand of average body weight 68.20±4.29gm were stocked in ponds and reared till they attain brood stock size. Induced breeding was performed during March-May 2009. Seeds (fry stage: 1.13±0.28gm) were stocked in culture ponds at a stocking density of 62,500 fry/ha. After stocking, supplementary feeding was done with floating pelleted feed containing 30 per cent crude protein @ 4-10 per cent of body weight twice daily. After 120 days of rearing, the fishes were harvested from ponds. Mean body weight at harvest was recorded to be 69.25±11.35gm. Gross fish production was 4,051±185kg/ha. Comparison was performed on growth of Thai variety *A. testudineus* with native/normal *A. testudineus;* fry of size 1.09±0.30gm of the latter were stocked in same stocking density and at the end of culture period of 120 days, mean body weight of the native species was recorded to be 33.38±8.74gm. Its gross production was 1,733±168.47kg/ha, much lower than that of Thai variety (Kohinoor *et al.* 2012). In a culture duration of 150 days, Thai *A. testudineus* production to the tune of 6,480-6,617kg/ha could be obtained; initial stocking of fry had been maintained at three densities from 50,000 to 1,25,000nos./ha (Kohinoor *et al.* 2007).

For getting higher growth rate in grow-out ponds, at least 35 per cent protein-rich supplementary feed should be provided to Thai variety *A. testudineus*. The feed may be prepared by mixing fish meal (50%), soyabean meal (10%), wheat bran (20%), corn meal or rice bran (10%) and mustard oil cake (10%).

Arrival of Thai *A. testudineus* in India

Since 2009, huge appearance and availability of Thai variety *A. testudineus* (Thai koi) in fish markets of Tripura have been noticed, which was mostly imported from Bangladesh both in live and frozen (iced) form, which in turn reduced the market rate of the fish. The selling price of native/local variety of *A. testudineus* (standard size of 40-60gm) in live condition is around Rs. 400-500/- per kg which are mostly collected from natural water bodies. Selling rates of Thai koi in live and in iced conditions are Rs. 200-300/- and Rs. 100-200/- per kg respectively. Those are imported from Bangladesh which is affordable for the normal/semi-elite consumers. Not much difference was perceived in taste between the local and Thai varieties of *A. testudineus* and hence was preferred by the consumers. Thai variety *A. testudineus* is also being gradually supplied to other north-eastern states specially Assam from the same source.

Culture of Thai koi in India

Though originated, cultured and bred in Thailand and subsequently cultured in Bangladesh with success and popularity and with good market demand, however till date Indian fish farmers are not well acquainted with the Thai variety of *A. testudineus*; rather the farmers and consumers misunderstood it and popularly termed it as 'hybrid koi'. As great deal of advancement has not been made in commercial seed production and culture of local variety of *A. testudineus* in India, hence market arrival of the fish is limited and mostly from natural sources. Major hurdle faced by the interested farmers is the non-availability of seed in adequate quantity required for monoculture. Based on the spectacular success exhibited by the Bangladeshi farmers in breeding, seed production and cultivation of Thai koi and arrival of the same regularly in niche markets, interested farmers of Tripura and adjoining states have started obtaining stockable-sized seeds of Thai variety *A. testudineus* from Bangladesh and adopted monoculture practices of this special exotic fish from the year 2012 with varied success level. Farmers are using formulated commercial carp feed for the Thai koi due to non-availability of koi-specific formulated feed. However farmers are also using farm-made mash feed with higher animal protein. Hatchery for Thai *A. testudineus* is yet to be established in India.

Body fat is produced after they attain seven months in age and above 250gm body weight, that is why younger Thai *A. testudineus* of 90-100gm body weight is somewhat inferior in taste in comparison to native *A. testudineus*, which attains body fat at 40-50gm size. In words of renowned fish farmer Sri Bablu Kumar Ghosh, whose residence is very near to Rajendrapur-Battala fish seed market in Naihati, presently at the renowned Rajendrapur-Battala fish seed market in Naihati, Dist. 24 Pgs. North, West Bengal, four licensed seed traders out of above 500 traders in the seed market are selling seeds of Thai variety *A. testudineus* after obtaining the same from seed traders of Bangladesh. Those are sold at individual size of 500mg in weight (2000 pieces weighing 1kg) and 22-24mm in length, selling price being Rs. 4/- per piece. If such fry stage of Thai variety *A. testudineus* is stocked in culture ponds (with fencing on all sides, provision of outlet channel, water depth maximum three feet initially beginning from one foot) @ 5nos./sq.mt. (it can be increased to 10-12nos./sq.mt.), then it will attain 250-275gm body weight at the end of 7-8 months of culture duration in West Bengal conditions. Commercially prepared pelleted feed (containing GNOC, omega-3 fatty acid, fish meal and other ingredients) has to be provided to them, containing 33 per cent protein costing Rs. 90/- per kg. A home-made pelleted feed may be prepared and fed to growing Thai *A. testudineus*, which will cost Rs. 65/- per kg. A progressive fish farmer at Barasat, Dist. 24 Parganas North has initiated this practice of Thai koi farming since 2009 in addition to grow-out farming of normal/native *A. testudineus*. For both native and Thai koi, he is stocking seeds @ 8nos./sq.mt. He has procured native koi seeds from Rajendrapur-Battala fish seed market @ 80-150 paisa per piece (200-250mg weight; 18mm length).

Introduction of Vietnam Variety *Anabas testudineus* in West Bengal

Since 2011, some fish farmers in West Bengal particularly in Hili Block of Dakshin Dinajpur district have started farming of yet another species - it is the 'Vietnam koi' or the Vietnam variety of *A. testudineus* (Sri Amrita Das, pers. comm.). It has also gained popularity in Patiram Gram Panchayat of Balurghat Block in same district. Remarkably it has been reported to attain 400-450gm body weight in ponds. During July-August 2012, a progressive fish farmer in Kushmandi Block of Dakshin Dinajpur district had procured 0.5 inch sized seeds of Vietnam koi from a seed trader in Hili Block, 1000 pieces costing Rs. 400/-. He had procured total 45000 seeds and stocked in a 1acre cultivable pond. In addition to CP brand pelleted feed, he used to prepare a home-made supplementary feed mixture comprising boiled Suji (3kg), fish meal (1kg), salt and boiled broken rice (1kg). He used to provide 10kg feed for every 100kg fish everyday, in two installments once in 12 hours. In four month period, his fishes attained 100gm body weight and within 7-8 months of culture, fishes weighed 275gm on an average with 80 per cent survivability and 15-20 per cent of the fishes were observed to attain 400-450gm body weight.

At Rajendrapur-Battala fish seed market in Naihati, seeds of Vietnam koi are available; each seed of 500mg size (2000 pieces weighing 1kg) are sold at Rs. 0.80-1.20/-. In North 24 Parganas, for short time and longer duration of culture period, farmers stock such seeds in pond @ 15 piece/sq.mt and 8 piece/sq.mt respectively. Three types of feed are fed in succession to the growing stages @ 15 per cent of total body weight daily: crumble-type pelleted feed (Rs. 98/- per kg), 1mm diameter pelleted feed (Rs. 68/- per kg) and 2mm diameter floating pellet (Rs. 48/- per kg). In this district, farmers have reported body weight of Vietnam koi to be 125-150gm at the end of 5-6 months of culture and 350-450gm at the end of eight months. Since it is a highly-priced fish, it is sold in lesser quantity in retail markets in comparison to major carps; progressive farmers as beginners in Vietnam koi farming are buying lesser quantity of seeds from Rajendrapur-Battala fish seed market. Seed traders in the market will be able to sell 1,00,000 seeds of Vietnam koi in one month period. In South 24 Parganas, recently two farmers from villages namely Canning and Muipith (Kultali) have procured 7000 pieces and 2000 pieces of Vietnam koi seeds respectively from the market. Partial harvesting of the bigger ones is done first from ponds; a high amount of produce of Vietnam koi after harvest cannot be sold at one time, so periodic harvesting is done in small quantity.

Farmers of Hili Block (adjacent to Bangladesh border and connected by roadway), Dakshin Dinajpur, West Bengal procure seeds (10-12mm stage) from hatchery owners of nearby Mymensingh and Bogura districts of Bangladesh in oxygen-packed containers and rear them to advanced fry stage of 1.5 inches. These are then sold to interested fish farmers of this state in nearby and distant places at Rs. 3/- per piece. A fish farmer of Trimohini village of this Block had procured 1,20,000 pieces Vietnam koi seeds (0.25gm individual weight; 5000 pieces weighing 1kg, 50-60paisa per seed) in oxygen-packed condition from a Bangladeshi person and stocked in his 0.26ha pond having water exchange facility. With 75 per cent survivability, he could obtain 8000kg marketable size Vietnam koi from his pond at the end of three months of culture, with 100-120gm body weight attained by the fishes. Out of the entire harvest, 5-8 per cent attained 300-320gm body weight. If seeds of Vietnam koi of 250mg body weight are first reared in nurseries for 20-25 days period, they will be about 2.5 inches in length (with 150-200nos. weighing 1kg) and after that they should be stocked in grow-out ponds. In such a condition, there will be 90-95 per cent survivability at time of harvest in three months and fishes will weigh 100-150gm that will fetch a price of Rs. 200/- per kg and above. If reared for another three months, they will weigh 350-450gm. For the first 8-10 days, fishes will be fed mash (dust-type) feed of CP brand @ 100 per cent of body weight daily, it will have 38 per cent protein content and each 10kg sack costs Rs. 970/-. With more gain in weight, Vietnam koi will not grow in length but will be thick and body will be elliptical.

From 2012 onwards, farming of Vietnam koi has gained popularity in Dakshin Dinajpur and 24 Parganas districts. Another farmer in Hili Block stated that his fishes attained 150-200gm body weight within 72 days of culture. In words of farmers, seeds of 250mg weight should be stocked in ponds of size 0.4ha @ 250000-300000 pieces per ha. Water level should not exceed 2.5 feet. After the first one month of culture, 20-30 per cent water replacement has to be done at an interval of 15-20 days. Normally 1 lakh seeds are stocked in every 0.4ha pond. Boiled broken rice is good feed ingredient for Vietnam koi. Under good management practice, 2 inch sized seeds will attain almost 150gm body weight in three months. For every 100kg fish, 4kg pelleted feed should be provided and in the last month, it will be 2.5kg. Farmers are using pelleted feed of successive sizes: 0.8mm (Growmax), 1.2mm (Growel/Growfin), 1.8mm, 2.5mm (Growfin), 4mm (Growmax Nutrila) and 6mm. Another farmer in Hili belt has specified his feeding schedule of Vietnam koi with renowned CP Brand feed:

CP Feed Code	Period (days)	Mean Body Weight (gm)	Feeding Rate (%)	Frequency of Meals/day
9001	1-20	0.3-2.7	50-10	6
9001 and 9910S	21-30	2.7-8	10-7	4
9910S and 9910L	31-40	8-15	7-6	4
9910L	41-50	15-25	6	4
9910L	51-60	25-40	5.5	4
9910L	61-70	40-60	5	4
9951	71-80	60-80	4.5	3
9951	81-90	80-100	4	3

Distinguishing features of Thai koi and Vietnam koi are presented hereunder:

Vietnam koi	Thai koi
1. Prominent black circular blotch present near the origin of caudal fin and deep black mark (mole) on the edge of operculum.	No such black distinguishing marks present.
2. Body is elliptical-shaped, much bigger in size than Thai koi, may attain 400-450gm weight.	Body is lengthier, thinner in comparison to Vietnam koi, attains maximum 250gm body weight.
3. Body colour is faint golden or greenish-red, resembling native/normal *A. testudineus.*	Small black spots present all over body, body is blackish.
4. Upper lip and snout is slightly downturned and inferior.	Snout is straight.
5. During lightning, roaring of clouds and drizzle, fishes will not move out from culture pond (only gravid females of above 450gm will move out).	Fishes under culture will definitely escape out from pond on cloudy days.
6. It attains marketable size within 100 days.	It attains marketable size in 120-135 days.

Now we arrive in concluding remarks. In Bangladesh, Sharnalata Agro Fisheries Limited has introduced Vietnam koi *Anabas testudineus* in 2010 which has a very fast growth rate than Thai koi (Hosen, 2014). Although the Thai koi is presently used for production purposes by large number of farmers in Bangladesh but it is not widely accepted by consumers owing to its gray-coloured body, small black spots and lack of taste in comparison to native *A. testudineus*. To improve this situation, the other variety of koi 'Vietnamese *A. testudineus*' have been imported from Vietnam; which is believed to give higher production and faster growth than Thai koi. A recent Bangladeshi report made known that Vietnamese koi grows as big as 250-300gm within 4 months culture period with a good FCR and similar body color as native koi.

A comparison on the growth rates of native koi, Thai koi and Vietnam koi is mentioned below:

Culture Period and Stocking Density	Growth and/or Production of Native koi	Growth and/or Production of Thai koi	Growth of Vietnam koi	Reference
120 days, 62500fry/ha (1.5-2.0 inch size)	1,733±168.47kg/ha (Average body wt.: 33.38±8.74gm)	4,051±185kg/ha (Average body wt.: 69.25±11.35gm)		Kohinoor *et al.* 2012
5 months, 50,000fry/ha	1916±125kg/ha	4800.40± 348.09kg/ha		Kohinoor *et al.* 2009
100 days, 2,50,000nos./ha (0.25-0.50gm size)	16381.2±106.12kg/ha (Average body wt.: 78.25±6.11gm)		22063±104.57kg/ha (Average body bwt.: 99.5±4.81gm)	Chakraborty and Haque, 2014
90 days, 37500fry/ha, (1gm size)			4500kg/ha (Average body wt.: 121.92gm)	Ahmed *et al.* 2015
8 months, 300000 piece/ha (250-300mg size)		250-275gm	300-450gm	Sri Amrita Das and Sri Bablu Kumar Ghosh, progressive fish farmers: pers. comm.
90 days, 300000 piece/ha (250-300mg size)		80-90gm	100-120gm	Sri Amrita Das, progressive fish farmer: pers. comm.

In West Bengal conditions, Thai koi will attain 90-100gm body weight within four months of culture but Vietnam koi will be of size 150-200gm within the same period. Even Vietnam koi of size 250gm has been reported in 100 days culture duration at Goltala fish farm, Salt Lake, North 24 Parganas. During the last 3-4 years, the latter is more preferred by the farmers in this state. Within 3-4 months, 9-12 tonne production of table-size Vietnam Koi is obtainable from a 1acre pond. In retail fish markets of Kolkata city, Vietnam koi are frequently found of size 150-250gm, it is sold at Rs. 250-300/- per kg. Bigger sized fishes of more than 300gm costs Rs. 450/- per kg. Though widely cultured in Bangladesh commercially, till this time December 2015, farming of Vietnam koi in West Bengal is considered unauthorized and is not permitted officially. It is little inferior in taste in comparison to indigenous *A. testudineus*. Recently, first author had an opportunity to discuss with Dr. K.K. Lal, Genetics and Biodiversity Coordinator at NACA, Bangkok, who opined that this Vietnam koi is neither hybrid nor a selectively-bred fish.

Many consumers said that the flesh of Vietnam koi is more oily than that of indigenous one. Though several fish species have been introduced in India both officially and unofficially in culture systems due to their merits, mostly due to rapid growth, hardly nature and easy seed availability, and so far there are reports to have ecological impact from escapement to open water, niche competition or cannibalistic habit on native species, still the use of exotic species has shown to be highly beneficial from production as well as socio-economic point of view. Hence Thai variety *A. testudineus* and Vietnam variety *A. testudineus* as air-breathing fishes in culture system of eastern India will have an impact in the fish market from consumers' point of view.

Normal/native *A. testudineus* (50-60gm)

A group of native *A. testudineus*

Vietnam variety *A. testudineus* (200-250gm)

A group of Vietnam *A. testudineus*

Vietnam koi (100gm)

A group of Thai variety *A. testudineus*

Thai variety *A. testudineus*

Vietnam *A. testudineus* (300gm)

Vietnam koi in market (1)

Vietnam koi in market (2)

Combined Farming of Scampi and Tiger Shrimp

In tiger shrimp *Penaeus monodon* farming, farm ponds connected to estuaries, brackishwater rivers and creeks are considered ideal since pond water salinity of 12-20ppt is one of the favourable parameter and basic requirement. The giant freshwater prawn *Macrobrachium rosenbergii*, which has become an important cultured species in freshwater aquaculture system requires pond water conditions as like Indian major carps. Recently it has been experienced by present authors that remarkably both *M. rosenbergii* and *P. monodon* could be cultured simultaneously in the same environment, *i.e.*, freshwater ponds. Sri Chandra has worked extensively as technical supervisor to commercial shrimp and Scampi producers in brackishwater and freshwater farms respectively in Purba Medinipur district in West Bengal.

Sri Mrityunjoy Bal, S/o Sri Bishnupada Bal, residing at Vill. Gorbhera under Dighanagar Mouza, P.O. Gurgram, Block Bhagabanpur-1 under PS Bhagabanpur, Dist. Purba Medinipur, West Bengal is a moderately resource-rich professional prawn farmer, who is involved in nursery rearing and grow-out monoculture of *M. rosenbergii* since 2004-2005. He owns three scientifically-managed, perennial and rain-fed grow-out ponds of 26 decimal (250 decimal = 1 hectare), 55 decimal and 90 decimal in area, having 4-6 feet depth. Since March-April 2013, he has been practicing farming of both these shell fish species together in his first two freshwater ponds. During March-April, he procures seeds of *M. rosenbergii* (5-8mm; paddy grain size, counted by spoon) and *P. monodon* (PL-15; 14-15mm size) from professional riverine prawn/shrimp seed capturists; seeds of such size of these two species are available in river Rupnarayan (captured at Kolaghat, distance of 65km from Gorbhera village) and river Keleghai (at Sabang) in this district during March to July. Mainly Scampi seeds are available in river Keleghai. Seeds are transported at his pond site either in aluminium Hundi or empty Dalda oil plastic containers of 15lit capacity, with pores on lid, each containing 5000-5500 pieces. Each seed of *M. rosenbergii* and *P. monodon* costs Rs. 2.00-2.50 and 40-50 paisa respectively. Scampi seeds available during July-August are not much preferred for farming.

During April, in a 10 decimal nursery pond (400mt^2), he normally stocks 10,000nos. of *M. rosenbergii* and 20,000nos. of *P. monodon* seeds and rears them together for 35-45 days, within which *M. rosenbergii* and *P. monodon* attain 1.5-2.0 inches and 3.0-3.5 inches (3gm) in body size respectively, suitable for grow-out farming. Combined stocking density in nursery ponds: 30,000 seeds/10 decimal water area. Since pond soil pH in this region is between 4.5-5.0, a higher dosage of lime is applied before seed stocking. Commercially available granular-type feed is provided to both species @ 80-100gm/10000 seeds everyday during 1st ten days of rearing, 100-140gm/10000 seeds during 2nd ten days, 140-480gm during 3rd ten days and 480-880gm/10000 seeds everyday during 4th ten days till day-40. Although it is Scampi feed, but it is given to both species and *P. monodon* accepts it.

In the end of June and onset of monsoon, in his 55 decimal grow-out pond, Sri Mrityunjoy had stocked 10,000 nos. of *M. rosenbergii* juveniles obtained from nursery pond and 4000nos. of *P. monodon* of size 3.0-3.5 inches. *P. monodon* is harvested in the end of September or early October before Durga Puja and in this four month period of grow-out culture, tiger shrimp attained 40gm body weight on average, almost of same size with only 5gm size variation and 70-75 per cent survivability. It fetches him a farm gate price of Rs. 400-450/- per kg. Protein-rich pelleted feed 'Waterbase Magnum XL Premium Prawn Feed' (25kg sack, Rs. 80/- per kg; 1.5-2.0mm pellet diameter) is provided to both Scampi and tiger shrimp in the pond four times a day; a strict feeding schedule is maintained beginning with 7 per cent feed application everyday in 1st week of culture {considering 2.5-3.0gm average body weight (abw)}, 6 per cent feed everyday in 2nd week of culture (considering 4-5gm abw), 5 per cent feed everyday in 3rd week of culture (6-7gm abw); it continues and ends up with 1.5 per cent feed everyday in 13th week of culture (considering 35-37gm abw), 1.2 per cent feed everyday in 14th week of culture (38-40gm abw); in the continuation period of culture beyond 90 days, the final schedule is maintained. Sri Mrityunjoy uses 'Grower' type feed (1-2mm dia pellet) to Scampi and tiger shrimp upto 25gm size and 'Finisher' type feed (2-3mm pellet) is used thereafter till time of harvest.

M. rosenbergii is harvested from his pond in the end of January next year (*Pous - Magh*) and in this seven month period of grow-out culture, beginning from June-July, Scampi attains 45gm body weight on average, with wide variation in size from 25gm to 90gm. Farm gate price of such Scampi is Rs. 500-550/- per kg and Rs. 600/- for those above 100gm weight. In days of insufficient rainfall, tubewell water/groundwater is let into culture ponds. Sri Mrityunjoy's elder brother Sri Gangadhar Bal is also a professional Scampi producer and practices monoculture of *M. rosenbergii* only.

Farm pond of Mrityunjoy Bal

Another farm pond

Scampi of Sri Bal's pond

Tiger shrimp of Sri Bal's pond

Both of them mentioned that occurrence of *P. monodon* seeds in river Rupnarayan at Kolaghat and nearby areas is less in comparison to *M. rosenbergii* seeds and also demand of hatchery-bred *P. monodon* seeds is much more in comparison to wild riverine seeds. Seed collectors more prefer to capture and segregate *M. rosenbergii* seeds. According to them, hatchery-produced *P. monodon* post larvae will not survive in Scampi culture ponds; it will require brackishwater conditions. Only riverine *P. monodon* seeds can be cultured in association with *M. rosenbergii*. Although present, availability of tiger shrimp seeds in river Rupnarayan at Kolaghat (salinity: assumedly maximum 4-5ppt, in March-April) is not sufficient and those are mainly found in Ramnagar canal, Mandarmoni canal, Pichhaboni canal, which are naturally-occurring creeks in the same district, much nearer to estuary and Bay of Bengal and have 12-18ppt salinity. Sri Mrityunjoy mentioned that *P. monodon* seeds collected from these creeks will not be able to survive in his freshwater Scampi ponds, those are ideal for brackishwater ponds. Kolaghat station in Rupnarayan river is located at a distance of 135 km from seaface.

Harvested Scampi and shrimp from same pond

Haul of Scampi and tiger shrimp

Sri Mrityunjoy Bal with sampled specimens

Sri Gangadhar Bal at his farm

Sri Mrityunjoy applies Dolomite and Triple super phosphate in recommended dosages during culture period and uses Mini Pump (drawing up pond water and forced release/flushing out upto a distance from pond dyke) to maintain DO_2 level in pond water. He has not faced any problems of viral infection (WSSV or MBV) in growing *P. monodon* in his freshwater Scampi culture ponds in last three years. There is much less risk of occurrence/ outbreak of devastating viral diseases in farmed *P. monodon,* when cultured in freshwater conditions in low density and seeds obtained from regions like river Rupnarayan having less than 4-5ppt water salinity. It has been determined in previous studies that water salinity in Rupnarayan at Kolaghat is 0.01ppt in monsoon, 0.20ppt in post-monsoon, another study showed 0.22ppt, maximum salinity in year 1993 was 0.9ppt, salinity as mean of three seasons: 0.5ppt. Scampi farmers can also obtain *M. rosenbergii* seeds of 10-20mm size from river Shilabati at Ghatal in Dist. Paschim Medinipur during March-May. Juvenile-sized Scampi seeds are available in river Keleghai at Egra and Potashpur during July to October.

REFERENCES

Adhikary, R.K., Saha, A., Mostafa, Z.B. and Shah, M.S. (2009). Growth Performance of Thai Koi in Integrated Culture System. *Bangladesh Research Publications Journal*, Vol. 2 No. 1: 361-370.

Ahmed, G.U., Rahman, M.M., Mohammad, N.A., Md. Badrul Alam and Sarker, B. (2015). Impact of Stocking Density on Growth and Production Performance of Vietnamese koi *A. testudineus* in Semi-ientensive Culture System at Mymensingh District. *Research in Agriculture, Livestock and Fisheries*, Vol. 2, No. 2: 335-341.

Alam, M.A., Rahman, L., Khan, M.M.R. and Rahman, S.M.Z. (2006). Allozyme Marker for the Analysis of Genetic Variation of Cross koi (Native male and Thai female) *Anabas testudineus* with their Parents. *Molecular Biology and Biotechnology Journal*, Vol. 4, No. 1 and 2: 71-75.

Belton, B., Karim, M., Thilsted, S., Murshed Jahan, K., Collis, W. and Phillips, M. (2011). Review of Aquaculture and Fish Consumption in Bangladesh. Studies and Reviews. The World Fish Center: 76.

Bhuiyan, S., Kashyap, D. and Kalita, B. (2000). Seed Production of Climbing perch *Anabas testudineus* through Natural and Induced Breeding. Aquatic Fish Database.

Biswas, B. and Shah, M.S. (2009). Taxonomic Comparison of Local and Thai koi (*Anabas testudineus* Bloch) from Khulna, Bangladesh. *SAARC Journal of Agriculture*, Vol. 7: 19-28.

Biswas, B. and Shah, Md. S. (2011). The Incidence of Natural hybridization between Two Strains of Climbing Perch *Anabas testudineus* (Bloch). *J. Taxon. Biodiv. Res.*, Vol. 5: 9-14.

Biswas Ulka, S., Happy, F.S., Rashid, H. and Ahmed, G.U. (2012). Improved Hatchery Management through Identification of peak Breeding Season and Sexual Maturity Stages of Native, Thai, and Hybrid koi (*Anabas testudineus*). Bangladesh Fisheries Research Forum. Book of Abstracts. Fifth Fisheries Conference and Research Fair 2012. BFRF, Dhaka, Bangladesh. 182.

Chakraborty, B.K. and Haque, S.M. (2014). Growth, Yield and Returns to Koi, *Anabas testudineus* (Bloch, 1792) under Semi-intensive Aquaculture System using Different Seed Types in Bangladesh. *J Fisheries Livest Prod.*, Vol. 2:113. doi: 10.4172/2332-2608.1000113.

Dasgupta, M. (2004). Relative Length of the gut of some Freshwater Fishes of West Bengal in Relation to Food and Feeding Habits. *Indian J. Fish.*, Vol. 51 No. 3: 381-384.

Dehadrai, P.V., Yusuf Kamal, M. and Das, R.K. (1985). Package of Practices for Increasing Production of Air-breathing Fishes, *Aquaculture Extension Manual*, No. 3. ICAR Publication.

Devaraj, K.V. (1975). Culture of Air-breathing Fishes. *Seafood Export Journal*: 35-40.

Dooligindachapabron, S. (1994). Development of Optimal Rearing System for Climbing Perch (*Anabas testudineus*). Doctoral Thesis, University of Manitoba, Canada. 189.

Faruk, M.A.R., Mony, S.F.A. and Hasan, M.M. (2012). Status of Biosecurity and Health Management in Fish Hatcheries. *IRJALS*, Vol. 1 Issue 5: 15-26.

Hasan, M., Ahamad, A.K.S. and Khan, M.M.R. (2010). A Pre-liminary Investigation on the Production of Thai koi *Anabas testudineus* reared in nylon hapas in Bangladesh. *Bang. Res. Pub. Jour.*, Vol. 4, No. 1: 15-23.

Hossain, M. A., Basak, S., Kibria, A.S.M. and Kohinoor, A.H.M. (2013). Substitution of Dietary Fish Meal Protein by a Mixture of Protein Concentrate and Meat and Bone Meal in the Diet of Climbing Perch, *Anabas testudineus* (Bloch 1792). *Indian J. Fish.*, Vol. 60 No. 2: 115-121.

Jannat-Most, K., Rahaman, M.R., Bashar, M.A. and Hasan, M.N. (2012). Effects of Stocking Density on Survival, Growth and Production of Thai Climbing Perch (*Anabas testudineus*) under fed ponds. *Sains Malaysiana*, Vol. 41 No. 10: 1205-1210.

Khan, H.A. and Mukhopadhyay, S.K. (1972). On the Fecundity of Climbing Perch *Anabas testudineus*. *J. Inland Fish. Soc. India*, Vol. 4: 212-213.

Kohinoor, A.H.M and Zaher, M. (2006). Breeding of Exotic koi (*Anabas testudineus*) at BFRI. *Fisheries Newsletter*, Vol. 14 No. 1: 1-2.

Kohinoor, A.H.M., Islam, A.K.M.S., Jahan, D.A., Zaher, M. and Hussain, M.G. (2007). Monoculture of Climbing Perch, Thai koi, *Anabas testudineus* (Bloch) under different Stocking Densities at on-farm Management. *Bangladesh J. Fish. Res.*, Vol. 11 No. 2: 173-180.

Kohinoor, A.H.M., Jahan, D.A., Khan, M. M., Ahmed, S.U. and Hussain, M.G. (2009). Culture Potentials of Climbing Perch, *Anabas testudineus* (Bloch) under different Stocking Densities at Semi-intensive Management. *Bangladesh J. Fish. Res.*, Vol. 13, No. 2: 115-120.

Kohinoor, A.H.M., Islam, M.S., Jahan, D.A., Khan, M.M. and Hussain, M.G. (2012). Growth and Production Performances of Crossbred Climbing Perch koi, *Anabas testudineus* in Bangladesh. *Int. J. Agril. Res. Innov. and Tech.*, Vol. 2 No. 1: 19-25.

Kumar, K., Mohanty, U.L., Gupta, S.D. and Sahu, A.K. (2010). *Journal of Inland Fisheries Society of India*, Vol. 42, No. 2: 8-13.

Mahmood, S.U., Ali, M.S. and Anwar ul Hoque. (2004). Effect of different Feed on larval/fry Rearing of Climbing Perch, *Anabas testudineus* (Bloch), in Bangladesh: II. Growth and Survival. *Pakistan Journal of Zoology*, Vol. 36: 13-19.

Md. Helal Hosen. (2014). Growth Performance of Vietnamese koi *Anabas testudineus* in a Commercial Farm. MS Thesis Submitted to Department of Aquaculture, Bangladesh Agricultural University.

Noor, A.M. (2005). Growth and Morphological Comparison between Local and Thai koi Anabas testudineus in Bangladesh. MSc Thesis, Department of Fishery Biology and Genetics. 25-42.

Rahaman, S. Monir, M.S. and Khan, M.H. (2013). Culture Potentials of Climbing Perch Thai koi *Anabas testudineus* under different Stocking Densities in Northern Region of Bangladesh. *Journal of Experimental Biology and Agricultural Sciences*, Vol. 1 No. 3: 201-207.

Saha, K.C. (1971). Fisheries of West Bengal. West Bengal Government Press, Alipore, West Bengal, India.

Sarkar, U.K., Deepak, P.K., Kapoor, D., Negi, R.S., Paul, S.K. and Singh, S.P. (2005). Captive Breeding of *Anabas testudineus* (Bloch, 1792) with Wova-FH for Conservation and Aquaculture. *Aquaculture Research*, Vol. 36: 941-945.

Suraiya, S., Haq, M. and Khan, M.M.R. (2012). Induced Breeding and Larval Rearing of Local and Thai koi (*Anabas testudineus*, Bloch, 1792). *J. Innov. Dev. Strategy.*, Vol. 6, No. 1: 63-68.

Thakur, N.K and Das, P. (1986). Synopsis of Biological data on Koi, *Anabas testudineus* (Bloch). Bulletin No. 40, Central Inland Fisheries Research Institute, Barrackpore, India: 47.

Trieu, N.V and Long, D.N. (2001). Seed Production Technology of Climbing perch (*Anabas testudineus*). A Case Study of Larval Rearing. Proceedings of the 2001 Annual Workshop of JIRCAS Mekong delta project. Cuu Long Rice Research Institute, Omon, Vietnam: 212-213.

Tuan, N.A, Hanh, H.M., Lan, L.M., Long, D.N., Tam, Đ.H., Lanh, N.V. and Thanh, L.T. (2002). Preliminary Results on Rearing of Climbing Perch (*Anabas testudineus*) in Concrete Tanks and Earthen Ponds. Proceeding of the 2002 Annual Workshop of JIRCAS Mekong delta project. College of Agriculture, Can Tho University, Vietnam: 227-230.

Van, K.V. and Hoan, V.Q. (2009). Intensive Nursing of Climbing Perch (*Anabas testudineus*) in Hapas using Pellet feed at different Protein levels, *J. Sci. Dev.*, Vol. 7 Issue 2: 239-242.

Waheduzzaman, Md. (2006). Induced Breeding Technique of Indian Major Carps and Thai Koi (*Anabas testudineus*). MSc Report submitted as a part of Aqua-Internship Programme. Asia Link Project, Faculty of Fisheries, Bangladesh Agricultural University, Mymensingh.

Yakupitiyage, A., Bundit, J. and Guhman, A. (1998). Culture of Climbing Perch (*Anabas testudineus*). A Review. Ait Aqua Outreach, Working paper, New Series No. T-8.

FARMING TECHNIQUES AND CROP PRODUCTION
Edited by : **Dr. Alka Chauhan; Dr. Anubhuti Sharma & Jaswant Ray**
Edition : **2017**
ISBN : 978-93-5056-855-2
Published by : **Discovery Publishing House Pvt. Ltd., New Delhi (India)**

5 Review on the Status of Local Chicken Management in Ethiopia

Nega Mekonnen[1*] & Cherenet Assfaw[1]

Abstract

Population, urbanization and anticipated income growth in Africa in general and in Ethiopia in particular is believed to influence the demand for food of animal origin. Such an increase needs substantial progress in the use of improved technologies, expanded use of inputs with favorable economic policies and with good interactions of holistic approaches Poultry in a particular with the ability to rapidly increase in number because the birds short generation interval, fertility, prolificacy and higher efficient of nutrient transformation in to high quality animal protein is one means of the small and marginal farmers and other low income groups could be improved. Ethiopia is one of the few African countries with significant large population of chicken which is estimated to be 56.5 million chickens out of which 99 per cent are local chickens producing 78,000 metric tonnes of eggs and 72,300 metric tonnes of meat per year. These chicken population in the country is non-descript indigenous which are adaptive but of low productivity in meat and egg. The egg production potential of local chickens is 30-60eggs/year/hen with an average of 38g egg weight in Ethiopia. Village chickens have been contributing a lot to increase food production and income for rural communities of Ethiopia.

Keywords: Local, Chicken, Ethiopia, Scavenging, Egg, Housing, Feeding.

INTRODUCTION

Chickens were domesticated in India and were being raised by the Chinese and Egyptians about 1400 b.c. Drawings of chickens have been found in Egyptian tombs dating from around 1400 b.c. Although poultry and eggs were used for food early in history, poultry rising has only recently become a major

1. Department of Animal Science, Assosa University, P.O. Box 18, Assosa, Ethiopia.

commercial enterprise. In the past, most poultry was raised on an individual family basis. The wild jungle fowl of India (*Gallus gallus*) may have been the early ancestor of most tame chickens. [1] Ethiopia is the first in Africa and tenth the world in livestock populations. Poultry species are originated from south East Asia and domesticated from red jungle fowl. [1] Poultry include all domestic birds such as: chickens, turkeys, ducks, geese, ostriches, guinea fowls, and pigeons. However, in Ethiopia except chickens the others are found in their natural habitat whereas geese and turkeys are not common. [2] Poultry contribute important socio-economic roles for food securities, generating additional cash incomes and religious/cultural reasons. [2]

In Ethiopia chicken populations are estimated to be about 49.3 million.[2] Indigenous chickens are largely dominated flock size and have good potential to adapt different agro-ecologies through habitual management systems. [2] But, they are non-descriptive types and vary in body size, conformation, plumage color and other phenotypic characteristics.[2] Still these large population indigenous chickens are found in traditional production systems. However, they are well adapted to the tropics, resistant to poor management, feed shortages, tolerate to diseases and provide better test of meat and eggs than exotic chickens [2] there is no well-developed breeding practice in chicken production in Ethiopia.

Poultry keeping [1] in Ethiopia is generally a back yard venture. Many people living in rural or urban area in one way or other engaged in this activity as side line activity in adaptation to their main occupation, aimed at producing eggs and meat for home consumption and to generate some adaptation house hold in comes, where as in pre-urban and urban settings people go for intensive commercial operations [2] using modern breeds, balanced feed, health care and housing system.

The chicken kept in the villages have no regular health control programme, may or may not have shelter and scavenge for most of their nutritional needs, according to [3] the low productivity of local scavenging hen's is not only because they are low producer of small sized eggs and slow growers but also the system is characterized by its high chicken mortality before they reach 8 weeks of age. However the local chickens are the results of uncontrolled breeding between various local chickens' ecotypes, which have not been selected by systematic breeding methods.[4]

Many poultry development projects have failed to meet their objectives, due to the in ability to identify appropriate technologies and define the poultry production practice. Low level of inputs and outputs characterize village poultry production systems. To harness the potential of village chicken, [5] suggest a new approach, aiming to increasing flock productivity through improved extension service, farmers training and preferential treatment of chickens. Therefore, the cause magnitude and consequent impact of the problem for the poultry productivity under traditional management must be studied and well documented before attempting any technological intervention to improve the village or traditional poultry production.

Systems of Poultry Production in Ethiopia

Three production systems can be seen in Ethiopia. One production system may be important in one agro-ecology but may not be important in the other. These production systems are characterized mainly by the objectives of the producer, the input used and number and types of birds kept on the farm, these systems are: *(i)* traditional (backyard) production system; *(ii)* commercial and *(iii)* small scale intensive production system. Ethiopian poultry production sector can largely be characterized as backyard system of production. Most people keep some chickens typically between 2-12 which scavenge around their compound and in their gardens. This statement is not to over simplify poultry production but simply to stress that back yard chicken rearing is the most common and accounts for the majority (98-99%) of poultry production in Ethiopia. [6] The backyard poultry production is high risk venture in the sense that it is quite likely that most of one's stock could die in any year. New castle disease (NCD) often kills off whole flocks every few year. Predators take their own share too. Because of the high risk associated as with the backyard poultry by the male and left to women. [6]

In Ethiopia there are about 56 million chickens of which about 99 per cent are indigenous chickens. The traditional production system is practiced almost by every family in the rural, urban and pre-urban dwellers. It is estimated that an average of seven indigenous birds are kept by every family. This system is characterized by minimum input with birds scavenging for most of their food and no investment other than the cost of the birds and for simple night time shelter. Village chicken production system is characterized by their low input-low output levels. Aarrange of factor such as: sub optimal management, lack of supplementary feed, low genetic potential and high mortality rate are the cause of the apparent low output level. However, village chickens play important role in supplying high quality protein to balance the family food supply and provide small disposal cash income in adaption to the socio-religious function that are important in the rural people's lives. [7]

The most noted features of village poultry production recurrently high level of mortality and other Common characteristics is that the input output relationship is low input low output system. Indigenous hens lay on the average 40-60 eggs per hen per year. [6] Moreover, the eggs size is small (35-40gm) and chick survival rate are very poor. Village hen brood and hatch their own eggs, if no supplementary feed, brood itself is often unsuccessful and all these factors in combination lead to low egg production and productivity. Given high mortality rate, high off take and short life span of chicken, flock size tends to shift substantially with in the years. It's difficult to pin down a single number for typical flock size; however, one can say that the variability is bounded by a common range. [8] Currently, Commercial poultry production system is a sector that involves both private and government enterprises. It is still in its early development stage. It contributes only about 1 per cent of the country's poultry production. Small scale intensive production system is a newly emerging system in urban and pre-urban areas particularly along the roads from Addis Ababa - Debrezeit - Nazareth and Addis Ababa Sebeta roads. It is characterized by small flock size (usually 50-500 birds). It is organized along commercial line.

General facts on Management of different Chicken Categories

- *Raising Laying Pullets:* Replacement pullets for laying flocks may be raised in confinement or onrange. The trend is toward confinement rising. Less land and labor is needed for confinement systems. Losses from parasites and predators are lower in confinement production. Pullets may be raised in the same house that is used for brooding, or they may be moved to a growing house. Pullets should be culled when they are moved to the growing house. They may be grown in cages, using one of two systems: partial cage growing or complete cage growing. Partial cage growing is floor brooding for the first 6 to 10 weeks and then moving the pullets to cages. Complete cage growing is brooding and growing entirely in cages. Light affects the age of sexual maturity and the rate of egg production. The length of the day is the controlling factor. Thus, increasing day length speeds upsexual maturity, and decreasing day length slows down sexual maturity. If pullet search sexual maturity too early, they will lay small eggs for several months. Several systems of controlling light during the growing period are used. The basic principle involved is not to grow pullets between 12 and 22 weeks of age under conditions of increasing light. Dark, windowless houses are used in some systems to permit total control of light. Some systems reduce the light gradually during the growing period. Others maintain a constant day length during the growing period. Day length is increased when the pullets are moved into the laying house. Less feed is required for growing pullets on range. However, more labor is required and there are greater problems with disease and predators. Clean range must be used and must be rotated. One acre can carry from 300 to 500 birds. Birds of different ages should not be mixed on range. Range shelters and shade are needed. Range growing of pullets is better adapted to small flocks than large commercial operations.
- *Laying Flock Management:* Laying flocks may be housed in open-floor systems or caged systems. Smaller flocks often use open-floor systems. The trend in large commercial flocks is toward using some system of caged layers. Laying houses must be cleaned and disinfected before

pullets are moved in the laying house should remain empty for at least 1 week after cleaning before moving the pullets in. The house and equipment should be in good repair and new litter put in the house. Handle pullets gently when moving them to the laying house. They are easily frightened. Moving them in the dark will excite them less. Watch the pullets for a few days to make sure they do not pile up and smother. Nests should be cleaned regularly and new nesting material added when needed. Keep waterers and feeders clean. Keep the litter stirred and add new litter when needed. Do not allow the litter to become wet and caked over. Several types of cages are used for cage laying systems, including single cages, multiple-bird cages, and colony cages. Multiple-bird cages contain 2 to 10 birds. Colony cages contain 11 to 40 birds. Single cages may be arranged in single rows, back-to-back, stair-step, or double deck. Single row is two rows of cages separated by an aisle. This system is generally used in narrow houses. The back-to-back system uses two rows of single cages placed back-to-back. This permits a sharing of common water and feed troughs.

The capacity of the house is increased by the use of this system. A stair-step system is created by offsetting one tier of single cages below another. Manure drops to the floor rather than on dropping boards. Double-deck systems place one row of cages directly on top of another. Dropping boards are used to catch the manure. Problems with this system include the difficulty of removing the manure and providing enough light to the chickens in the lower cages. Most multiple-bird cages house two to five birds per cage. Cost per bird is lower than with single cages. Cage arrangements are the same as with single-birdcages. The stair-step arrangement is considered to be the most profitable. Advantages of colony cages include lower housing and labor costs. Problems include higher death loss, lower production, and more dirty and broken eggs. As more hens are placed in the colony cage, the production level decreases. Feeding in cages may be done by hand or automatically. Watering may be done by the use of continuous flow troughs, drip nipples, or automatic cups. Laying hens require a minimum of 14 hours of light per day. Many controlled lighting systems use a maximum of 17 hours of light per day. Artificial lighting must be used as the length of available natural light decreases with the season. Several types of lighting systems are used. These include all-artificial lights, morning light, evening light, a combination of morning and evening light, and all-night lighting. Light is increased to 12 hours at 20 weeks of age. It is then increased gradually (15 to 20 minutes per week) until the maximum desired light is reached. Lights are generally controlled by automatic time clocks. All-artificial lighting is used in windowless houses. Morning lighting systems turn on lights 2 to 5 hours before sunrise and turn off at daybreak. Evening lighting systems turn on in the evening. Dimmers are used to prevent a sudden change from light to dark. Morning-evening systems use lights at each end of the day. All-night lighting is generally used only for second-year laying flocks. Low-watt age bulbs are used in this system.

- *Managing Chickens for Meat Production:* Chickens raised for meat production are brooded in the same way as laying chickens. Chickens for meat production are generally raised in confinement, although range can be used. Broilers require 1 square foot (0.09 m2) of space from 2 weeks of age to market. Capons and roasters require 2 to 3 square feet (0.18 to 0.28 m2) of floor space from 10 to 20 weeks of age. After 20 weeks of age, provide 4 to 5 square feet (0.37 to 0.46 m2) of floor space per bird. Broiler producers usually use lights 24 hours a day. One 60-watt bulb per 200 square feet (18.6 m2) of floor space provides adequate light. No nests or roosts are used in producing meat-type chickens. A capon is a male chicken that has been surgically castrated. The operation is usually performed when the birds are 3 to 5 weeks of age. Capons produce meat that is tenderer than that produced by broilers. However, they require more labor and investment to produce. Hormone implants can be used to produce the same results as caponizing.
- *Breeding Flock Management:* Hatching eggs are produced under agreements with a hatchery. The hatchery generally provides the farmer with the breeding stock having the special bloodlines that the hatchery wants produced. Ten to 14 cockerels (males) per 100 pullets should be started. These are later culled down to 8 to 12 cockerels at 10 weeks of age. Leghorn breeds require one cockerel for each 15 to 17 hens at mating time. Heavier breeds require one cockerel for each 12 to 15 hens. Brooding is done in the same way as for laying flocks. Raising the chickens requires the management practices outlined for laying flocks. Breeding stock is often revaccinated for Newcastle disease and bronchitis about 1 month before breeding begins. This gives the newly hatched chicks a temporary immunity to these diseases. Mating begins at least 2 weeks before the eggs are to be delivered to the hatchery. Do not put too many birds in one mating pen. This will reduce the mating. Hatching eggs should be gathered three or four times per day. Gather more often if the weather is very hot or cold. Handle hatching eggs in the same careful way that other eggs are handled. Store hatching eggs at 50°F to 60°F (10°C to 15°C) and at 80 per cent humidity. Always pack hatching eggs with the large end up. If eggs have to be held more than 1 week, tip the crate sharply to prevent the yolk from sticking to the shell. Hatching eggs must be fumigated within 2 hours after they are gathered. This will help prevent the spread of egg-borne diseases such as: pullorum, fowl typhoid, paratyphoid, Para colon, and navel infection. Formaldehyde or potassium permanganate is used to fumigate the eggs. Chlorine dioxide may be used as a spray or dip instead of fumigation. It is easier to use and gives better results.

Purpose of Local Chicken Production in Ethiopia

Poultry in Ethiopia are kept for the main purpose of generating-income, obtaining food (egg and meat), to use as gift for religious success and social obligations, Study undertaken in the central high land of Ethiopia [6] indicated that the main objective of village poultry keeping is the production of eggs for hatching (52%), sale (23%), home Consumption (20%) and as gift (5%), similarly, birds are kept for sale (27%) for sacrifice or healing ceremonies (25%), for replacement stock (20%) and for home consumption (20%). In some case farmers give live birds (9%) as a gift and invite special gusts to eat the popular dish 'doro watt' which contains both chicken meat and egg and are considered to be one of the most exclusive national dishes. [3] Indicated that farmers sell live birds and eggs, particularly during holydays and festivals; they also sell at the onset of local disease out brake to prevent expected financial loss. In such circumstance, price fall dramatically due to high supply of birds relative to demand. In another study conducted in five agro-ecological zone of Ethiopia by [7] live birds and eggs are usually sold in local market to civil servants and occasionally to middle man for retail in the larger town and cities of the market shed.

General facts on Advantage and Disadvantages of Local Chicken Production

Raising poultry has a number of advantages, among which is high feed efficiency, fast return on investment, spreading income throughout the year, high return compared to feed costs, low land requirements, adaptability to both small part-time enterprises and large commercial enterprises, the operation can be highly mechanized, with high output per hour of labor. There are some problems involved in raising poultry, among which are serious problems with diseases and parasites, need for a high level of management ability, especially for large commercial flocks, need for large amounts of capital for large operations, limitations of zoning on the location of flocks, death losses may be high due to predators and stampeding, quality of product must be controlled carefully, careful marketing is required, high volume is needed for an economical enterprise, problems of waste disposal and odor.

Feeds and Feeding of Local Chicken in Ethiopia

The most common chicken feed resources in Ethiopia include grains, house hold wastes; industrial by products, market left over, feed items obtained from scavenging , green leaves and etc., the domestic birds requires the same type of nutrients as other farm animals, carbohydrates, protein, vitamins, fats, minerals and water. The same is true that as all other farm animals, domestic birds kept for the productive benefits (meat and egg). Improvements in performance standards coupled with intensive methods of production have served to focus attention up on price knowledge regarding nutrients requirement for growth and reproduction. In common with all other classes of livestock, the domestic chicken requires food for optimal growth efficiency of feed utilization that its ration contains a certain specific quantity and balance of each dietary constitute [10] Poultry production in tropical countries is based on the traditional scavenging system and characterized by low output per chicken.

According to [4] the village chicken production in Ethiopia drives the major proportion of the feed through scavenging. Birds are usually kept in free range system which means that they are allowed to roam more or less ferly the main scavenging chicken feed resources base was thought to be insect, warms, seeds, plant material with very small amount of grain and house hold table left over supplements [11] mentioned that there are three distinguishable system for managing village poultry production, namely the extensive system free range and backyard and small scale intensive system. In the free range and backyard system, a bird can certainly not find all nutrients it need for optimal production all the year round. During the dry season poultry can quickly develop vitamin deficiency because of the scarcity of succulent vegetable on the range. There is thus a need to supplement the scavenge chicken with sources of minerals and vitamins.

Most of the materials available for the scavenging are not concentrated enough in terms of energy because they contain a lot of crude fiber. There is need to supplement scavenging poultry with energy sources. That is why grains are given to poultry in the traditional village poultry system. Small holders using extensive system adopt cafeteria choose of feeding of nutrients. Energy supplements such as: maize, sorghum and millet are offered every in the morning and late in the evening. Birds scavenge during the day season mostly for protein (insect, worms, larvae,) and vitamins (green leaves, paper etc.), minerals (stone, grits, shell etc.,) in between the meals. It has been estimated that about 35 gm grains supplement per hen per day is given to local chickens in the free range system in the south western Nigeria [12]

General facts on Poultry Feeds and Feeding

The cost of feed is about two-thirds of the total cost of producing eggs and meat from chickens. All management practices affect profits in chicken production. Feeding practices must meet the needs of the chickens and still allow room for profit. Rations for the chickens must supply the protein, carbohydrates, minerals, vitamins, and water that poultry require. In addition, some additives and unidentified growth factors are oft en used in chicken rations. Tables that give the nutrient requirements of poultry and the composition of common feeds for poultry are found in the appendix of this book. Most of the energy in poultry diets is supplied by grains, grain by-products, and animal and vegetable fats and oils. Poultry only have a limited ability to use high-fiber feeds such as: roughages because of their relative inability to digest the fiber. Grains make up from 50 to 80 per cent of the total ration for chickens. Corn is the most commonly used grain in poultry rations. Other grains such as: oats, wheat, grain sorghum (milo), and proso millet may be substituted for part of the corn in poultry rations.

When poultry are fed ad libitum (given all they will eat), they tend to eat enough to meet their energy requirements. Chickens fed low-energy diets will eat more feed than those fed high-energy diets. Therefore, the amount of required nutrients in a poultry ration must be adjusted in relation to the energy level in the ration in order to ensure that the birds consume the right amount of the needed nutrients. The concentration of nutrients must be increased in high-energy diets because the birds will eat less of the ration per day. The concentration of nutrients should be reduced in low-energy rations because the birds will eat more of these rations per day. High-energy rations usually result in higher efficiency in converting feed to meat or eggs as compared to low energy rations. Pelleted feeds contain more nutrients per volume of feed; this results in a higher intake of nutrients with the consumption of a given amount of feed as compared to non-pelleted feeds. Adding fat to the ration increases the amount of energy in the diet. When substituting other grains for corn in poultry diets, care must be taken to ensure that the level of required nutrients in the ration is adjusted to compensate for the difference in energy level and feed intake. Corn has a higher energy level than other grains that can be used in poultry rations. Generally, other grains should be substituted for only part of the corn in the ration because of their lower energy level and higher fiber level.

For example, oats or barley should be limited to no more than 10 to 15 per cent of the ration. When preparing poultry feeds, corn should be coarsely ground. Oats, barley, and millet should be finely ground. Wheat and grain sorghum should be processed through a roller mill. If wheat is ground, care must be taken not to grind it too fine. Fats may be used to increase the energy level of low-energy rations. Animal and vegetable fats should be limited to no more than 5 to 10 per cent of the diet. Fats will increase the palatability of the diet, decrease dustiness, and improve the texture of the feed. Fats are used more oft en in broiler rations to increase the energy level of the diet. In hot weather, feed containing added fat may become rancid unless it has been properly stabilized. Proteins supply the essential amino acids needed by chickens. The amino acids most commonly deficient in chicken rations are: arginine, glycine, lysine, methionine, and tryptophane. Common sources of protein for chickens include: soybean meal, meat scraps, and fish meal. Balancing the ration on the amino acid needs rather than crude protein content assures that the nutritional needs of the chickens are met. This practice may also result in a lower-cost ration.

From 55 to 78 per cent of the egg and the chicken's body weight is water. Younger chickens have the highest water content. Chickens need a fresh, clean supply of water at all times. The daily water consumption of chickens varies with the type of chicken, the temperature, and type of diet fed, rate of growth, egg production, and type of watering equipment used. It shows the daily water consumption of chickens at moderate temperatures (68°F to 77°F [20°C to 25°C]). Water consumption will increase at higher temperatures. On very hot days, chickens may consume as much as three times the water used on cooler days. The mineral requirements of chickens include: calcium, phosphorus, manganese, iodine, sodium, chlorine, and zinc. Calcium can be supplied by the addition of oyster shell or limestone. Current recommendations for calcium are that it makeup 3.4 per cent of the ration for laying hens.

It is especially important for laying hens because the formation of the shell of the egg requires a great deal of calcium. Commercial mineral mixes can be used to supply the other minerals needed in the ration. Vitamins required by chickens include A, D3, E, K, riboflavin, B12, niacin, pantothenic acid, and choline. Grains, protein sources, and green feeds will supply some of the vitamin needs. However, it is common practice to use a vitamin premix when preparing chicken rations. This ensures that the necessary vitamins are present in the ration. The use of additives in poultry rations is discussed in Chapter 7. Proper management practices must be followed whenever feed additives are used in the ration. Unidentified substances found in dried whey, marine and packing-house by-products, distillers' soluble, green forages, soybeans, corn, and other natural materials have been found to be beneficial to chickens. These factors stimulate growth, increase reproduction, improve egg quality, or reduce the toxicity of some minerals. Many poultry rations for young birds and breeders contain some of these feeds to add these factors to the diet.

Chickens have no teeth. Gritin the ration helps the gizzard in grinding feed. Grit is usually small particles of granite. Research indicates that grit may or may not improve the use of feed with all-mash (completely ground and mixed) rations. It is definitely needed when other types of rations are fed. Grit comes in small, medium, and large sizes. Feed the small size to chicks, the medium size to growing chickens, and the large size to hens. Young chicks should be fed the grit by sprinkling it on the feed twice a week. For growing chickens and hens, feed grit free-choice in hoppers. The different kinds of chicken feeds are all available as commercially manufactured feeds. Commercial feeds are available in the form of mash, pellets, or crumbles. Pellet and crumble forms cost more than mash. Chickens may produce slightly better with the pelleted or crumble forms. Pellet and crumble feeds reduce feed waste and the chickens may eat them a little better. The manufacturer's directions for use must be followed closely. Always follow feed tag directions closely when using feeds containing additives. Four systems that may be used for preparing rations are:

- Use a complete commercial feed.
- Use a commercial protein concentrate and mix with local or homegrown grains.
- Buy all the individual ingredients and mix the ration.
- Use a commercial vitamin-mineral premix and soybean meal and mix with local or homegrown grain.

The choice of system depends on the age of the chickens being fed, the relative costs, the size of the enterprise, and the equipment available for grinding and mixing feeds. Farmers with small flocks generally find it more economical to use a complete commercial feed. Large commercial poultry enterprises generally use some system of mixing either at a local mill or on the farm. For large operations, mixing the feeds usually results in a lower feed cost per tonne.

Phase feeding is a system of making specific feeds to be used to meet the changing nutritional requirements of chickens. A number of factors, such as: rate of lay, egg size, body maintenance needs, and temperature, are used to determine the content of the feed. The purpose is to lower feed cost. There are some problems in the use of phase feeding. The procedure for taking into account all of the factors when making up a ration is a complicated one. When more than one age group of chickens is being fed, more feed storage bins and feeders are needed. It requires a high level of management ability on the part of the producer. Phase feeding is more practical for large commercial operations than it is for small farm flocks. Chickens should be fed only fresh feed. Overfilling feeders results in wasted feed. Hanging feeders should be filled only three-fourths full. Trough feeders should be filled only two-thirds full. Fill feeders in the early morning and refill during the day as needed. Keep the feed clean and never supply moldy or dirty feed. Feeders should be cleaned periodically. Feed should be stored in a dry place where rats or mice cannot get at it. Feed should be handled and stored in bulk for large operations.

A good manager watches the feed consumption of the flock closely. A drop in feed intake is oft en the first sign of trouble. Stress, disease outbreak, molting, or other management problems are oft en first indicated by a drop in feed consumption. Feed intake is also influenced by the energy level of the ration, level of protein intake, environmental temperature, body size, amount of feather coverage, and rate of growth or egg production. Feed intake is greater when high-energy rations are fed and lower when a low energy ration is fed. Feed intake is also lower at higher environmental temperatures and higher at lower environmental temperatures. Feed intake will change about 1.5 per cent for each 1.8°F (1°C) above or below 68°F to 70°F (20°C to 21°C). While temperature is the major factor that affects the level of feed intake, a low intake of protein may cause a higher total feed intake. The other factors mentioned above also have some influence on the level of feed intake.

- *Feeding for Egg Production:* Chicks must be given feed and water as soon as they are put into the brooder house. Starter rations should contain 18 per cent protein. Complete starter feeds should be used for chicks and they should be fed without grain until they are 6 weeks old. About 40 pounds (18 kg) of starter mash per 100 chicks is required for the first 2 weeks. From 2 to 6 weeks, 250 to 300 pounds (113 to 136 kg) of starter mash are needed per 100 chicks. Chick-size grit should be provided when the birds are young and a medium size given as they become older. For chicks up to 2 weeks of age, 100 linear inches (2.4 m) of feeder space is required for 100 chicks. Two hundred linear inches (5 m) of feeder space is needed per 100 chicks from 3 to 6 weeks of age. Up to 2 weeks of age, 25 linear inches (64 cm) of waterer space is needed per 100 chicks. From 3 to 6 weeks of age, 50 linear inches (1.3 m) of waterer space is required per 100 chicks. At 6 weeks of age, the feed should be changed to a growing ration. From 6 to 14 weeks the ration should contain 15 per cent protein. The ration should contain 12 per cent protein from 14 to 20 weeks. Grain may be fed from 6 weeks on.

Grain and mash should be fed in separate feeders. Begin with 10 pounds (4.5 kg) of grain to 100 pounds (45 kg) of mash. Gradually increase the amount of grain until the ration is one-half grain and one-half mash. At 18 to 20 weeks of age change the ration to a laying mash. The change should be made over a 2-week period of time. From 7 to 12 weeks of age, 250 linear inches (6.4 m) of feeder space and 50 linear inches (1.3 m) of waterer space are needed per 100 birds. From 13 to 20 weeks, 300 linear inches (7.6 m) of feeder space and 100 linear inches (2.5 m) of waterer space are needed per 100 birds. A laying ration should contain 14.5 per cent protein. The cost per dozen eggs produced should be used in deciding which the most economical ration to use is. Egg production, body size, health, and temperature all affect the amount of feed A laying hen eats. Light breeds eat about 24 pounds (10.9 kg) per 100 hens per day. A hen of the light weight breeds eats a total of 85 to 90 pounds (38.6 to 40.8 kg) of feed per year. A heavy-breed hen eats 95 to 115 pounds (40.8 to 52.2 kg) per year. About 2 to 5 pounds (0.9 to 2.3 kg) of oyster shell and 1 pound (0.45 kg) of grit per year per hen are required.

Light weight breeds require 300 linear inches (7.6 m) of feeder space and 50 linear inches (1.3 m) of waterer space. Heavy weight breeds need 400 linear inches (10.2 m) of feeder space and 100 linear inches (2.5 m) of waterer space per 100 birds. The ration for the laying flock should not be changed suddenly. This creates stress in the hens that will result in a drop in egg production. Even changing from a coarse-ground feed to a fi ne-ground feed may create stress and a drop in production. Three systems of feeding are commonly used for laying hens: *(i)* all mash; *(ii)* mash and grain and *(iii)* cafeteria. The all-mash system is the use of a complete ground feed. This system is well adapted to use with mechanical feeding systems. It is oft en used by commercial egg producers. In the mash and grain system, grain and mash are fed separately. A 20 to 26 per cent protein supplement is fed with a light grain feeding in the morning. Corn is fed in the evening. Some of the grain may be fed in the litter. This causes the hens to stir up the litter and help keep it drier. The cafeteria system allows the birds to balance their own rations. Grain is fed in one feeder and a 26 to 32 per cent protein supplement is fed in another feeder. Feed is kept in the feeders at all times. Older hens may tend to eat too much grain and not enough protein supplements when this system is used. About one fourth of the feeders should contain a protein supplement and three-fourths of the feeders should contain grain.

- *Feeding Efficiency:* Is the number of pounds (kms.,) of feed required to produce a dozen eggs. Records must be kept of the amount of feed used and the egg production in order to calculate feed efficiency. Divide the total pounds (kms.,) of feed fed by the number of dozen eggs produced to calculate how many pounds (kms.,) of feed it took to produce one dozen eggs. Feed efficiency should be about 4.3 pounds (1.95 kg) of feed per dozen eggs. Wasted feed, low rate of lay, health problems, or other management problems lower feed efficiency.
- *Feeding Broilers:* For chicks from day-old to 6 weeks, use a broiler starter ration with at least a 23 per cent protein level. Replacement chick starters, designed for egg production type birds, should not be used for broiler starter rations. Broiler starter rations should contain 3 per cent added fats and a coccidiostat. The protein level is adjusted to the energy level of the ration. Use chick-sized grit scattered on top of the mash or feed in separate hoppers. At 3 to 6 weeks of age, broilers should be fed a ration containing 20 per cent protein. Broilers need 100 linear inches (2.5 m) of feeder space and 25 linear inches (64 cm) of waterer space per 100 birds up to 2 weeks of age. Provide 300 linear inches (7.6 m) of feeder space and 50 linear inches (1.3 m) of waterer space for birds from 3 to 6 weeks of age. Feed a finishing ration of 18 per cent protein to birds from 6 weeks old to market age (usually, about 8 to 9 weeks of age). The finishing ration should contain 3 per cent or more of added fat. Broiler rations are fed as complete mixed feeds and never as separate grain and protein supplement, as rations for laying hens might be.

Provide 350 linear inches (8.9 m) of feeder space and 75 linear inches (1.9 m) of waterer space per 100 birds from 6 weeks to market age. Broilers are full fed at all times to obtain the fastest possible gains. Capons and roasters are fed to heavier weights than broilers. They are fed the same ration as broilers up to 6 weeks of age. After 6 weeks, grain is added to the ration in addition to the finishing mash until it is being fed as one-half of the ration. Vitamins and trace minerals are included in rations in small amounts. Broiler rations must be mixed properly and the quality carefully controlled. This is the responsibility of the feed mill where the mixing is done. Inventory control, assaying of mixed feeds (analysis for content), and assaying of ingredients are methods of ensuring proper mixing and quality control. Feed conversion in broilers refers to the amount of feed needed to produce 1 pound or 1 km of live weight. It is found by dividing the total weight of feed fed by the total weight of broilers marketed. Feed conversion after condemnations is found by subtracting the weight of the condemned meat from the weight of the birds marketed before dividing into the total weight of the feed used. Feed conversion is affected by a number of factors, including:

- Genetic background of the strain being fed.
- Type of feed used.
- Temperature, amount of feed wasted.
- Additives used in the feed.
- General management of the operation.

Other factors also affect feed conversion, but those mentioned here are the major ones. Current feed conversion in the broiler industry averages about 1.85 pounds (0.84 kg) of feed per 1 pound (0.45 kg) of gain for males and 1.95 pounds (0.88 kg) of feed per 1 pound (0.45 kg) of gain for females.

- *Feeding the Breeding Flock:* A special mash is made for use with breeder flocks. It contains 14.5 per cent protein and is fortified with extra vitamin A, D, B12, riboflavin, pantothenic acid, niacin, and manganese. This mash is more expensive than laying-henmash. The breeding flock should be started on breeder mash about 1 month before hatching eggs are to be kept. Breeding flocks may be fed a ration that is one-half mash and one-half grain. The breeding flock is fed in much the same way as is the laying flock. Replacement pullets for breeding flocks of meat-type chickens tend to grow too fast and develop sexual maturity too early. This results in too many small eggs that are not good for hatching purposes. Egg production tends to be at too low a level at its peak. Several methods may be used to slow down the rate of growth and sexual maturity. These include limiting feed intake, skip-a-day feeding, low-protein diets, and low-lysine diets. A limited-feed intake programme is based on feeding at the rate of about 70 per cent of the normal feed level. This programme is begun when the birds are from 7 to 9 weeks of age and is continued until they are 23 weeks old. They are then full fed on a laying mesh. A skip-a-day programme involves full feeding every other day. On alternate days, only 2 pounds (0.9 kg) of grain is fed per 100 birds. This feeding programme is followed from the seventh or ninth week to the twenty-third week.

A low-protein diet is one in which the protein level of the ration is 10 per cent. This programme is also followed from the seventh or ninth week to the 23rd week. A low-lysine diet will also slow down rate of growth and sexual maturity because of the amino acid imbalance. The diet contains 0.4 to

0.45 per cent lysine and 0.6 to 0.7 per cent arginine. It is followed from the seventh or ninth week until the twenty-third week. The protein level of this diet is 12.5 to 13 per cent.

Genetic Diversity and Distribution of Chicken Breeds

Almost all birds kept under traditional production system in Ethiopia are non-descript indigenous breeds of low performance. Broodiness is highly pronounced, egg production is estimated at 40-60 per bird per year. Egg weight is low ranging from 39 to 42 gm. The weight of male to an age of 12 months is about 1.52 kg., and for female it is much less than this. Few exotic breeds are imported and kept in commercial poultry keeping centers. Government is distributing exotic chicken breeds to farmers. The purpose of distribution is for up grading performance of local chicken breeds for the purpose of the Improvements of the genetic potential of the local chickens would done through selection in and or upgrading with exotic breeds thus, for the last for decades, scientists and government Have promotic schemes in which exchange or cockerels from selected strain or breed could improve the performance of local chickens. The intention of the scheme was to enable farmers to handle pure breeds as wells as cross breed chicken [13]. There is no well-developed breeding practice in chicken production in Ethiopia. However, farmers in the view to increase meat and egg production follow their own breeding practice. According to [6] the breeding practices of farmers were allowing cocks and hens to mate indiscriminately without systematic mating. The other practice was the use of improved exotic breeds crossing with local ecotypes. Nevertheless, their effects on upgrading of the village chicken performances have been minimal. This is because the programmes were usually planned without participation of farmers, with no parallel improvement of feeding, housing and health care and typically lasts for short time [2] there is no well-developed breeding practice in chicken production in Ethiopia. However, farmers in the view to increase meat and egg production follow their own breeding practice according to [11] the breeding practices of farmers were allowing cocks and hens to mate indiscriminately without systematic mating. The other practice was the use of improved exotic breeds crossing with local ecotypes. Nevertheless, their effects on upgrading of the village chicken performances have been minimal. This is because the programmes were usually planned without participation of farmers, with no parallel improvement of feeding, housing and health care and typically lasts for short time. [2] There is no well-developed breeding practice in chicken production in Ethiopia. However, farmers in the view to increase meat and egg production follow their own breeding practice according to [10]. The breeding practices of farmers were allowing cocks and hens to mate indiscriminately without systematic mating. The other practice was the use of improved exotic breeds crossing with local ecotypes. Nevertheless, their effects on upgrading of the village chicken performances have been minimal. This is because the programmes were usually planned without participation of farmers, with no parallel improvement of feeding, housing and health care and typically lasts for short time [3] there is no well-developed breeding practice in chicken production in Ethiopia. However, farmers in the view to increase meat and egg production follow their own breeding practice according to (Nigussie 2011). The breeding practices of farmers were allowing cocks and hens to mate indiscriminately without systematic mating. The other practice was the use of improved exotic breeds crossing with local ecotypes. Nevertheless, their effects on upgrading of the village chicken performances have been minimal. This is because the programmes were usually planned without participation of farmers, with no parallel improvement of feeding, housing and health care and typically lasts for short time. [8]

General facts on Temperate Chicken Breeds

Chicken in general are divided into breeds, varieties, types, and classes. A *breed* is a group of related fowls that breed true to a number of given traits that identify the breed. Breeds are subdivided into varieties based on certain traits, such as: color of plumage and comb type. *Type* refers to the purpose for which the poultry are bred. The two general types are egg-type and meat-type. *Class* generally refers to the geographic origin of the poultry. Four classes generally used for chickens in the United States are: *(i)* mediterranean; *(ii)* american; *(iii)* english and *(iv)* asiatic.

Most chickens used for egg and meat production are produced by cross-mating, breed crossing, or inbreeding. Very few pure strains of chickens are used commercially. Cross-mating is crossing two or more strains within the same breed. Breed crossing is crossing different breeds to get the desired traits. Inbred chickens are produced by inbreeding and crossing the inbred lines to get the desired traits. Most commercial egg-producing flocks are made up of White Leghorn strain crosses because of their superiority in egg production. Hybrid (inbred) crosses are also popular for egg production. The Leghorns and the Hybrids are white egg layers. Brown egg layers are Rhode Island Reds New Hampshires, and Barred Plymouth Rocks These are larger than the Leghorn strains and therefore have higher feed costs per dozen eggs produced. They are not as popular for large commercial flocks. Smaller farm flocks sometimes use these breeds because they produce more meat for home use and are considered to be dual-purpose breeds. However, they are not as efficient in either egg or meat production as breeds that are bred for one purpose.

Commercial crosses that are bred for meat production are generally used for broiler production operations. A common cross is White Plymouth Rock females mated to Cornish males. These crosses do not have a high rate of egg lay, but are highly efficient as meat producers. Characteristics of some typical breeds of chickens in four classes are shown in. There are a number of different varieties of most chickens. Color of plumage, type of comb, and size identify the different varieties. There are a number of different types of comb found in chickens. Some of these are: *(i)* single; *(ii)* rose; *(iii)* pea, *(iv)* cushion; *(v)* buttercup; *(vi)* strawberry and *(vii)* V-shaped. The single comb is the most common type. The other comb types mentioned are mutations. It shows some of the comb types of chickens. Bantamsare small chickens, usually weighing from 16 to 30 ounces (0.45 to 0.85 kg) as adults. There are nearly 150 varieties of bantams. Most of them are of the same breeds as the larger chickens. Bantams are generally used for show and as pets. They are not generally bred for egg or meat production.

Commercial hatcheries supply almost all of the chickens produced in the United States. Commercial hatcheries obtain hatching eggs from foundation breeders who raise parent flocks. Foundation breeders usually produce hatching eggs under some type of contract with the hatchery. Large commercial egg and meat producers buy chicks or started pullets from the hatchery. Small farm flock owners may obtain chickens from *(i)* a hatchery as day-old chicks; *(ii)* a grower who produces ready-to-lay pullets or *(iii)* as second year layers from a commercial flock. It is possible, although not too practical, to hatch chicks on the farm.

Day-old chicks should be bought from a reputable hatchery that is U.S. Pullorum-Typhoid Clean. The chicks should be secured from a hatchery that is as close to home as possible. The less distance the chicks have to travel, the lower the loss. Day-old chicks require brooding facilities, which increases the costs of raising them to production age. Day-old chicks can be bought as straight-run or sexed chicks. Straight-runchickscost less than sexed chicks. Straight-run chicks are about one-half pullet (female) and one-half cockerels (male). Sexed chicksare sorted into pullets and cockerels. (Sex-linked characteristics may be used to sort chicks by sex at the hatchery. Sexing chicks by visual inspection is a specialized occupation requiring special training and practice.) The decision as to which to buy depends on how the chickens are to be used. Straight-run chicks will provide some birds for meat. If birds are wanted only for egg production, then pullets should be purchased. If only meat production is desired, cockerels should be purchased. Started chickens may be available from a grower who specializes in this type of operation. These chickens require less equipment and care than day-old chicks. Started pullets are generally sold at about 6 to 8 weeks of age. Ready to-lay pullets are sold at about 16 to 20 weeks of age. Started chickens cost more than other chickens because of the feed, care, culling, and management that has already been invested in them. Most commercial flocks of laying hens are replaced after 12 to 15 months. They go through a molting period and will then lie again. A small farm flock owner could get cheaper chickens with a bred-in potential for high rate of lay from this source. Farm flocks used for meat production are usually started from day-old chicks. Straight-run chicks are usually bought. Meat-type breeds should be used.

General facts on Tropical Chicken Breeds

The majority of breeds used today by commercial poultry-keepers are hybrids that have been bred by the large scale international poultry-breeding corporations, and fertile eggs, day-old chicks or parental breeding stock are imported into tropical countries, primarily from temperate climates. Under good management the productivity of these hybrids can be very high. Fowls lay 250270 white shelled eggs per annum, weighing 62 g on average. Body size in 1.25 kg at sexual maturity and 1.7 kg at conformation maturity. Male broilers weigh 1.9 kg at 44 days with a feed conversion of 1.9:1.0. Females show a somewhat lower productivity. Those interested in purchasing hybrid breeding stock should consult their extension organization or representatives of the international corporations who are established in many tropical countries.

If for some reason hybrid breeding stock is not available from the international corporations then the improved pure breeds most commonly used are of three types: those developed for high egg production, those bred specifically for meat production, and dual-purpose breeds. The breeds used for high egg production are mainly of Mediterranean origin and the most popular are the *Leghorn, Ancona* and *Minorcan*. The *White Leghorn* is the most widely used white egg producing breed. Mature cockerels and hens weigh approximately 2.7 kg and 1.8 kg, respectively. The hens do not go broody very easily so that it is necessary to set the eggs under a hen of another breed or to incubate them artificially. Hens are very good layers with a high efficiency of feed conversion, but birds of this breed do not produce good carcasses. They appear to be more heat tolerant than other commercial breeds, although in other ways they are not particularly hardy. Meat-producing types are typified by the *Orpington, Cornish* and *Jersey Black Giant*. These are heavy breeds, mature cockerels of the three breeds weighing 3.9 kg, 3.9 kg and 5.0 kg, respectively. These breeds are not normally economical egg producers or particularly heat tolerant. Apart from the White Leghorn, dual-purpose, brown egg producing breeds such as: the *Rhode Island Red* (RIR), *New Hampshire* and *Australorp* are the most popular breeds used in tropical countries. Mature RIR cockerels and hens weigh approximately 3.6 kg and 2.7 kg respectively. The RIR hens are good layers and meat producers, but they possess a yellow-skinned carcase, unliked by some consumers. They go broody very easily, but thrive well in the humid tropics. The New Hampshire is an early maturing breed. Mature cockerels and hens weigh 4 kg and 2.6 kg, respectively. Australorps have been extensively used in Southeast Asia, although hens of this breed do not lay as well as some of the other breeds mentioned and quickly go broody. The breed crosses well with the White Leghorn. Mature cockerels and hens weigh 3.6 kg and 2.7 kg., respectively. In some countries the government imports selected pure lines of poultry and breeds from them large numbers of exotic purebreds or crossbreds for use in village upgrading programmes or by commercial producers. The Government Poultry Breeding Programme in India is an example of such a scheme. Where fowls have to hatch their own brood, scavenge for the major part of their food and are unprotected against predators and endemic disease, then indigenous breeds should be used. There are innumerable types.

In those countries where the main functions of domestic fowl in the past were to supply meat and provide fighting cocks, body-size and vigor have been the traits for which they have been selected. There are many such breeds; the Indian *Aseel* being a typical example. These fowl grow very slowly. Even under the best of managerial conditions they only achieve a live weight of approximately 1.8 kg in 6 months, but cockerels and hens grow on to achieve mature live weights of 4.5 kg and 3.23.6 kg, respectively. The breast and thighs of the cockerels are particularly well developed and the pullets are also valuable meat producers. The average egg production of this breed is 35 per annum. Some indigenous breeds produce a relatively.

Egg Handling

Good poultry husbandry and management are essential for profitable egg and meat production, growth rate, egg weight, feed intake proportion of second class eggs, egg shell quality, percentage production and mortality rate are the key factors that determine profitability for the farmer. Good poultry management needs that the poultry man should have a wide knowledge of feeding, housing, disease control, record keeping, breeds and breeding.

To ensure egg safety and quality, home producer should manage chicken properly. Eggs that spend more time in the nest have an increased chance of becoming dirty, broken or lower in quality. Collecting eggs at least twice daily is recommended profitable before noon. Coated wire.

Baskets or plastic egg plates are good containers for collecting [15]. Dirty eggs can be cleaned with fine sand paper brush or emery cloth. Eggs need to be wash temperature of the water should be at least 20°F warmer than the egg. This prevents the egg contents from contaminating and producing microscopic bacteria [16].

Local Chicken Ownership Pattern and Gender Role

Among house hold members in Ethiopia chicken can be owned by children, wife or husband. In the rural sub-Saharan Africa including Ethiopia more than 70 per cent of chicken owners are women [17] they look after the birds as earnings from sale of eggs chickens are often significant sources of their income. Women dominated most of the activities around chicken production. The women dominated in feeding (37.7%), watering (51.2%)

and cleaning (37.2%) [18]. Men dominated shelter construction (60%) and treatment of chicken (40.5%). In the study conducted in five agro-ecological zones of Ethiopia [19] reported that women have better knowledge about poultry and poultry production than their men counterpart. Flock is mainly managed by women. Hence helping women to boost rural production, increase equitable distribution of food in the house hold.

Housing of Local Chicken in Ethiopia

Poultry housing should provide adequate shelter, a healthy and comfortable environment and reduce labor requirements to a minimum. Requirements for housing differ from one region of the tropics to another. In the wet tropics protection is required against rain, high humidity and moderately high ambient temperatures, whereas in the dry tropics protection is required against very high and quite low ambient temperatures and possibly dust storms. There is a variation in forms of housing of chicken across different areas of Ethiopia. Some poultry keepers in Ethiopia keep chicken in family house at night, where as some others use different shelter in the same roof and the rest use separate shelter, respectively. The sharing of the same roof with human being might be due to the small flock size per household and/or giving low emphasis for their birds or lack of facilities to construct separate houses. Sharing the same roof with people particularly overnight might be also associated with the protection from predators, which is very severe in the night than during daytime. This is in agreement with the findings of [5] indicated that in Ethiopia and in Kenya, where it is reported that no separate housing for the chickens rather generally housed in the living room or in the kitchen where they scavenge for feed. But [21] from Zimbabwe reported that most farmers (>90%) had some structures that were especially constructed for poultry housing without internal facility like egg laying nests.

The housing forms were not uniform across the different age groups and vulnerability of village chicken. Broody hen with chicks was given more care but simple roost was provided to other groups of chicken. In areas where there was high risk of predators, households were giving more care for all groups of chicken in nighttime. In addition to this, such housing systems only targeted to protect chicken from predators without giving consideration to negative-impact of harsh production environment on poultry productivity.[22] reported that, the most serious problem facing birds at early age is inadequate environments. Till most of the farmers are not aware of the importance of separate poultry-house construction for better production and this trend might be resulted in low productivity and predations of chicken. Moreover these bird-quarters lack internal facilities like: egg laying nest, roosts and feeder. Similar findings were reported by [21]. However, daytime housing was not recommended by [23] who found that, daytime housing was not economical in areas where there is no enough feed supply. Housing of village chickens in properly constructed house would facilitate for good productivity.

Usually there is no special housing provided for birds in the rural village of Ethiopia. In most case (88.5%) of the birds roost inside the family dwelling at night. A few house hold (11.5%) have constructed a small enclosure outside the house and the poultry night shelter is occasionally cleaned by the house wife, depending on her work load [6]. A study conducted in north western part of Ethiopia. [21] Also revealed that only 50.77 per cent of farmers kept their chickens outside the main house in shades built for the birds. [10] Reported that in Rushing a district of Zimbabwe, all farmers provide housing to their chickens. Brick and liter types were the most popular house because farmers felt that they provide more warmth's and security from both thieves and predators than other type of housing. Proper housing must not only provide environment that moderates environmental impacts but also must provide adequate ventilation to the birds lay eggs nest boxes and to feed sleep in comfort security. Lack of adequate housing can partly explain chicken mortality and thus good housing is a prerequisite for any viable and sustainable poultry production.

General facts on Poultry Housing

Poultry housing should provide adequate shelter, a healthy and comfortable environment and reduce labor requirements to a minimum. Requirements for housing differ from one region of the tropics to another. In the wet tropics protection is required against rain, high humidity and moderately high ambient temperatures, whereas in the dry tropics protection is required against very high and quite low ambient temperatures and possibly dust storms.

- *Location:* If there is a choice of location all buildings should be sited on the highest ground not subject to flooding and where advantage can be taken of any prevailing breezes. All buildings should if possible face in the same direction and preferably be east west orientated. There should be a distance of at least 12 m between individual buildings in order to reduce the possibilities of disease and parasite transference from house to house. If possible the brooder house should be completely separate from other buildings. The feed room should be centrally sited and the egg-storage room located adjacent to egg-laying units.
- *Floors:* The most suitable material for the floor is concrete, but wooden or rammed earth floors can be used.
- *Walls:* In the wet tropics the walls of all except environmentally controlled houses should be open. Heavy-gauge nettingwire or expanded metal grilles are the most suitable materials with which to screen buildings. Screening is essential as it keeps out the larger vermin and wild birds. The screened walls should be provided with some form of protective cover that would normally be rolled up or pulled to one side, but which can be used during the rainy season to protect the birds and, in the case

of deep-litter houses the litter, from driving rain. Split bamboo, reedcurtains or blinds are very suitable or heavy-duty plastic sheeting can be used. In dry climates the walls should be solid, at least to above the door level. Brick or clay and straw are very suitable materials. In such houses it is necessary to make adequate provision for ventilation. Although external temperatures may rise rapidly during the day time, internal temperatures will rise more slowly in such houses.

- *Roofs:* In the wet tropics high-pitch roofs are required that will shed heavy rain. They should overhang the eaves by at least 1.0 m. The height of the roof should be at least 3.7 m at the eaves. In the dry tropics the roofs can be flat or have a low pitch, but they should be as high off the ground as is practice a bleat least 3.7 m. The main roofing materials available are corrugated iron and thatch, although in a few tropical countries such as: Mauritius and Indonesia clay tiles are cheap and can be used for roofing. Corrugated iron is the least suitable, and if it is used it should be painted with aluminum paint on the upper side and with black paint on the lower side. Thatch is very suitable, but as it has to be replaced quite frequently maintenance costs are high. It also has the disadvantage that it harbors vermin. A wide variety of thatching materials are available in the tropics, including all types of grasses and reeds and many types of palm thatch, including doum palm (*Hyphaenethebaica*) in the dry areas of East and Northeast Africa, coconut palm and nipa palm (*Nypafruticans*) in Southeast Asia and oil palm (*Elaeisguineensis*) in West Africa, Southeast Asia and elsewhere. A corrugated iron roof can be combined with thatch which acts asan insulating material under the corrugated iron. There should be a gap of approximately 10 cm between the corrugated iron and the thatch.
- *Dimensions:* The dimensions of houses will obviously vary in accordance with the needs of the poultry farmer. In general, houses approximately 10 m wide and with 1.2 m internal passages have been found to be practical and useful. They can, of course, be any length that is required. Methods of Reducing Heat Stress Where environmentally controlled houses cannot be utilized for economic reasons or because adequate services are not available, the poultry farmer should still attempt to reduce the possibility of heat stress in housed birds. The first consideration is adequate ventilation. In the wet tropics houses without walls should provide adequate ventilation and some degree of alleviation of heat stress on birds from improved air circulation. In the dry tropics, where the birds are enclosed, proper ventilation of the house is essential. As hot air rises, ridge ventilation is a necessity. If economic and service circumstances allow it, forced-air fans should be used.

- *Fold Houses and Pens:* The runs are made of 1.3 cm mesh 14-gauge wire netting set on a framework of light but tough wood. To house 50 birds the frame should have a floor space of 9 m2. The house can be of the slatted ark type that is widely used in the temperate zone, modified for use in the tropics. It should stand 30 cm above the ground. The floor is made of slats approximately 2.5 cm wide and spaced 2.5 cm apart. A moveable wire netting floor is fitted 10 cm below the slats to prevent the entry of vermin. The walls, which also form the roof, converge steeply to the ridge about 1.2 m above the slats. The one wall can be enclosed, but the other should consist of a door made from a frame covered with 1.3 cm mesh, 14-gauge netting in order to permit free circulation of the air. A bamboo or plastic roll-up flap or curtain should be attached to the open wall so that protection can be provided during heavy rain. The wall-roof can of course also be made of thatch. Fold houses are only practical in areas devoid of major predators.
- *Semi-Intensive Houses:* It is advisable under tropical conditions to utilize houses that accommodate approximately 50 adult birds The wire out-runs should be at least 1.8 m in height and be made of 1.3 cm heavy-gauge galvanized wire netting. The top-most 13 cm should be left slack so that it does not provide birds with a steady foothold, and the wire should be buried 30 cm into the ground to stop vermin burrowing under. This precaution is particularly necessary where the mongoose is a local predator.
- *Deep-Litter Houses:* For the small poultry-keeper who cannot afford a controlled-environment deep-litter house the main considerations are that the house should be cheap to construct, that birds are not over-crowded in the house and that the litter is not allowed to become damp. The maximum depth of the litter should be no more than 30 cm. The normal requirements of mature birds are litter with a depth of 10.13 cm accumulating to 2023 cm. For chicks the initial depth of the litter should be no more than 58 cm, but it can gradually be built up as the chicks grow. As stated previously the floor of the deep-litter house can be rammed earth, wood or concrete, but concrete is preferable. There must be a retaining wall of concrete or brick around the floor at least 30 cm high. If division walls are required inside the house the most suitable material to use is expanded metal grilles, as these allow for ventilation but are also quite rigid. Many materials can be used as a litter including peat moss, wood shavings, sawdust, rice husks, chopped maize, sorghum or millet stalks, chopped rice straw, dried leaves, groundnut shells, or even dried cow manure. If damp patches occur in the litter it should be turned and treated with burnt lime or superphosphate at the rate of 1 kg for every 1.5 m2 of litter.

- *Battery House:* Data on the cages have already been provided. Requirements are that the house should be well ventilated, lighted and vermin-proof. On small farms a house with a concrete floor, a roof and wire-mesh or expanded metal sides would meet these requirements, but the birds will not perform quite as efficiently as they will in an insulated, controlled-environment house. In such a house the batteries of cages can be serviced by automatic watering, feeding and cleaning devices that if powered from a reliable source and properly serviced are very labor saving and efficient.
- *Controlled-Environment Houses:* These are houses in which the optimal environment is provided for whatever form of production is planned. Ambient temperature, humidity, air movement and light must all be controlled. The building must therefore afford effective insulation from the external environment.

Constraints of Local Chicken Management in Ethiopia

In most African countries including Ethiopia, the chicken kept in the villages have no regular health control programme, may or may not have shelter and scavenge for most of their nutritional needs. According to [3], [24] and [25] the low productivity of the local scavenging hens is not only because they are low producers of small sized eggs and slow growers but also the system is characterized by its high chick mortality before they reach around 8 weeks of age. Moreover, the local chickens are the results of uncontrolled breeding between various local chicken ecotypes, which have not been selected by Systematic breeding methods.

Many poultry development projects have failed to meet their objectives, due to the inability to identify appropriate technologies and define the poultry production practices and constraints. Low levels of inputs and outputs characterize village poultry production systems. Different categories of the people in Ethiopia are constrained from consuming poultry product at home due to unavailability of the poultry products, giving priority for income-generation and expensiveness to prepare the dish, respectively than other factors. Chicken and eggs from poor households and owned by children's in the family were more likely to be sold as a sources of cash income.

Disease, Parasite and Predator Problem

G The Incidence of Disease, Parasite and Predators in Ethiopia

Disease, parasite and predators are the main causes for loss of chicken in Ethiopia. Viral (Newcastle), protozoal (coccidiosis) and bacterial diseases are the most common health problems of local chicken in Ethiopia. Among all disease problems the major problem impairing the existing production system in Ethiopia is the high incidence of new castle disease which is named locally 'fengle' [2]. Another report in southern part of the country by [14], Indicated that fowl cholera is major problem followed by new castle disease. [18] Report that in rushing district of zimbabuwe; disease attributed 20 per cent of the total death of the birds. [6] Reported that among the diseases of village chicken in Ethiopia. *Newcastle disease* was ranked as the most economically important one because of reducing both the number and productivity of birds. The cause for New castle disease *(NCD)* was Paramyxo virus, transmitted by sick birds and other species of wild birds. Incubation period of this disease is from 2 up to 15 days. The symptom of this disease is: Coughing, gasping and raspy breathing and/or extreme nervousness and distended crop, inactivity, inco-ordination, drowsiness, huddling near heat source, dropping head partial paralysis coma death. The second most important chicken disease in Ethiopia is coccidiosis. It is a disease caused by nine species of coccidiosis (Protozoan parasites), spread through contaminated food, water or litter. Each species attacks a different portion of the intestine or ceca. It is extremely difficult to isolate chickens from cocidiosis. It's Symptom Vary with type of coccidian, but general signs are decrease in feed intake, birds hunch backs, droop tails and ruffle feather. Diarrhoea may start and the loose droppings may be bloody (reddish brown), following diarrhoea mortality may increase. It can be treated if a confirmed outbreak among chickens 1 to 12 weeks of age and if it is severe, treat immediately with locally recommended coccidiostat.

Other important poultry diseases in Ethiopia include: fowl pox, fowl chlera, infectious coryza and pllorum.

- *Fowl pox:* Cause of this disease are Viruses spread by insects especially mosquitoes and then by direct contact with infected birds and wild birds. It generally attacks birds in the age of 3 to 5 months. Symptoms of this disease are of -two forms: Dry pox or modular form usually appear as a wart or insect bite causing swelling of combs wattles, face and sometimes eyes. By itself, this form doesn't cause much mortality. Wet or diphtheritic form starts with discharges from the eyes and nostrils, then cheesy material form in the mouth which can cause suffocation.
- *Fowl choler:* Fowl cholera was recognized as a disease of poultry 200 years ago. It still remains an important and poorly controlled disease of poultry it is caused by etiologic agent is pasteurella multocida which can be destroyed by many disinfectants and by sun light, heat and drying, conversely, the organism persists for months in decaying carcasses and moist soil. It is mostly transmitted through contaminated drinking water or feed, rats and mice. There are two types of fowl cholera these include: *(i)* per acute or server cholera: infected birds may suddenly be found dead even though they looked perfectly healthy the day before. *(ii)* Acute and chronic: Sudden unexpected deaths occur. Laying birds may found dead on the nest. Sick birds show anorexia, depression, nasal or oral discharge of mucus, white watery or green mucoid diarrhoea. The course of the illness is short and often followed by death.

- *Infectious coryza:* Infectious coryza is an acute or sub-acute disease. All ages of chickens are susceptible although most natural outbreak occurs in chickens that are half grown or older. It is caused by Homophilus gallinarum which is a fragile bacterium can stay outside of the host for only a few days. Easily destroyed by many disinfectants and by environmental factors. It is transmitted through Sick or apparently healthy carrier birds which are major reservoir of infection and easily transmit the disease.
- *Pullorum:* it is a disease Caused by Salmonella bacilli transmitted through the egg from one generation to another if the parents are not free of the disease. Transmission can also occur by visitors feet animals, contaminated feed, water equipment and wild birds. Symptoms of this disease include: Sudden death in chicks, other chicks droop wings, huddle near heat source. Diarrhoea is white sticky and forming. Chicks may have 50 per cent mortality, adults in acute outbreaks are weak and depressed may have greenish diarrhoea. It can be Treated by Sulpha based drugs. Do not use infected birds for breeding. It can be prevented by Buy only certified pullorum free chicks and implement sanitary management.

The most common *parasites* that attack chicken in Ethiopia include: *(i)* Internal parasites (Round warms, Tape warmas, Cecal warms) *(ii)* External *(a)* (Lice on Body and Head. *(b)* Mites (Red, Scaly leg, Feather, Depluming). Both internal and external parasites get their food from the host and they may carry diseases which can affect host. Good sanitation is important in order to prevent them.

The problem of disease in village poultry production is compounded by the interaction of the different factors that are significant important to disease epidemiology. At village level; contacts between flocks of different households; exchange of birds as gift or process of sale and purchase are the main source of infections for disease transmission [18], [18]. According to[13] the losses attributable to mortality are not known; however it has been estimated that more than 750 million chickens in Africa die each year as a result of various infection and chick mortality due to disease. This represents a major loss in village chicken production system. Predator attributed to 40.5 per cent of the total death of the birds [22] Predators were listed as a major cause of premature death and many households had suffered serious losses due to predation. This predation was strongly associated with the rain season because of the high density of vegetation which attracted and provided cover for predator animals [6] Although predator were blamed for the majority of losses combination of poor nutrition predator and various diseases factor made significant contribution. The highest mortality of village chicken was seen up to 2 weeks of age groups followed by one up to two months of age groups. This mortality rate may not only due to diseases but also other factors like harsh production environment where they scavenge on. Similarly, mortality during brooding stage (up to 8 week of age) was high for village chickens [5], [9], [23] and [20]. These authors further explained that this (mortality) represents the major loss in the scavenging system of production, but most of the losses were not clearly known.

General facts on Disease and Parasites of Chicken

Health is the condition in which all organ systems and body structures are working in full harmony. *Disease* is a deviation from normal health. It is a condition where the harmony in function of organs and body structures is upset and normal life is disturbed. *Stress is* an additional burden on an organism which tends to produce disharmony. Stress can arise from any of a number of internal and external factors. All factors of stress cause hormone change in which the adrenal glands and the pituitary gland play a part. Birds under stress produce less and more prone to disease condition.

There are internal and external factors that influence an outbreak of disease. There are internal and external factors that influence an outbreak of disease.

- *Internal Factor:* Include: heredity, sex and immunity when we come tohereditybirds have natural hereditary protection against certain diseases whereas other are more susceptible to the same disease. When we see age, some diseases occur at a certain age *e.g.,* coccidsosis of the ceca is a typical disease of the young bird. Marek's disease although contracted as a chick shows no symptoms until 4 to 5 months. Only fully grown adult birds suffer from leucosis complex or tuberculosis. When we see sex, some diseases appear more in one sex than the other does. In the case of immunity, some birds have more immunity to certain diseases. Immunity can be stimulated either by vaccination or by natural recovery from diseases. In a few diseases short lived immunity may be passed from hen to chick through the egg.
- *External Factors:* Include: feed, water, climate temperature, relative humidity, hygiene, composition of air and stocking density of the birds. When we see stocking density of the birds, with increased stocking density there is more contact between birds and the possibility of infection is increased. Lack of enough space for each bird for feeding and exercise expose the birds to diseases in the case of feed, with proper feeding birds can resist diseases, more than when there is poor feeding, some feeding practices will lead to increased infection. In case of water, insufficient and impure water will cause a drop in production and will expose birds to disease attack, continuous supply of fresh water is essential.
- *Hygiene:* Disease is always a hazard in poultry rearing with the establishment of large farms the risk of disease increases. The first requirement for good hygiene is effective cleaning with good cleaning

one can eliminate more than 90 per cent of all disease. The following hygienic measures are used to protect poultry against diseases.

1. Isolation of the farms. Locate them as far away from other poultry farms as practical. No admittance of visitors. The poultry house has to be closed properly. If any person is to be admitted to the poultry house he must be made to change his footwear and clothes and should disinfect his hands. Get feed in bulk transport or in proper houses and Prevent entry of wild birds into poultry house.
2. Keep one category of poultry on the farm at any one time and if possible keep birds of one age. Young chicks are more sensitive to diseases than older birds. Microorganisms can be transmitted easily from adults to chicks and vice versa. Prevent children, dogs, cats or other animals from entering poultry house. Poultry house personnel should not be allowed to keep poultry at home.
3. All poultry equipment in the poultry house should be cleaned and disinfected before use. Good housing solid floor *e.g.,* cement and smooth walls are essential for cleaning and disinfection. All insects' rats and mice should be destroyed since they are carriers of diseases. Rats are vicious predators of young chicks. Good ventilation is essential to maintain temperature and humidity. Use of healthy stock all the time is very important. A scheme of vaccination based on sound veterinary advice is essential. Cull all sick birds at the first sign of disease. An immediate removal of dead birds is necessary and all dead birds should be disposed of either by burning or by burial.
4. Avoid overcrowding and overheating of the birds. Buy chicks or hatching eggs from pullorum free flocks. Give well balanced and adequate feed from a reputable mill or give fresh home mixed concentrate. Provide a footbath of disinfectant at the entrance of poultry houses.

Egg Incubation and Hatching Process in Ethiopia

A study conducted in Ethiopia revealed that there is higher egg hatchability rate at wet season than dry season because high temperature that occurs during dry season most commonly affected incubation of egg by the hen because at hot temperature condition it was difficult for the hen to sit on the egg for long period of time. With good hatchability in most traditional systems, keeping the flock number constant requires eight to ten eggs for production living at average of 35-40 per cent eggs for sell and consumption [21].

General facts on Egg Incubation and Hatching Processes

- *Collection and Storage of Hatching Eggs:* Hatching eggs should be collected as frequent as possible at least four times a day. With respect to storage one of the required quality characteristics for hatching eggs is freshness.

In most cases it cannot be avoided to store the eggs for a few days before putting them in the incubation. It is therefore important to know how eggs best can be stored. During storage of hatching eggs two main processes have to be prevented as much as possible Development of the embryo and Evaporation of water out of the eggs. Can be achieved by a proper temperature and humidity. After lying the egg gradually cools down from 41°C (hens body temperature) to house temperature. As long as the egg temperature is higher than 27°C the embryonic development continues. The embryos have the highest chances to survive a storage period if they are cooled down below 27°C within five to six hours after lying. When eggs are stored for a few days to even two or three weeks it is necessary to lower the temperature. A relationship exists between the length of the time eggs are stored and the optimum temperature for best hatchability. So the longer the storage period, the lower the storage temperature should be. On the other hand, storage of eggs at lower temperature may cause condensation of moist from the air on the shell when they suddenly taken from the storage room to a room with a higher temperature.

- *Effects of Storing Hatching Eggs:* Storage prolongs incubation time. On average beyond 2 days adds one hour to incubation time. It depresses hatchability. There is a loss of 0.5-1 per cent per day after the first period of 7 days (more evaporated) Depresses weight of broiler hatched from eggs stored for 14 days. For this reasons hatching eggs should not be stored for more than 7 days.
- *Selection of Hatching Eggs:* Do not include dirty floor eggs. Use first class eggs, all eggs with obvious abnormalities should be rejected. Avoid malformed eggs sine they do not hatch well. Avoid broken or cracked eggs, because they do not hatch since they dry out in the incubator. Small and extra-large eggs should not be used. Long eggs are usually 'double yolks' which do not hatch. Do not use abnormally coloured eggs since they are usually the result of genetic defect.
- *Position and Turning of Eggs in the Incubator:* Eggs should be turned regularly at least twice a day starting 24 hours after setting until the 18th day. There are two reasons for turning. To prevent the embryo sticking in one side for equal temperature distribution. When turning avoid shocking and jolting. Regarding position it is important to place the eggs the small end pointing down ward. If the blunt end is placed down ward hatchability will be decreased by about 15 per cent.
- *Fundamental Points of Incubation*: In addition to quality of hatching eggs the following factors are major importance to achieve good result. Temperature, Humidity, Ventilation and Hygiene.

- *Temperature:* The optimum temperature for the development of the avian embryo varies in relation to the type of incubator. Distinction is made between incubators with a fan and without a fan. The development of a fertile hen egg into a young chick requires: A temperature of 37.5-39°C (100-103°F) for three weeks, A supply of fresh air allowing the embryo to breathe, Enough humidity to prevent the egg content from drying out and Some movement of the egg to prevent the embryo from sticking to one side of the egg. An incubator must therefore have Source of heat, Thermostat to maintain the temperature at 37.5-39°C, Tray which holds the egg steady but allows the movement of air around the eggs, Supply of water to humidify of (to moisten) the air in the incubator and Ventilator to provide fresh air and to remove stale air.

General facts on Natural Incubation of Eggs

It is by natural incubation that most chicks of indigenous breeds are produced in the villages. The village hen, sitting on the usual clutch of some eight to ten eggs, needs little food and even less attention. However, the results are usually rather poor, and if the incubating hen was only given a fraction of the care normally bestowed on an artificial incubator, major benefits would accrue. The principal requirements for a 'sitting hen' are a plentiful supply of clean drinking water, a subsistence feed supply, protection against insect pests and vermin, and on hatching, protection of the chicks from predators. The nest should be placed in some quiet, shaded cool corner at ground level and should be enclosed so that the hen can leave it only when permitted. This should be each morning, for about 10 minutes as soon after dawn as is convenient, and again in the evening. During these times the hen should be fed grain and provided with fresh water to drink and a sand-bath in which to dust her. She should be left undisturbed after the eggs have started to chip and be allowed to move off the nest into her breeding quarters at will. Chaff, sawdust or sand makes the best bedding. In very dry climates the nest should be dampened daily. Before the hen sits on the nest, both she and it should be liberally dusted or sprayed with an insecticide.

Chick Growing/Brooding

Chick Brooding in Ethiopia

Average natural brooding period in Ethiopia was estimated to be 2.5-3 month. [19] Estimated that under scavenging conditions after incubation phase a 56 days brooding period will follow. Almost All farmers in Ethiopia brood their chicks naturally most of the farmers loss their chicks during brooding. The cause for loss is disease and predators /rat cat and wild birds/ local hen is used for brooding and incubation.

General facts on Chick Brooding

Brooding refers to the period when young chicks require a lot of care. The period ranges from one-day of age to about four weeks in the tropics.

During this period supplementary heat is provided for the chicks comfort. It is the most critical period in the life of the birds and there can be more deaths during this short period than throughout the rest of the birds' lives. Great care must be taken during brooding. There are two methods of brooding chicks namely natural brooding and artificial brooding.

- *Natural Brooding*: Is the method whereby a broody hen takes care of the chicks she hatched. The local fowls are more suitable for natural brooding. A good sized broody hen can brood up to 12 chicks in colder weather and up to 15 during hot weather. The system is suitable for small number of chicks. Under backyard conditions the hatched chicks are reared and protected by the broody hen.
- *Artificial Brooding:* In this case use is made of equipment and facilities which provide conditions similar to those of the broody hens like: adequate warmth, protection against harsh conditions and predators. Proper feeding watering and veterinary care are provided. The type of brooder used will depend on location and financial resources of the farmer. The most important thing is that the brooder supplies enough heat without fumes which could harm the chicks. Brooder operations in the temperate climate require heating of a whole house. In the tropics heat may be provided to a particular area in the house. Artificial heat sources are (brooders can be made of).
    1. Electric brooder (infra-red heat bulbs).
    2. Kerosene brooders.
    3. Hot air hot water or radiant heat.
- *Battery Brooder:* Battery brooders are designed to accommodate large number of chicks in a limited space for short period of time. It is not used to raise chicks to maturity. It is not commonly used in Africa except for research.
- *Management of Chicks from 1 day to 8 week of Age:* Poor management as well as disease can result in high mortality. Therefore, it is essential to provide proper growing conditions for the chicks. Before the day old chicks are received. Make sure that the following are in order. If it has been used remove old litter. The floor, walls and roofs thoroughly cleaned. All holes and cracks should be patched. Disinfect the house, allow the house to dry. Add at least 5cm litter material for the first time, the litter should be clean and dry.
- *Cleaning of the House and Equipment:* Soon after the birds are removed the house should be cleaned disinfected and made ready for the next batch. After cleaning the house must be left empty for at least 15 days.
- *Cleaning Procedure:* Remove all old litter from the house and haul it away from the house, clean the house and disinfect it, clean the equipment, clean and fumigate feed bin, clean areas around the house, Place good

litter material on the floor at 5-10 cm depth, check light, check water (20°C), Check brooder temperature that: 1st day = 33-34°C, 2nd day = 32°C, 1st week = 30°C, 2nd week = 30-25°C, 3rd week = 8-25°C and 4th week = 25-20°C. Every time check the temperature under the brooder canopy. In the absence of thermometer it is possible to estimate the intensity of heat under the canopy by observing the condition of the chicks as follows: When the temperature is too high we see that: The chicks sit with spread out wings and open beaks, sit as far as possible away from the heat source, there is less feed intake, the chicks drink more water and this often cause wet litter. When the temperature is too low we see that the chicks Come close together, are less active, will raise their feather cover and will stay close to the heat source.

- *Light*: The chicks will eat when there is light. As eating must be stimulated especially early in the brooding period artificial lighting is a must. However gradual reduction of the light is recommended.
  0-1 week: 23 hours light (including day light).
  1-2 weeks: 20 hours (ditto).
  2-4 week: 16 hours (ditto), from 4 weeks onward a constant day length of 14 hrs is advisable.
- *Feeding:* When the chicks are day old flat feeders cut out from chick boxes egg trays and flats can be used. As they grow up the feeders should be changed to deeper and longer containers. Shallow drinkers must be used during this period.
- *Confinement:* To confine the chicks around the source of heat source, feed, and water and to prevent drought it is necessary to erect a so called brooder guard around them. A cardboard or any similar material with a height of about 15cm can be used. Space provision will be a maximum of 500 chicks per brooder, 75 chicks per fount, 100 chicks per feeder plate or 50 chicks per egg tray. Density at one day, 40-50 chicks per m^2, remembers to expand the guard a little every day. Allow 2cm/bird and 7cm/bird feeding spaces of round and long feeders respectively, 1.5cm/bird drinking spaces of round and long drinkers. Standard for heating capacity brooders is 5 kcal/hr./chick. Standard for lighting capacity are: bulbs 3-4 w/mtube, lights 0.8-1w/m^2. Light an electrical heating reflector lamp is 150W = 129 Kcal /hr. Males can be recognized at 6-8 weeks of age in unsexed flocks by the following characteristics: Cocks usually have a bigger comb, Cocks stand in a more upright position than hens, in cocks the feathers are more pointed than in hens whose feathers are smaller and rounded.
- *Causes of Early Mortality in Brooder Chicks:* The aim of the poultry farmer is to raise all his chicks if possible, so he should try to identify the causes of early mortality in the chicks during the brooding period and eliminate

them. The possible causes of early mortality in baby chicks are many and varied but can be any one or a combination of the following:

- *Hatching mishaps:* Diseased and badly hatched chicks are common in some hatcheries. The navel of such chicks may be bloody the fluff and down feathers still moist some chicks may have crossed beaks and curled toe due to poor hatchery hygiene or caused by faulty techniques such as: low or high incubator temperatures low or high humidity or poor ventilation. Affected chicks may only survive a few days.
- *Chilling:* This is caused by poor brooding and is often more common during cold weather. The chicks cluster in heaps and many die from crushing. Provide brooder guards and sufficient heat during brooding.
- *Suffocation and Choking*: Death can occur from suffocation and choking when there is poor ventilation or when brooding lamps given off fumes. Chicks can be choked to death by eating too finely milled feeds without enough water.

- *Lack of Water:* This can cause death when the attendant is negligent and does not provide water to the chicks regularly.
- *Lack of Feed:* Death can occur from starvation caused by insufficient feeder space incorrect brooding space or by failure of attendants to feed the chicks.
- *Improper Housing:* Death from overcrowding, poor ventilation or heat prostrations are common when management is poor. Inadequate equipment can cause overcrowding, starvation, pecking and cannibalism.
- *Injuries:* Death can occur very early in life from injuries from pests, damaged equipment and rough handling of chicks during sexing and vaccination.
- *Diseases:* There are many diseases that can cause deaths in chicks. It is advisable to vaccinate and medicate chicks promptly and regularly. Good management and quality feed is important.

Infertility, Poor Hatchability and Temperature Problems

Egg infertility and poor hatchability are among of the problem encountered in village chicken production that undertake in Ethiopia. [23] indicated that fertility and hatchability of village chicken may be affected by many factors, but the main once are, male to female ratio, mating efficiency of cocks and competition of cocks for mating .In most cases of infertility in poultry has been observed that the males are blamed once. Quality and quantity of feeds, eggs storage time, before incubation, egg quality, numbers of eggs given to hen for hatching and temprature of incubating nests may contributed for low efficiency of hatchability. Hatching eggs should be collected as frequent as possible at least four times a day. With respect to storage one of the required quality characteristics for hatching eggs is freshness. In most cases it cannot be avoided to store the eggs for a few days before putting them in the incubation. It is therefore important to know how eggs best can be stored. During storage of hatching eggs two main processes have to be prevented as much as possible Development of the embryo and Evaporation of water out of the eggs. After lying the egg gradually cools down from 41°C (hens body temperature) to house temperature. As long as the egg temperature is higher than 27°C the embryonic development continues. The embryos have the highest chances to survive a storage period if they are cooled down below 27°C within five to six hours after lying. When eggs are stored for a few days to even two or three weeks it is necessary to lower the temperature. A relationship exists between the length of the time eggs are stored and the optimum temperature for best hatchability. So the longer the storage period, the lower the storage temperature should be. On the other hand, storage of eggs at lower temperature may cause condensation of moist from the air on the shell when they suddenly taken from the storage room to a room with a higher temperature.

The growth rate and food intake of starter chicks aged between three and eight weeks is affected in linear manner by ambient temperature between 7°C and 21°C, both growth and food intake decrease by 0.12 per cent for each degree rise in environmental temperature 21-26°C. During 5-7 days after hatching the young bird is very dependent on care takes to provide an optimum temperature for survival and growth particularly during the first few days of brooding. Ventilation is critical element in poultry production. Excessive ventilation waste fuel and less ventilation allow litters wet. Generally during the first day of brooding keeping litters dry is recommended. The effect of relative humidity on performance of chicken is much more interrelated with temperature. At 21°C relative humidity within the range 48 to 90 per cent has no effect on growth.

Conclusion

Generally poultry production in Ethiopia is a chain of interrelated economic activities under taken with a social context. A vast number of house hold women and children actively participate in poultry production using their own indigenous breed and local knowledge of poultry management to generate income and or to compliment the protein requirement of the households.

The most dominant chicken production system in the rural area is the backyard extensive system based on the local indigenous birds scavenging with occasional seasonal supplementary feeding of home grown grains and house hold food refusal and with no specific poultry house. On the country women engaged in major management activities pertinent to poultry production. Improvement of the genetic potential of the local chicken would do through selection with in or upgrading exotic breeds. Many people living rural or urban area in one way or the other engaged in this activity as side line activity in adaptation to their main occupation and to generate some adaption house hold incomes. Village chicken production system is characterized by their low inputs – low output levels.

Indigenous hens lay on the average 40-60 eggs per hen per year. To insure egg safety and quality, home producers should manage chicken properly, otherwise that spend more time in the nest have an increased chance of becoming dirty, broken or lower in quality. The major problem impairing the existing production system in Ethiopia is the high incidences of new castle disease which is named locally as 'fengle'.

The attention given to poultry, particularly in breeding management, supplementary feeding, health care and housing practices, was very low in all the surveyed locations. Hence better breeding management, improving the health of poultry, practicing Supplementary feeding could increase the productivity of birds. Continuous location based training and awareness creation should be done on feeding, housing, health and breeding management of poultry so as to enhance the productivity and bring meaningful change in the livelihood of small holders by exploiting the existing poultry resource in the three areas. To solve the problem of feed shortage, efforts should be made to promote access to industrial by products and production of grains. Establishing animal health clinics and equipping them with the necessary facilities, drugs and animal health professionals could be important to identify, control and monitor poultry diseases in all locations.

REFERENCES

1. Payne, W.J.A. and Wilson, R.T. (1999). An Introduction to Animal Husbandry in the Tropics. 4thed. Longman Singapore Publisher, Singapore.
2. Solomon Demeke, (2004). Growth Performance and Survival of Local Chicken under Scavenging and Intensive System of Management in Ethiopia, Jima Collage of Agriculture Ethiopia.
3. Tadelle Dessie, (1996). Studies on Village Poultry Production System in the Central High Lands of Ethiopia. Msc thesis Swedish University of Agricultural Science.
4. Alganesh, *et al.* (2003) Survey on Traditional Livestock Production System.
5. Kitalyi, A.J. (1998). Village Chicken Production System in Rural Africa House Hold Food Security.
6. Tadelle D. and B. Ogle (2001). Village Poultry Production Systems in the Central High Lands of Ethiopia. Tropical Animal Health and Production, 33 (6): 521-537.
7. Tadelle Dessie 2003(b) Village Chicken Production System in Ethiopia. Paper (2) uses Parents and Performance Evaluation of Chicken Products Socio-economic Function of Chicken Livestock Research for Rural Development. http//www. cipau.org.co / irrd /irrd17 /10/map 17115.
8. Hailemariam. B (2006). Analysis of Traditional Grain Scavenging Based Poultry.
9. Tadelle Dessie and B. Ogle, (2001). Village Poultry Production System in the Central High Lands of Ethiopia. *Tropical Animal Health and Production J.* 33:521-537.
10. Ashenafi .k and Abera. M, (2007) on the Characterization of Local Chicken in South Ethiopia Producing Held in Awassa, March 16-19.

11. Sonaiya E.B. and Gueye E.F, (1998) The First Electronics Conference on Family Poultry. FAO, Rome. Italy http://www.fao,org /ag/laga/agap/lpa/fampol/intropap.
12. Sonaiya E.B and Obi, O.O (1995). Gross Margin Analysis of Small Holder Rural Poultry Production in Osun State *Nigeria Journal of An. Production*, 22:99-105
13. Sonaiya E.B, (1990). Towards Sustainable Poultry Production in Africa.
14. Thomsen, K., (2005). Poultry as Development. An Ethnography of Small Holders and Technical Development Assistance in Benin. MSc thesis, Institute of Anthropology, University of Copenhagen, Copenhagen, Denmark.
15. Bunning. M. and Avenes. J, (2010) Eggs Safety and Quality in Village Chicken Production.
16. Dereje Duressa (2004). Storage and Duration on Egg Quality in Rural Area.
17. Guye E.F, (1998) Approaches to Poultry Development Processing of the 21st Words Poultry, Congruence, Montreal Canada.
18. Mapiye. C and Sibanda. S. (2005). Constraints and Opportunities of Village Chicken Production System in Small Holder Sector of Rushinga District of Zimbabwe, Livestock Research of Rural Development Harege, Zimbabwe, http: //www.cipau.org co/ irrd/ irrd17/10map 17115.
19. Smith, A .J., (1990b). The Integration of Rural Production into the Family Food Supply System. CTA-Seminar Proceedings on Small Holder Rural Poultry Production 9-13 October 1990, Thessloniki, Greece, 1: 15-128.
20. Tadelle Dessie, (2003(a)). Village Chicken Production System in Ethiopia. Paper (1) flock Characteristics and Performances, Live Stocks Research for Rural Development.
21. Maphosa T., Kusina J., Kusina N. T., Makuza S. and Sibanda S. (2004) A Monitoring Study Comparing Production of Village Chickens between Communal (Nharira) and Small-scale Commercial (Lancashire) Farming Areas in Zimbabwe. University of Zimbabwe. Livestock Research for Rural Developments16/7/2004. (mkhonto@avu.org).
22. DhiAlchalabi (2001). Monitoring Poultry House Environments. Poultry International, Production, Processing and Marketing Worldwide. 40(10): 29-35.
23. Hallima Hussen (2007). Phenotypic and Genetic Characterization of Indigenous Chicken Population in North Western Ethiopia.
24. Alganesh Tola, Matewos Belisa and Gizaw Kebede (2003). Survey on Traditional Livestock Production System. pp. 141-150. Proceeding 11th Annual Conference of Ethiopian Society of Animal Production, Addis Ababa, Ethiopia, August 28-30, 2003.
25. Negussie Dana, Alemu Yami, Tadelle Dessie and Samual W/Hana (2003). On Farm and on Station Evaluation of the 'hay box chicken brooder' using different Insulation Materials at the Debrzeit Agricultural Research Center and Denbi Village AdaaWoreda. pp. 211-216. Proceeding Annual Conference of 10th Ethiopian Society of Animal Production, August 21-23/2003.

Page 123-140

FARMING TECHNIQUES AND CROP PRODUCTION
Edited by : **Dr. Alka Chauhan; Dr. Anubhuti Sharma & Jaswant Ray**
Edition : **2017**
ISBN : 978-93-5056-855-2
Published by : **Discovery Publishing House Pvt. Ltd., New Delhi (India)**

6

Evapotranspiration and Crop Production

Alok Kumar Patra[1] & Pulak Kumar Patra[2]

Abstract

Evapotranspiration is an important phenomenon in crop production and in many cases it is directly related to the crop yield. Evapotranspiration depends upon soil moisture availability. The amount of water required to compensate the evapotranspiration loss from the cropped field is the crop water requirement. The irrigation water requirement basically represents the difference between the crop water requirement and effective precipitation. Crop evapotranspiration is a tool to calculate the water requirements of the crops and plants. Using the crop evapotranspiration data, correct amounts of water can be provided to the crops. This conserves water, reduces waste and increases water use efficiency. Sometimes overwatering can be a bigger problem than under watering. Based on rainfall and crop evapotranspiration, the water availability period can be worked out. This is useful for selection of suitable crops and planting time of that crop in a locality. In this paper an attempt is made to define evapotranspiration concepts like: reference crop evapotranspiration, actual evapotranspiration and crop evapotranspiration, to enumerate the importance of evapotranspiration in crop production.

INTRODUCTION

Crop water requirement is the water required by the crop plants for their survival, growth, development and to produce economic parts like: grain, fruit, tuber etc. This requirement is applied either naturally by

1. Professor (Agronomy), All India Co-ordinated Research Project on Integrated Farming Systems, Orissa University of Agriculture and Technology, Bhubaneswar - 751 003, Odisha, India.
2. Associate Professor, Department of Environmental Studies, Institute of Science, Visva-Bharati, Santiniketan - 731 235, West Bengal, India.

precipitation or artificially by irrigation. Hence the crop water requirement includes all losses like: transpiration loss through leaves, evaporation loss through soil surface in cropped area and amount of weather used by plants for its metabolic activities which is estimated to be less than 1 per cent of the total water absorption. These three components of water loss from a vegetated area cannot be measured separately so easily. Hence the evapotranspiration loss is taken as crop water use or crop water consumptive use. *Evapotranspiration* is the combination of two separate processes named evaporation and transpiration. Evaporation accounts for the movement of water to the air from sources such as: the waterbodies and soil. Transpiration accounts for the movement of water within a plant and the subsequent loss of water as vapour through stomata in its leaves. So evapotranspiration is a bio-physical process.

Evaporation

The change of state of water from liquid to the vapour and its diffusion into the atmosphere is referred to as evaporation. Water evaporates from a variety of surfaces, such as: lakes, rivers, pavements, soils and wet vegetation. Energy is required to change the state of the molecules of water from liquid to vapour. Direct solar radiation and, to a lesser extent, the ambient temperature of the air provide this energy. During evaporation, water molecules absorb energy which gives them the motion required to escape from the surface of liquid and become a gas. Since a certain amount of energy is consumed in the process of evaporation, the remaining liquid is cooled by an equivalent amount. Thus, the process of evaporation is always accompanied by a cooling effect.

As evaporation proceeds, the surrounding air becomes gradually saturated with water vapour and the process will slow down and might stop if the wet air is not transferred to the atmosphere. The replacement of the saturated air with drier air depends greatly on wind speed. Hence, solar radiation, air temperature, air humidity and wind speed are meteorological parameters to be considered when assessing the evaporation process.

In agrometeorology, evaporation is defined as the maximum possible loss of moisture from a wet, horizontal, flat surface exposed to weather parameters, which exist in the vicinity of plants. Evaporation is an essential part of the water cycle. It is the primary pathway through which water moves from the liquid state back into the water cycle as atmospheric water vapour. The oceans, seas, lakes and rivers provide nearly 90 per cent of the moisture in the atmosphere *via* evaporation, with the remaining 10 per cent being contributed by plant transpiration. A very small amount of water vapour enters the atmosphere through sublimation, the process by which water changes from a solid (ice or snow) state to a gaseous one, bypassing the liquid phase.

Where the evaporating surface is the soil surface, the degree of shading of the crop canopy and the amount of water available at the evaporating surface are other factors that affect the evaporation process. Frequent rains, irrigation and water transported upwards in a soil from a shallow water table wet the soil surface. Where the soil is able to supply water fast enough to satisfy the evaporation demand, the evaporation from the soil is determined only by the meteorological conditions. However, where the interval between rains and irrigation becomes large and the ability of the soil to conduct moisture to the surface is small, the water content in the topsoil drops and the soil surface dries out. Under these circumstances the limited availability of water exerts a controlling influence on evaporation. In the absence of any supply of water to the soil surface, evaporation decreases rapidly and may cease almost completely within a few days. The evaporation from the soil is an important factor deciding the irrigation water requirements of a crop. The evaporation from the soils is also an important factor in modifying the microclimate of a crop.

Factors Affecting the Evaporation

Evaporation losses from a fully exposed water surface are essentially the functions of several factors.

1. *Temperature:* Evaporation is directly proportional to the temperature of the evaporating surface. The warmer the evaporating surface, the more is the energy available for evaporation and more is its rate. With an increase of temperature, the kinetic energy of water molecules increases and surface tension decreases with a resultant increase in evaporation. The maximum amount of water vapour that can exist in any given space is a function of prevailing temperature.
2. *Wind:* Evaporation increases with increasing wind speed. When wind speed is more, turbulence is set up in the air and moisture evaporated from the ground is mixed upward. Thus, dry wind replaces the moist air near water. The process of evaporation takes place continuously when there is a supply of energy to provide latent heat of vaporisation.
3. *Relative Humidity:* When the air above water is dry or has low relative humidity, the evaporation will be greater than when air has high relative humidity over the water.
4. *Area of Evaporation:* Evaporation is more where more water is available. It is greater over oceans than over continents. If the area of the exposed surface of water is large, the rate of evaporation will be high.
5. *Pressure:* Lower atmospheric pressure on open surface of the liquid results in higher evaporation and *vice versa*.
6. *Composition of Water:* Evaporation is inversely proportional to the salinity of water. The dissolved salts and other impurities decrease the rate of evaporation. Therefore, the rate of evaporation from the surface of the

sea is less than that of fresh water in rivers. Under equivalent conditions ocean water evaporates 5 per cent less than fresh water in rivers.

Transpiration

Transpiration is the loss of water by the plants, predominantly by means of leaves, although in woody plants a tiny loss might also occur through the lenticels of the bark of branches. Water loss from plant surfaces is a complex process. Transpiration consists of the vaporisation of liquid water contained in plant tissues and the vapour removal to the atmosphere. It occurs when vapour pressure in the leaf cells is greater than the atmospheric vapour pressure. Most of the water absorbed by plants is lost to the atmosphere through this process and only a tiny fraction is used within the plant. Crops mostly lose their water through stomata. The stomata are small openings on the plant leaf through which gases and water vapour pass.

Transpiration plays an important role in dissipation of radiant energy by plant parts, translocation of water in the plants and translocation of minerals in the plant. The opening of the stomata for transpiration process allows the diffusion of carbon dioxide gas from the air for photosynthesis. Transpiration also cools plants, changes osmotic pressure of cells, and enables mass flow of mineral nutrients and water from roots to shoots.

During a growing season, a leaf will transpire water many times more than its own weight. The transpiration ratio is the ratio of the mass of water transpired to the mass of dry matter produced; the transpiration ratio of crops tends to fall between 200 and 1000 (*i.e.*, crop plants transpire 200 to 1000 kg., of water for every kg., of dry matter produced).

Desert plants have specially adapted structures, such as: thick cuticles, reduced leaf areas, sunken stomata and hairs to reduce transpiration and conserve water. Many cacti conduct photosynthesis in succulent stems, rather than leaves, so the surface area of the shoot is very low. Many desert plants have a special type of photosynthesis, termed crassulacean acid metabolism or CAM photosynthesis, in which the stomata are closed during the day and open at night when transpiration will be lower. Some xerophytes reduce the surface of their leaves during water deficiencies and if temperature becomes cool enough and water levels are adequate the leaves expand again.

Factors Affecting the Transpiration

The amount of water that plants transpire varies greatly geographically and over time. There are a number of factors that determine transpiration rates. Some plants adopt physiological modifications to check the excess transpiration. Some other plants modify their structure for this purpose, thereby withstand drought. Such characters greatly affect the transpiration.

1. *Air temperature:* Increase in the temperature results in opening of stomata leading to high rate of transpiration. Temperature has significant effect on the permeability of the wall of the guard cells and therefore greatly

affects the osmotic phenomenon. This phenomenon is responsible for the movement of water molecules.

2. *Light:* Light plays a predominant role in transpiration both directly and indirectly. The direct effect of light is on the opening and closing of stomata. Bright light is the main stimulus which causes stomata to open. It is because of this reason that all plants show a daily periodicity of transpiration rate. The indirect effect of light is that the increasing light intensity raises the temperature of leaf cells. This increases the rate at which liquid water is transformed into vapour.
3. *Humidity:* The rate of transpiration is almost inversely proportional to atmospheric humidity. It is greatly reduced when the atmosphere is very humid. However, as the air becomes dry, the rate of transpiration also increases proportionately. It is easier for water to evaporate into dryer air than into moisture saturated air.
4. *Wind Velocities:* The velocity of wind affects the rate of transpiration to a greater extent. Fast moving wind and air currents bring fresh and dry masses of air in contact with leaf surfaces. So, increased movement of the air around a plant will result in a higher transpiration rate.
5. *Soil-moisture Availability:* With very low moisture absorption due to any reason, plants begin to senesce (premature ageing, which can result in leaf loss) and transpire less water. If there is little water in the soil, the tendency for dehydration of leaf causes stomatal closure and a consequent fall in rate of transpiration. This situation occurs during periods of drought or at a temperature so low that water is not absorbed by roots.
6. *Plant Characteristics:* Plants transpire water at different rates. Some plants such as: cacti and succulents, which grow in arid regions, conserve water by transpiring less water than other plants. In these plants, leaves are altogether absent and their function is taken up by the stem. The water need of a crop varies with its height. In general, the rate of transpiration of a tall crop will be more than when the crop is cut or clipped. Crop plants with more number of leaves (or spines, or other photosynthesising organs) mean a bigger surface area and more stomata for gaseous exchange. This will result in higher transpiration rate. A leaf with a larger surface area will transpire faster than a leaf with a smaller surface area.

Evapotranspiration

Evaporation and transpiration occur simultaneously from a vegetated surface and there is no easy way of distinguishing between the two processes. It is difficult to separate water evaporated from the soil, intercepted moisture remaining on vegetation surfaces after precipitation with subsequent evaporation and the moisture lost through transpiration. Therefore, a compound term evapotranspiration is used to refer to the total loss.

Apart from the water availability in the topsoil, the evaporation from a cropped soil is mainly determined by the fraction of the solar radiation reaching the soil surface. This fraction decreases over the growing period as the crop develops and the crop canopy shades more and more of the ground area. When the crop is small, water is predominately lost by soil evaporation, but once the crop is well developed and completely covers the soil, transpiration becomes the main process.

Thus, evapotranspiration (ET) is defined as the loss of water from a vegetated surface through the combined processes of soil evaporation and plant transpiration. Both soil evaporation and plant transpiration represent evaporative processes. The difference between these two processes rests in the path by which water moves from the soil to the atmosphere. Water lost by transpiration must enter the plant *via* the roots, and then pass to the foliage where it is vaporised and lost to the atmosphere through stomata in the leaves. In contrast, water lost through soil evaporation passes directly from the soil to the atmosphere. Evapotranspiration data are usually presented as a depth of water loss over a particular time period in a manner similar to that of precipitation. The evapotranspiration rate is normally expressed in millimetres per unit time. The rate expresses the amount of water lost from a cropped surface in units of water depth. The time unit can be an hour, a day, a month or even an entire growing period or a year.

Crop Water Need

Evapotranspiration is also called water use (WU) or consumptive use (CU). The sum of volume of water taken by vegetation for transpiration and evaporation from soil, plus water used by the plant for metabolic processes is termed as water use or consumptive use. Since the water requirement for metabolic processes in crop plants is very little and insignificant the ET is considered to be same as CU or WU.

The crop water need is defined as the depth (or amount) of water needed to meet the water loss through evapotranspiration. In other words, it is the amount of water needed by the crops to grow optimally. The crop water need always refers to a crop grown under optimal conditions, *i.e.*, a uniform crop, actively growing, completely shading the ground, free of diseases, and favourable soil conditions. The crop water need mainly depends on climate, crop type and growth stage of the crop. The highest crop water needs are found in areas which are hot, dry, windy and sunny. The lowest crop water needs are found when it is cool, humid and cloudy with little or no wind. The influence of the climate on crop water needs is given by the reference crop evapotranspiration (ET_o). Grass has been taken as the reference crop.

Factors Affecting Evapotranspiration

Weather parameters, crop characteristics, management and environmental aspects are factors affecting evapotranspiration.

Crop Factors

Plant characters such as: root/shoot ratio, leaf characteristics, plant type and stage of plant development affect ET rate.

1. *Plant type:* Plant type refers to the species or variety of plant being grown. Grass and many non-native plants require considerable water when grown in the desert. In contrast, many native plants are adapted to the desert and require much less water. This factor is also related to the foliar architecture (spatial distribution of the leaves), internal resistance of the plant to water transport, and other morphological aspects (number, size, and distribution of stomata, etc.), which exert a direct influence on ET.
2. *Growth stage:* Stage of plant development also plays a critical role in determining ET. Plant development encompasses both the relative activity of the plant and plant size. Small plants and areas with sparse plant canopies use far less water than large plants and areas with dense plant canopies. When the crop is small, water is predominantly lost by soil evaporation, but once the crop is well developed and completely covers the soil, transpiration becomes the main process of water loss. Such a factor is also directly related to the size of transpiring foliar surface, for the larger leaf area the larger the transpiring surface, and the higher the potential for water use will be.
3. *Reflection coefficient (albedo):* Radiation reflection influences directly net radiation availability for the ET process. The darker the vegetation, the lower the reflection coefficient and the higher net radiation will be.
4. *Plant height:* Taller and rougher plants interact more efficiently with the atmosphere in motion, extracting more energy from the air and, therefore, increasing ET.

Weather Factors

Weather conditions dictate the amount of energy available for evaporation and therefore play a crucial role in determining ET rate. Solar radiation, wind speed, humidity and temperature are the four major weather parameters that affect the rate of ET.

1. *Solar radiation:* Solar radiation contributes huge amounts of energy to vegetation and this is the main source of energy for the evapotranspiration process. The evaporation from a cropped soil is mainly determined by the fraction of the solar radiation reaching the soil surface. This fraction decreases over the growing period as the crop develops and the crop canopy shades more and more of the ground area. Net radiation is the primary climatic factor controlling ET when water is not limiting,

especially in subhumid and humid climates. In cold humid climates, only 50 to 60 per cent of net radiation may be converted to latent heat. In hot, arid climates, latent heat may exceed net radiation by 10 to 50 per cent with sensible heat derived from the air and converted to latent heat. In spite of these relationships, the heat energy balance approach employed to determining or estimating ET is recognised as a reliable and conservative method. A thorough understanding of the factors controlling the energy balance of a cropped soil enables making accurate estimates or predictions of evapotranspiration and irrigation water requirements. It also facilitates more effective irrigation water management (Allen *et al.* 1989).

2. *Wind speed:* The wind has two major roles in determining ET rate. It transports heat that builds up on adjacent surfaces. Wind also serves to accelerate evaporation by enhancing turbulent transfer of water vapour from moist vegetation to the dry atmosphere. In this case, the wind is constantly replacing the moist air located within and just above the plant canopy with dry air from above.
3. *Temperature:* Temperature impacts ET through its impact on vapour pressure deficit. When all other factors are equal, ET will be higher for warm as compared to cool vegetation because less energy is required to evaporate water from the warm vegetation. Temperature also impacts the relative effectiveness of the radiant energy and wind in evaporating water. Radiant energy is more effectively utilised for ET when temperatures are high. In contrast, wind has more impact on ET when temperatures are low.
4. *Humidity*: Humidity and temperature work in concert with each other to determine the dryness of the atmosphere. The vapour pressure deficit (VPD) is the meteorological variable used to quantify the drying power of the atmosphere. The VPD estimates the difference in vapour pressure between the moist vegetation and the drier atmosphere above.

Management and Environmental Factors

Factors such as: soil salinity, poor land fertility, limited application of fertilisers, the presence of hard or impenetrable soil horizons, the absence of control of diseases, pests and weeds and poor soil management may limit the crop development and reduce the evapotranspiration.

1. *Soil moisture:* Evapotranspiration simply cannot take place if there is no water in the soil. Moisture retentive capacity of the soil, available moisture in the crop root zone, water contribution from subsurface water table and soil surface characteristics greatly influence the rate of evapotranspiration. As long as the rate of root uptake of soil moisture balances the water losses from the canopy, evapotranspiration continues to occur at its potential rate. When the rate of water uptake by roots

falls below the transpiration demand, actual transpiration begins to fall below the potential rate. This is either because the soil cannot supply water to roots quickly or the plant can no longer extract water to meet the evaporation demand. The effect of soil water content on ET is conditioned primarily by the magnitude of the water deficit and the type of soil. On the other hand, too much water will result in waterlogging which might damage the root and limit root water uptake by inhibiting respiration.

2. *Spacing and crop stand*: Closer spacing results in an intensive competition for water and this causes the radicular system to deepen into the soil to enhance the volume of available water. More generous spacing allows for a more superficial radicular system, but also brings about more heating to the soil and plants and promotes a freer circulation of wind among the plants, causing an increase on ET. Soil evaporation in a young orchard, where trees are widely spaced, can be reduced by using a well-designed drip or trickle irrigation system. The drippers apply water directly to the soil near trees, thereby leaving the major part of the soil surface dry, and limiting the evaporation losses.
3. *Orientation of the crop main line:* Crops oriented perpendicularly to predominant winds tend to extract more energy from the air than those oriented in parallel. For regions with constant winds, a solution to prevent the stomata-closing would be the use of windbreaks. A windbreak reduces wind velocities and decreases the ET rate of the field directly beyond the barrier. The effect can be significant especially in windy, warm and dry conditions although evapotranspiration from the trees themselves may offset any reduction in the field.
4. *Water storage capacity:* Clay soils have a higher water storage capacity than sandy soils, and are capable of maintaining a more constant ET rate for longer. However, in sandy soils the radicular system tends to be quite deeper, compensating for lower water retention.
5. *Tillage and irrigation scheduling:* Tillage operations and the type of irrigation method and its scheduling can alter the micro climate, affect the crop characteristics or affect the wetting of the soil and crop surface.

Evapotranspiration Concepts

Depending on the vegetation conditions, size of the vegetated area, and soil water supply, different conceptions are to be defined, such as: reference crop evapotranspiration (ET_o), actual evapotranspiration (ET_a) and crop evapotranspiration (ET_c). Distinctions are also made between reference crop evapotranspiration (ET_o), crop evapotranspiration under standard conditions (ET_c) and crop evapotranspiration under non-standard conditions ($ET_{c\ adj}$). ET_o is a climatic parameter expressing the evaporation power of the atmosphere. ET_c refers to the evapotranspiration from excellently managed, large, well watered fields that achieve full production under the given climatic conditions. Due to suboptimal crop management and environmental constraints that affect crop growth and limit evapotranspiration, thus, ET_c under non-standard conditions generally requires a correction (Allen *et al.* 1998).

Reference Crop Evapotranspiration (ET_o)

The evapotranspiration rate from a reference surface is called the reference crop evapotranspiration or reference evapotranspiration and is denoted as ET_o. The reference surface is a hypothetical grass reference crop with specific characteristics. Reference evapotranspiration represents the maximum rate of evapotranspiration from an extended surface of 8-15 centimetres tall green grass cover, actually growing and completely shading the ground under unlimited supply of water.

ET_o was introduced to study the evaporative demand of the atmosphere independently of crop type, crop development and management practices. As water is abundantly available at the reference evapotranspiring surface, soil factors do not affect evapotranspiration. The only factors affecting ET_o are climatic parameters. Consequently, ET_o is a climatic parameter and can be computed from weather data. ET_o expresses the evaporating power of the atmosphere at a specific location and particular time of the year. Differences in leaf anatomy, stomatal characteristics, aerodynamic properties and even albedo cause the crop evapotranspiration to differ from the reference crop evapotranspiration under the same climatic conditions.

Actual or Real Evapotranspiration (ET_a)

Actual evapotranspiration is the amount of water actually utilized by an extensive surface vegetated with grass, at an active growth stage, covering completely the soil surface, however with or without water restriction conditions. Whenever there is no soil water restriction, $ET_a = ET_o$. Thus, ET_a d" ET_o. At this point it is important to emphasize that, by definition, the concepts of ET_a and ET_o are applicable only to a surface vegetated with grass (Pereira and Pires, 2011).

Crop Coefficient (K_c)

The ratio between the actual evapotranspiration (ET_a) and the reference evapotranspiration (ET_o) gives the crop coefficient (K_c). In other words, the relationship between the reference grass crop and the crop actually grown is given by the crop factor or crop coefficient, Kc.

$K_c = ET_a/ET_o$

or, $ETa = K_c \times ET_o$

Due to variations in the crop characteristics throughout its growing season, K_c for a given crop changes from sowing till harvest. In case of annual dryland crops, the K_c value is mostly 0.3 to 0.6 from the time of sowing to its establishment. It increases to a maximum of 1.0 to 1.3 when the whole ground surface is covered by the crop canopy. Crop coefficient declines to about 0.5

when the crop attains the physiological maturity. The seasonal crop coefficient of rice crop varies between 1.0 and 2.0 depending upon the climatic conditions of the area where the crop is grown. The crop coefficient of a particular crop may vary from year to year as the weather variables change.

Crop Evapotranspiration (ET_c)

Crop evapotranspiration is the amount of water used by a crop at any growth stage, since the sowing/planting date up until the harvest, whenever there is no water restriction in the soil. This process is also called crop maximum evapotranspiration. ET_c is a function of leaf area (transpiring surface), because the bigger the leaf area, the higher ET_c will be for the same atmospheric demand. ET_c might be obtained from ET_o by means of the following expression.

$$ET_c = K_c \times ET_o$$

K_c is the crop coefficient (or crop factor) and varies with the phenological stage of the crop, and also among species and varieties, being a function of leaf area index.

Thus, the crop evapotranspiration under standard conditions is the evapotranspiration from disease-free, well fertilized crops, grown in large fields, under optimum soil water conditions, and achieving full production under the given climatic conditions. The amount of water required to compensate the evapotranspiration loss from the cropped field is defined as crop water requirement. Although the values for crop evapotranspiration and crop water requirement are identical, crop water requirement refers to the amount of water that needs to be supplied, while crop evapotranspiration refers to the amount of water that is lost through evapotranspiration. The irrigation water requirement basically represents the difference between the crop water requirement and effective precipitation. The irrigation water requirement also includes additional water for leaching of salts and to compensate for non-uniformity of water application (Allen *et al.* 1998).

Where field conditions differ from the standard conditions, correction factors are required to adjust ET_c. The crop evapotranspiration under non-standard conditions ($ET_{c\ adj}$) is the evapotranspiration from crops grown under management and environmental conditions that differ from the standard conditions. When cultivating crops in fields, the actual crop evapotranspiration may deviate from ET_c due to non-optimal conditions such as: the presence of pests and diseases, soil salinity, low soil fertility, water shortage or waterlogging. This may result in scanty plant growth, low plant density and may reduce the evapotranspiration rate below ET_c. The crop evapotranspiration under non-standard conditions is calculated by adjusting K_c for all kinds of stresses and environmental constraints on crop evapotranspiration (Allen *et al.* 1998).

Both ET_c crop and ET_o are expressed in the same unit; usually in mm/day (as an average for a period of one month) or in mm/month. The crop factor, K_c, mainly depends on the type of crop, the growth stage of the crop and the climate.

Determination of K_c

With its large leaf area a fully developed maize crop will be able to transpire more, and thus use more water than the reference grass crop. So K_c of maize is more than 1. But in case of fully developed cucumber crop, less water will be used than the reference grass crop and thus K_c of cucumber is less than 1. A certain crop will use more water once it is fully developed, compared to a crop which has just recently been planted. The climate influences the duration of the total growing period and the various growth stages. In a cool climate a certain crop will grow slower than in a warm climate. Thus, to determine the crop factor K_c, it is necessary, for each crop, to know the total length of the growing season and the lengths of the various growth stages.

The total growing period is the period from sowing or transplanting to the last day of the harvest. It is mainly dependent on the type of crop and the variety, the climate and the planting date. As the growing period depends on local circumstances it is better to obtain these data locally. In general, the growing period for a certain crop is longer when the climate is cool and shorter when the climate is warm.

Once the total growing period is known, the duration of the various growth stages has to be determined. Mainly the total growing period is divided into four growth stages.

1. The initial stage is the period from sowing or transplanting until the crop covers about 10 per cent of the ground.
2. The crop development stage starts at the end of the initial stage and lasts until the full ground cover has been reached (ground cover 70-80%). It does not necessarily mean that the crop is at its maximum height.
3. The mid-season stage starts at the end of the crop development stage and lasts until maturity. It includes flowering and grain-setting.
4. The late season stage starts at the end of the mid-season stage and lasts until the last day of the harvest. It includes ripening.

The approximate duration of the various growth stages for some of the major field crops is presented in Table 6.1. For each crop the minimum and maximum duration of total growing period have been taken and sub-divided into the various growth stages. In Table 6.2 the K_c values for each of the four growth stages (initial stage, crop development stage, mid-season stage and late season stage) of some these crops are presented.

Table 6.1: Approximate duration of Growth Stages for Various Field Crops

	Total	Initial Stage	Crop Development Stage	Mid-season Stage	Late Season Stage
1	2	3	4	5	6
Barley/Oats/Wheat	120	15	25	50	30
	150	15	30	65	40
Bean/green	75	15	25	25	10
	90	20	30	30	10
Bean/dry	95	15	25	35	20
	110	20	30	40	20
Cabbage	120	20	25	60	15
	140	25	30	65	20
Carrot	100	20	30	30	20
	150	25	35	70	20
Cotton/Flax	180	30	50	55	45
	195	30	50	65	50
Cucumber	105	20	30	40	15
	130	25	35	50	20
Eggplant	130	30	40	40	20
	140	30	40	45	25
Grain/small	150	20	30	60	40
	165	25	35	65	40
Lentil	150	20	30	60	40
	170	25	35	70	40
Lettuce	75	20	30	15	10
	140	35	50	45	10
Maize, sweet	80	20	25	25	10
	110	20	30	50	10
Maize, grain	125	20	35	40	30
	180	30	50	60	40
Melon	120	25	35	40	20
	160	30	45	65	20
Millet	105	15	25	40	25
	140	20	30	55	35
Onion/green	70	25	30	10	5
	95	25	40	20	10
Onion/dry	150	15	25	70	40
	210	20	35	110	45
Groundnut	130	25	35	45	25
	140	30	40	45	25

Contd...

1	2	3	4	5	6
Pea	90	15	25	35	15
	100	20	30	35	15
Pepper	120	25	35	40	20
	210	30	40	110	30
Potato	105	25	30	30	20
	145	30	35	50	30
Radish	35	5	10	15	5
	40	10	10	15	5
Sorghum	120	20	30	40	30
	130	20	35	45	30
Soybean	135	20	30	60	25
	150	20	30	70	30
Spinach	60	20	20	15	5
	100	20	30	40	10
Squash	95	20	30	30	15
	120	25	35	35	25
Sugarbeet	160	25	35	60	40
	230	45	65	80	40
Sunflower	125	20	35	45	25
	130	25	35	45	25
Tomato	135	30	40	40	25
	180	35	45	70	30

Source: http://www.fao.org

Table 6.2 shows average Kc values for the various crops and growth stages. In fact, the Kc is also dependent on the climate and, in particular, on the relative humidity and the wind speed. The values indicated above should be reduced by 0.05 if the relative humidity is high (> 80%) and the wind speed is low (< 2 m/sec). The values should be increased by 0.05 if the relative humidity is low (< 50%) and the wind speed is high (> 5 m/sec).

Hydrologic Cycle and Evapotranspiration

The hydrologic cycle can be defined as the pathways of water as it moves in its various phases through the atmosphere, to the earth, over and through the land, to the ocean, and back to the atmosphere. During this cycle, which has no beginning or end, water molecules may assume various states, returning to a hydrologic pathway as new chemical compounds that are mixed with various solid and liquid substances. In the cycle, water evaporates from the oceans, ponds, rivers, and various land surface to become part of the atmosphere; water vapour is transported and lifted in the atmosphere until it condenses and precipitates on the land or oceans; precipitated water may be intercepted by vegetation, become overland flow over the ground surface, infiltrate into the ground, flow through the soil as subsurface flow, or discharge into streams as surface runoff.

Table 6.2: Values of the Crop Factor (K_c) for Various Crops and Growth Stages

Crop	Initial Stage	Crop Development Stage	Mid-season Stage	Late Season Stage
Barley	0.35	0.75	1.15	0.45
Bean, dry	0.35	0.70	1.10	0.30
Bean, green	0.35	0.70	1.10	0.90
Cabbage	0.45	0.75	1.05	0.90
Carrot	0.45	0.75	1.05	0.90
Cotton	0.45	0.75	1.15	0.75
Cucumber	0.45	0.70	0.90	0.75
Eggplant	0.45	0.75	1.15	0.80
Flax	0.45	0.75	1.15	0.75
Grain/small	0.35	0.75	1.10	0.65
Groundnut	0.45	0.75	1.05	0.70
Lentil/Pulses	0.45	0.75	1.10	0.50
Lettuce/Spinach	0.45	0.60	1.00	0.90
Maize, grain	0.40	0.80	1.15	0.70
Maize, sweet	0.40	0.80	1.15	1.00
Melon	0.45	0.75	1.00	0.75
Millet	0.35	0.70	1.10	0.65
Oats	0.35	0.75	1.15	0.45
Onion, dry	0.50	0.75	1.05	0.85
Onion, green	0.50	0.70	1.00	1.00
Pea, green	0.45	0.80	1.15	1.05
Pepper, fresh	0.35	0.70	1.05	0.90
Potato	0.45	0.75	1.15	0.85
Radish	0.45	0.60	0.90	0.90
Sorghum	0.35	0.75	1.10	0.65
Soybean	0.35	0.75	1.10	0.60
Squash	0.45	0.70	0.90	0.75
Sugarbeet	0.45	0.80	1.15	0.80
Sunflower	0.35	0.75	1.15	0.55
Tobacco	0.35	0.75	1.10	0.90
Tomato	0.45	0.75	1.15	0.80
Wheat	0.35	0.75	1.15	0.45

Source: http://www.fao.org

In a given watershed, discharge of water is primarily from ground-water withdrawals for irrigation, evapotranspiration where the water table is near land surface, overland flow (runoff), and seepage to streams and springs where the water table intersects the land surface. Recharge of water is primarily from precipitation; other sources of recharge are irrigation return flow and seepage from streams, canals, and reservoirs. Large amounts of the intercepted water and surface runoff return to the atmosphere through evaporation. Infiltrated water may percolate to deeper soil layers to recharge groundwater, and later emerge in springs, or as seepage into streams, to form surface flow. Finally, this water may flow to the larger rivers and, eventually to the sea and/or evaporate into the atmosphere. Throughout this cycle, water is usually subject to evaporation of one kind. Types of vegetation, management and land use, and climatic conditions significantly affect evapotranspiration, and therefore determine the amount of water lost through evapotranspiration from a watershed.

Importance of Evapotranspiration in Crop Production

Evapotranspiration is an important phenomenon in crop production and in many cases it is directly related to the crop yield. Evapotranspiration depends upon soil moisture availability. Under unlimited soil water availability actual evapotranspiration (ET_a) almost equals to crop evapotranspiration (ET_c). Actual evapotranspiration gets reduced with the depletion of soil water.

The amount of water required to compensate the evapotranspiration loss from the cropped field is defined as crop water requirement. The irrigation water requirement basically represents the difference between the crop water requirement and effective precipitation. The irrigation water requirement also includes additional water for leaching of salts and water required to compensate for non-uniformity of water application. Crop evapotranspiration is a tool to calculate the water requirements of the crops and plants. Using the crop evapotranspiration data, correct amounts of water can be provided to the crops. This conserves water, reduces waste and increases water use efficiency. Sometimes overwatering can be a bigger problem than under watering (Patra, 2003).

Based on rainfall and crop evapotranspiration, the water availability period can be worked out. This is useful for selection of suitable crops and planting time of that crop in a locality (Reddy and Reddy, 2007). If rainfall exceeds the crop evapotranspiration, it is assumed that this is the best period for crop growth. However, if the surplus is huge, there is run off and a poor drainage may lead to waterlogging which restricts crop growth. For rainfed crops in arid and semiarid areas, the planting time should be so adjusted that early establishment and ripening phases should coincide with the period when rainfall is less than crop evapotranspiration (Patra, 2016). In humid regions usually *kharif* crops suffer from excess water in the soil since rainfall exceeds crop evapotranspiration. Proper drainage is to be ascertained to avoid crop failure. But in *rabi* and summer crop periods, usually crop evapotranspiration exceeds rainfall. Therefore, the crop should be irrigated (Patra and Panda, 2003). Evapotranspiration study helps.

- Understanding the critical need of water for different phenological stages of the crops and thereby planning irrigation schedules.
- Understanding the relationship between the crop yield and irrigation water.
- Quantifying the water needed by the plant at critical stages.
- Increasing water use efficiency through scientific irrigation management practices at the context of change in hydrological cycle due to climate change.
- Guiding for the production of a crop with a fully developed canopy.
- Demarcating soil climatic zones including the drought prone areas.
- Developing suitable soil and crop management practices, crop varieties, water conservation techniques, cropping pattern and ways to improve productivity of rainfed crops.

Conclusion

Evapotranspiration is the combination of two separate processes named evaporation and transpiration. Evaporation accounts for the movement of water to the air from sources such as: the waterbodies and soil. Transpiration accounts for the movement of water within a plant and the subsequent loss of water as vapour through stomata in its leaves. So evapotranspiration is a bio-physical process. Using the crop evapotranspiration data, correct amounts of water can be provided to the crops. This conserves water, reduces waste and increases water use efficiency. Based on rainfall and crop evapotranspiration, the water availability period can be worked out. If rainfall exceeds the crop evapotranspiration, it is assumed that this is the best period for crop growth. However, if the surplus is huge, there is run off and a poor drainage may lead to waterlogging which restricts crop growth. For rainfed crops in arid and semiarid areas, the planting time should be so adjusted that early establishment and ripening phases should coincide with the period when rainfall is less than crop evapotranspiration.

Evapotranspiration study helps in understanding the critical need of water for different phenological stages of the crops and thereby planning irrigation schedules and quantifying the water needed by the plant at critical stages.

REFERENCES

Allen, R.G., Jensen, M.E., Wright, J.L. and Burman, R.G. (1989). Operational Estimates of Evapotranspiration. *Agronomy Journal* 81:650-662.

Allen, R.G., Pereira, L.S., Raes, D. and Smith, M. (1998). Crop Evapotranspiration. Guidelines for Computing Crop Water Requirements. In: *FAO Irrigation and Drainage*, Paper No. 56. Rome, FAO.

Andre Pereira and Luiz Pires (2011). Evapotranspiration and Water Management for Crop Production, Evapotranspiration - From Measurements to Agricultural and Environmental Applications, Giacomo Gerosa (Ed.), In Tech Europe University Campus STeP Ri, Slavka Krautzeka, Rijeka, Croatia.

http://agropedia.iitk.ac.in/content/climatic-requirements

http://en.wikipedia.org

http://science-edu.larc.nasa.gov

http://www.climatechange.gc.ca

http://www.fao.org

http://www.imdagrimet.gov.in

http://www.indiaweather.gov.in

http://www.krishiworld.com/html/crop_pat

http://www.scientificpsychic.com/ atmosphere-composition.html

http://www.theweatherprediction.com/habyhints

http://www.worldwatch.org

Patra, A.K. (2003). Agromet Advisory Services in the service of the Farmers of WCTL Agro-climatic Zone of Orissa. *Gabesana Prabaha*, Silver Jubilee Souvenir, RRTTS, OUAT, Chiplima.

Patra, A.K. (2016). Principles and Applications of Agricultural Meteorology. New India Publishing Agency, New Delhi. pp. 434.

Patra, A.K. and Panda, M.M. (2003). Weather based Agro-advisory Services. RRTTS, OUAT, Chiplima.

Reddy, S.R. and Reddy, D.S. (2007). Agrometeorology. Kalyani Publishers, Ludiana, 313 pp.

Page 141-161

FARMING TECHNIQUES AND CROP PRODUCTION
Edited by : **Dr. Alka Chauhan; Dr. Anubhuti Sharma & Jaswant Ray**
Edition : **2017**
ISBN : 978-93-5056-855-2
Published by : **Discovery Publishing House Pvt. Ltd., New Delhi (India)**

7 Advances in Tissue Culture Techniques for Crop Improvement

R.R. Dhutmal

INTRODUCTION

Initially, crop improvement activities focused on selection, which exploited the variability existing in populations of the crop species. But it was soon recognized that genetic variability is a pre-requisite for selection to be effective and that, selection rapidly exhausts the genetic variability existing in the crop species. This realization has forced humans to continuously search for such tools that would create novel and useful genetic variation. Hybridization was perhaps the earliest such tool that has been, is being and is likely to continue to be the most widely used approach for cross ability. As a result, traits present only in some of the related species can be used for crop improvement, while those present in many related species remain inaccessible (Singh, 2006).

In this context, the developments in a seemingly unrelated discipline have offered several useful approaches to tackle some of the important issues and problems of crop improvement. Haberlandt, in 1902, initiated the *in vitro* culture of plant cells in an effort to find out if mature cells were totipotent, *i.e.*, could give rise to complete plants preferably through somatic embryogenesis. Complete plantlets were regenerated from mature plant cells through shoot bud regeneration and somatic embryogenesis during 1950s and 1960s But much earlier than this, in 1925, plant tissue culture technique was applied to solve a plant breeding problem: Labiach used a simple technique to successfully culture embryos excised from poorly developed

Asstt. Breeder, Vasantrao Naik Marathwada Krishi Vidyapeeth, Parbhani (M.S.), India seeds and recover progeny from interspecific cross of *Linum*. Subsequently, the tissue culture technique offered several other approaches to resolve specific plant breeding problems such as: protoplast fusion and *in vitro* pollination/ fertilization to overcome crossability problems, somaclonal variations to resolve useful mutants, anther culture to rapidly produce haploids and ultimately, doubled haploids (= homozygous lines) etc. These techniques have found useful applications in crop improvement as enumerated in detail by Brown and Thorpe (1990), Mortison (1991) Evans (1989) Various tissue culture techniques with their recent developments are discussed hereunder.

History of Plant Tissue Culture

The science of tiissue culture takes its roots from the discovery of cell followed by propounding of cell theory. In 1838, Schleiden and Schwann roosed that cell is the basic structural unit of all living organisms. They visualised that cell is capable of autonomy and therefore it should be possible for each cell if given an environment to regenerate into whole plant. Based on this remise, in 1902, a German physiologist, Gottlieb Habertland for the first tile attempted to culture isolated single palisade cells from leaves in knops salt solution enriched with sucrose. The cell remained alive for up to one month, increased in size, accumulated starch but failed to divide. Though he was unsuccessful but laid down the foundation of tissue culture technology for which he is regarded as the father of plant tissue culture. After that some of the landmark descoveries took place in tissue culture which are summerized as under:

1902 - Haberlandt proposed concept of in vitro cell culture.

1904 - Hannig cultured embryos from several cruciferous species.

1922 - Kolte and robbins successfully cultured root and stem tips respectively 1926 Went discovered first plant growth hormone-Indole acetic acid.

1934 - White introduced vitamin B as growth suppliment in tissue culture media for tomato root tip.

1939 - Gautheret, white and Nobecourt established endless proliferation of callus cutures.

1941 - Overbeek was first to add coconut milk for cell division in Datura.

1946 - Ball raised whole plants of Lupinus by shoot tip culture.

1954 - Muir was first to break callus tissues into single cells.

1955 - Skoog and Miller discovered kinetin as cell division hormone.

1957 - Skoog and Miller gave concept of hormonal control (auxin: cytokinin) of organ formation.

1959 - Reinert and Steward regenerated embryos from callus clumps and cell suspension of carrot (Daucus carota).

1960 - Cocking was first to isolate protolast by enzymatic degredation of cell wall.

Table 7.1: Different Techniques of Plant Culture and their Applications in Plant Improvement

Tissue Culture Techniques	Applications
Seed Culture	1. Increasing efficiency of germination and germinig production in seeds difficult to germinate in vivo. 2. Precocious germination by application of plant growth regulators. 3. Induction of multiple shoot formation and organogenesis by application of plant growth regulators. 4. Elimination of viruses as seed do not carry viruses.
Embruo culture	1. Overcoming embryo abortion due to incompatibility barriers. 2. Overcoming seed dormancy and self-sterility of seeds. 3. Embryo rescue in distant (interspecific and intergeneric) hybridization where endoplasm development is poor. 4. Production of monoploids.
Ovary or ovule culture	1. Production of haploid plants. 2. Recovery of hybrid embryos overcoming embryos overcoming embryo abortion at very early stages of development of zygote due to incompatibility barriers. 3. Achievement of In vitro fertilization.
Anther and Microspore culture	1. Production of haploid plants. 2. Production of homozygous diploid lines through chromosome doubling, thus reducing the breeding cycle. 3. Genetic transformation using microspores. 4. Production of useful gametoclonal variation. 5. Mutation investigations easier with single set of chromosomes. 6. Fixation of certain genetic characters from heterozygous source materials.
In vitro pollination	1. Production of hybrids difficult to produce by embryo rescue.
In vitro fertilization	1. Production of distance hybrids avoiding germination and pollen germination and pollen tube growth. 2. Production of transgenic by injecting exogenous DNA in the nuclei of gametes and zygotes.
Organ cuture	1. Mass production of plants of elite and rare germplasm. 2. Production of calli, shoot and roots for production of secondary metabolites.

Distant Hybridization

In crop improvement programme it is often desirable, or even necessary sometimes to cross individuals/lines/accessions belonging to two different individuals. Such crosses constitute distant hybridization and provides useful applications such as: transfer of useful genes for disease and insect resistance, quality, wider adaptation, mode of reproduction, yield, cytoplasm, development of new varieties (*e.g., Gossypium hirsutum* x *G. barbadense* hybrid varieties of cotton) and even, production of new crop species (Triticale of *Triticum x Secale*). In majority of the distant crosses success was poor.

The difficulties encountered in distant hybridization may be of the following three types. *Firstly,* there may be failure of zygote formation due to the inability of the pollen tube to reach the embryo sac for a variety of reasons; the mechanisms responsible for this failure are known as *prefertilization barriers. Secondly,* the zygote produced by fertilization may fail to develop into a mature embryo and give rise to hybrid seedlings (post fertilization barriers). These barriers can be overcome by embryo rescue, *in vitro* pollination, in vitro fertilization and somatic hybridization (Monnier, 1990).

Embryo Rescue

In this method young embryos are removed from developing seeds and are placed on a suitable nutrient medium to obtain hybrid seedlings when embryo fails to develop due to endosperm degeneration, this is called embryo *rescue.* Embryo culture has been widely used for this purpose. *Triticale (8x)* is produced by crossing Triticum *aestivum (6x)* with *Secaie cereale.* In any case, embryo development is slightly a regulated process and ordinarily, embryos germinate only after completing the development and maturation. But when excised and young embryos are cultured in vitro, they do not complete the normal embryogenic development characteristic of the in vivo process, Instead, they germinate into weak seedlings; this is called *precocious germination.* GA accelerates precocious germination of barley embryo even under those conditions that suppress the process, *e,g.,* high somolarity, elevated temperature and high light intensity.

In vitro Pollination

When pollen is applied to stigma of ovaries cultured in vitro or directly on to ovules cultured with or without placental tissue, it is called in vitro pollination. The first report of in vitro pollination was pollination was published in 1962 by Kanta and coworkers. They had cultured intact placenta with ovules of *Papaver somniferum* and pollen grains were dusted directly onto the ovules. Pollen grains germinated within 15 min., fertilization occurred within 1-2 days and fully differentiated embryos developed after 22 days of pollination. Since then, this approach has been used to recover hybrids from several sexually incompatible cross combinations.

Pollen grains are usually deposited directly on ovules, placenta or stigma depending on the type of culture. In such cases where pollen grains fail to germinate on the surface of cultured ovules, they may b germinated separately in a suitable medium, and then applied to the ovules; this approach has been successfully used in maize. Pollen grains of *Brassicaceae* are difficult to germinate in vitro. As a result, in vitro pollination is much less successful in this group of plants. However, in vitro pollination has been successful in many species, including some intergeneric crosses, *e.g., Melandrium album x Viscaria vulgaris, M. album x Minuartia laricifolia, M. album x Dianthus serotinus. N. tabacum x Penunia hybrids,* etc.. Still, in most interspecific combinations only nongerminable seeds were obtained.

In vitro Fertilization

In vitro fertilization may be defined as fusion of isolated male and female gametes in vitro to form a zygote, which ultimately would give rise to normal individuals. The first report of in vitro fertilization in case of plants was published in 1990 by Kranz and coworkers who succeeded in fusing isolated male and female gametes of maize.

Somatic Hybridization

In this method hybrid plants are obtained from unrelated species irrespective of their sexual compatibility. Production of hybrid plants through the fusion of protoplasts of two different plant species/varieties is called *somatic hybridization* and such hybrids are known as *somatichybrids*. The technique of somatic hybridization involves the following four steps: isolation of protoplasts, fusion of the protoplasts of desired species/varieties, selection of somatic hybrid cells. Culture of the hybrid cells and regeneration of hybrid plants from them. Therefore, somatic hybridization can be resorted to only when the following two criteria are satisfied: isolation of protoplasts in large quantities and tot potency of the isolated protoplasts. Somatic hybridization was conceived as a strategy to get around the problem of sexual incompatibility encountered in many interspecific cross combinations (Warra and Glimelius, 1995). Therefore, somatic hybrids may be expected to find the same range of applications, and suffer from similar limitations as do the sexually produced interspecific hybrids. In short, somatic hybridization can generate novel species which may themselves be of interest, or may serve as sources of useful genes and cytoplasms.

In addition, somatic hybridization provides two unique opportunities of combining chloroplasts of one species with the mitochondria of the other species and of recovery of mitochondria having recombinant genomes that combine some features from each of the two parents. Somatic hybrids with at least partial fertility have been produced in the families Cruciferae, Solanaceae and Gramineae or Poaceae; many of these hybrids are not obtainable by the sexual route. But at present the bulk of studies on various strategies of somatic hybridization are concerned with species of *Brassica, Nicotiana, Solanum* and *Lycopersicum*. In case of potato, the technique is already being used in commercial breeding progarmmes of the Netherlands and Germany. In general, somatic hybrids have a low pollen fertility and show genetic instability (Brown and Thorpe, 1995). Among the four methods, embryo rescue and somatic hybridization are practiced widely.

Somaclonal Variation

Callus and Suspension Cultures

When explants are cultured on a suitable growth regulator combination, many of its cells undergo division. Even mature and certain differentiated cells, *e.g.*, parenchyma and often collenchymas, cells undergo changes to

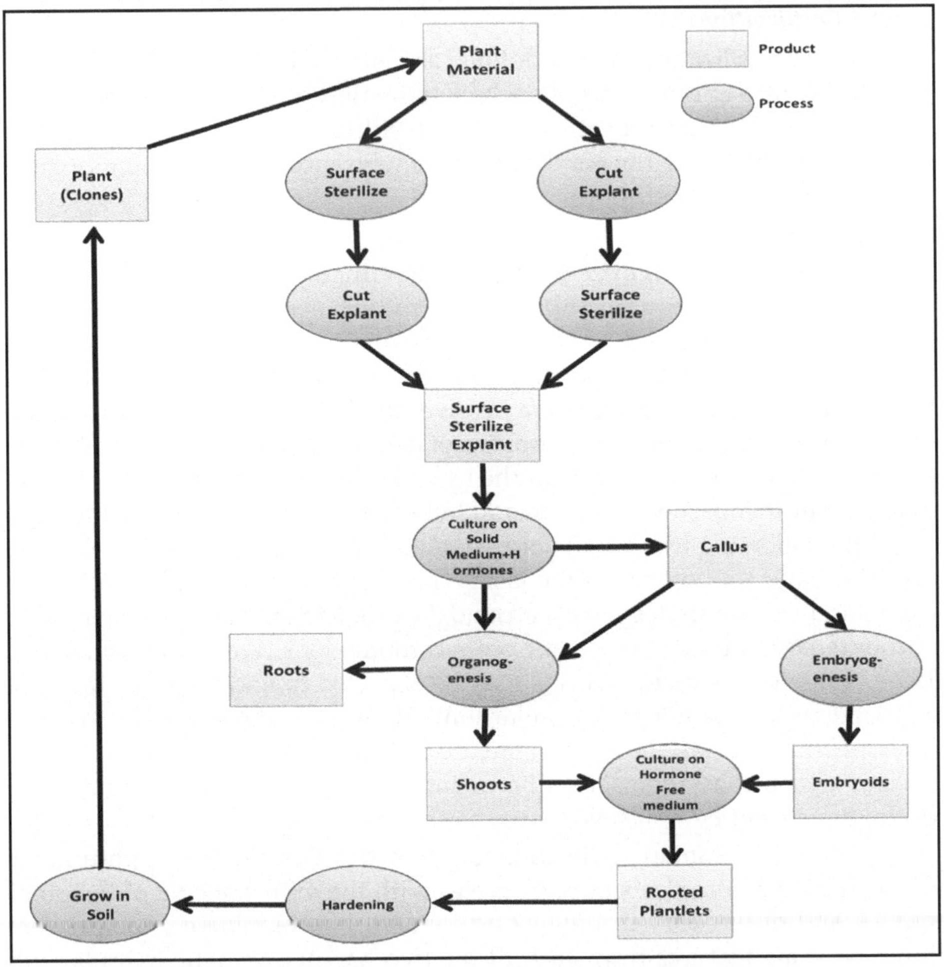

Fig. 7.1: **Flow chart summarizing tissue culture experiments**

become meristematic; This is called *dedifferentiation*. Dedifferentiation involves renewed and enhanced RNA and protein syntheses leading to the formation of new cellular components needed for meristematic activity. Initially, cell division is confined to the cut ends, but subsequently it covers the entire explants. The resulting cell mass (callus) is ordinarily unorganized, but it often consists of several cell thpes including fibers and vascular elements. Individual cells are isolated from the calli and cultured in liquid medium under aeration [suspension culture].

Changes in and Causes of Somaclonal Variation

Availability of efficient plant regenerating systems from cultured somatic cells, pollen and protoplasts and characterization of soma clones with molecular techniques have widened the potential use of somaclonal variation

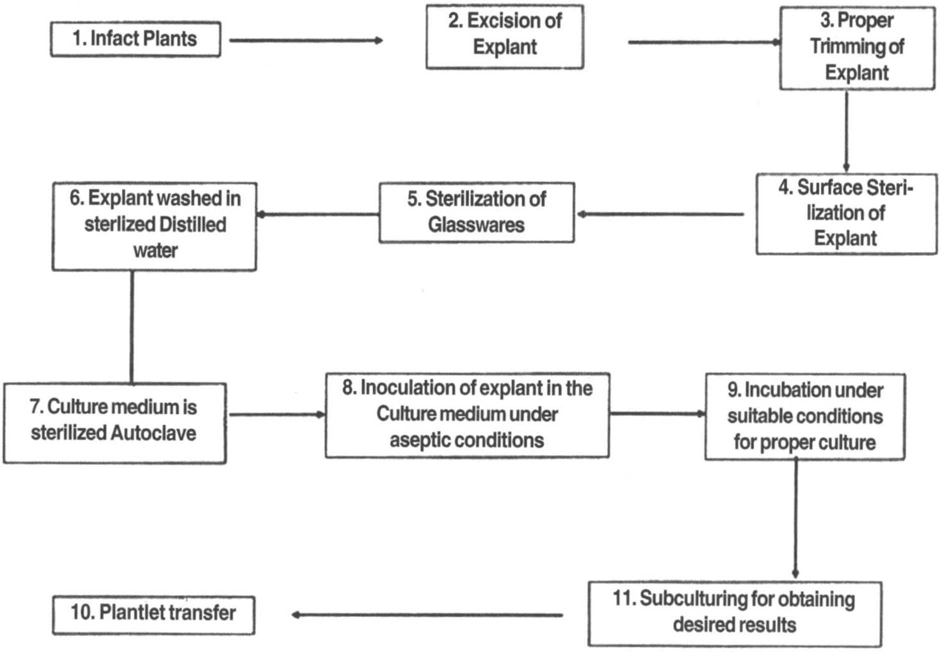

Fig. 7.2: **Steps in general technique of Plant tissue culture**

in crop improvement. Genetic instability and somaclonal variation have been recorded in callus, liquid suspensions, cultured protoplasts, adventitious roots, somatic embryos, regenerated plants (Larkin and Scowcroft, 1981) and among seeds. These variations are either genetic or epigenetic in origin and might arise either from pre-existing genetic variation within the explants or due to stress induced during in vitro passage.

Factors such as: nature of explant, genotype, age of culture, polyploidy, inter-chromosomal translocations, intra-chromosomal inversions, media composition, plant growth hormones, stresses, due to the method and specific growth conditions of in vitro cultures, nutritional factors, chromosomal changes (aneuploidy, deletions, duplications besides somatic crossing over and sister chromatid exchange) contribute to somaclonal variation. Variations may also be due to point mutation, gene amplification, gene rearrangements and other karyological aberrations. It creates additional variation in the species or developed cultivars.

Isolation and Evaluation of Somaclonal Variation

In vitro selection: Cell selection strategies have been devised for the isolation of useful variants such as: those for disease resistance, abiotic stress resistance, efficient nutrient utilization etc. Selection pressure can be applied

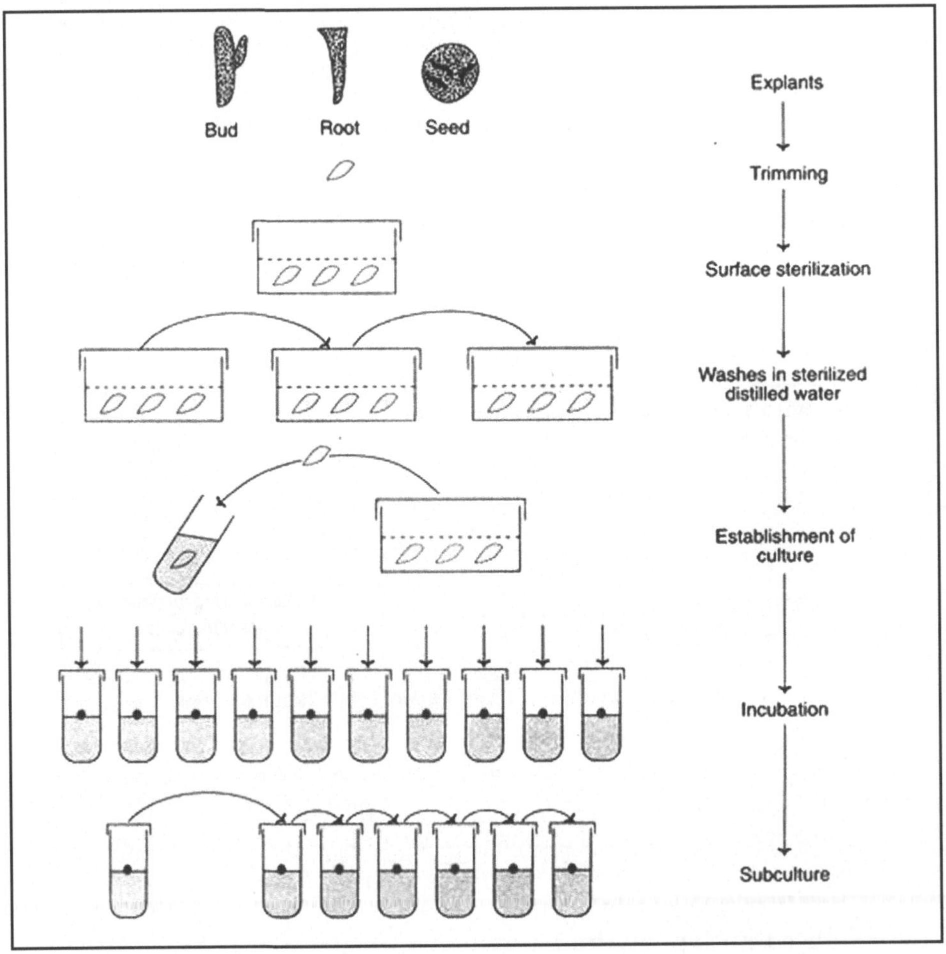

Fig. 7.3: **A diagrammatic outline of the basic procedure in plant tissue culture**

directly on explants, callus pieces, suspension cultures, protoplasts etc.. The calli pieces are treated with selection agents (toxin, NaCl) or mutagenic agents and the regenerants are evaluated. Use of suspension cultures permits a more uniform exposure of cells to the selection agent. The plody level also can be increased through incorporation of colchicines in vitro and it restores fertility in the wide hybrids as in *Saccharum* and *Sorghum* hybrids.

Field evaluation: The somaclones can be evaluated under field conditions. The phenotypic, cytological and molecular changes were studied and further selections were made. The plants regenerated from cultured cells constitute the R_0 generation while the sexual or asexual progenies of R_o are represented by $R_{1.}$

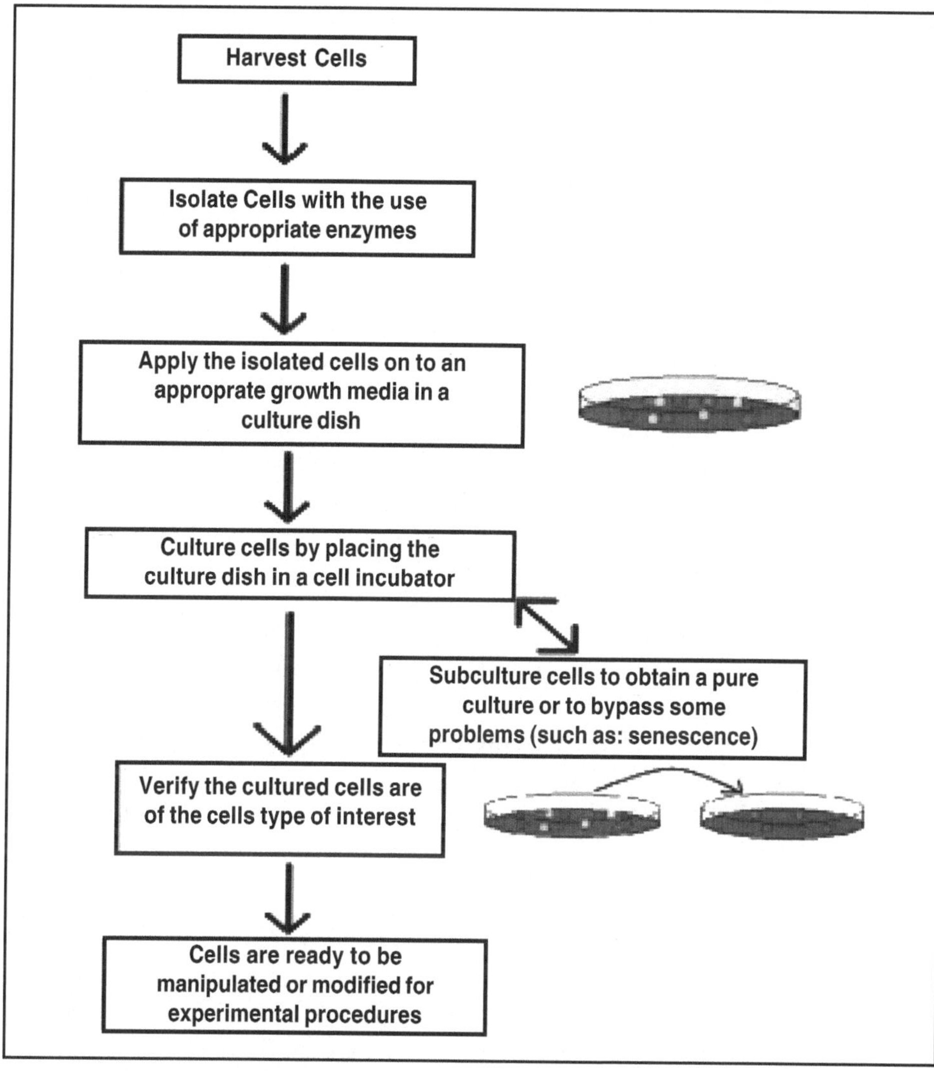

Fig. 7.4: **The process to culture cells**

In order to better understand the somaclonal variant rate in plant tissue culture, a statistical approach has been adopted (Cote *et al.* 2001). According to this approach, the variant percentage could be calculated by: per cent V = [1-(1-p)n] × 100, where per cent V is the percentage of variant, P the probability of variation and 1 the number of multiplication cycles.

Somaclonal Variation in Transgenic Plants

Somaclonal variation was well-known before the first plant genetic transformation had succeeded. Therefore, because tissue culture is a prerquest for most transformation protocols, it was generally regarded as the source of undesirable variation accompanying transformation. Untransformed but tissue culture regenerated vontrols have often been used in transformation experiments to observe somaclonal variation without the influence of transformation. Attempts to understand the sources of somaclonal variation and to modify transformation procedures to reduce its frequency during gene transfer are thus important especially in crops such as: sugarcane, where success of backcrosses to restore the original genotype is made difficult by the complex ploidy state of the plant.

Achievements

Somaclonal variation has been observed in more than 200 species, including most important crops. There are examples in wheat, maize, celery, tomato, banana, oil palm, sugarcane, potato, oats, rice, lettuce, tobacco, carrot, barley and alfalfa. The main selections from India include Bio -12 (*Citronella Java*) yielding 37 per cent more oil and 39 per cent more citrinellol than the contro, Pusa Jaikisan (*Brassica juncea*) showing 17.4 per cent yield advantage over the parent Varuna, Ratan a low neurotoxin variant of khesari, Co 94012 (sugarcane) developed from CoC 671 and released for the state of Maharashtra giving>13 per cent sugar recovery.

Somatic Embryogenesis

A somatic embryo (SE) is an embryo derived from a somatic cell, other than zygote, usually on culture in vitro. Somatic embryogenesis may be defined as the process of development of a bipolar structure like: zygotic embryo from a non-zygotic somatic cell.

Developmental Pattern of SEs

SEs generally originate from single cells, which divide to form a group of meristematic cells usually, this multicellular group becomes isolated by breaking cytoplasmic connections with the other cells around it and subsequently by cutinization of the outer walls of this differentiating cell mass. The cells of meristematic mass continue to divide to give rise to globular (round ball-shaped), heart-shaped, torpedo and cotyledonary stages. In general, the essential features of SE development, especially after the globular stage, are comparable to those of zygotic embryos. Somatic embryogenesis may occur directly from the explants without an intervening callus phase (direct somatic embryogenesis) or a callus phase may precede SE regeneration (indirect somatic embryogenesis). In practice, however, it is very difficult to differentiate these two events. Direct SE regeneration is most likely to occur from ovules, zygotic and somatic embryos and young seedlings. These SEs are useful for multiplication, cryopreservation, due to their genetic stability.

Several genes were found to be expressed at different developmental stages of SE. Carrot gene DC8 encodes a LEA protein, which is hydrophobic. DC8 is produced in only those tissues that are either derived from embryos and young seedlings. These SEs are useful for multiplication, cryopreservation due to their genetic stability.

Haploid Production through Tissue Culture Method

Haploid cells occur naturally in the gametophytic phases of higher plants, in their ovules and pollen. It is the cells of these tissues that are the main targets for doubled haploidy (DH). By manipulating the environment of the gametic cells it is possible to divert development to produce embryos rather than mature pollen grains or ovules. The microspores of developing pollen grains are of particular interest since plants generally produce pollen to excess. Microspore embryogenesis therefore has the potential to generate several hundred DH plants from a single anther. Induced or spontaneous chromosome doubling of haploid embryogenic cells produces doubled haploid plants. These are completely homozygous, true breeding, and consequently of great importance in genetics and plant breeding (Morrison *et al.* 1991 and Thomas, 2005).

The first haploids as noticed by A.D. Bergner in 1921 working with *Datura stramonium* L...Subsequently haploids were reported in many other species but at low and variable frequencies. The first attempt to use haploidy in breeding appears to be by Chase (1952) who selected the low frequency of parthenogenetic haploids in maize and then applied chromosome doubling treatments to produce in bred lines. The remarkable discovery that haploid embryos and plants can be produced by culturing anthers of Datura. (Guha and Maheswari, 1964: 1966) brought renewed interest to haploids. Subsequent to androgenesis (anther or microspore culture), the other methods gynogenesis (culture of ovules or ovaries) and the bulbosum method (using wide hybridization followed by chromosome elimination) were developed.

Androgenesis

Culture of anthers has been a popular and effective technique for haploid induction. Immature anthers containing Uninucleate microspores or isolated microspores are induced for haploid development. Critical stages of androgenesis include: growing conditions, pre-treatment of floral parts (before and after collection of material for culture), physiology of donor plants, genotype, media composition, isolation, incubation, regeneration, and chromosome doubling. Microspore culture has more potential than anther culture in view of large number of microspores per anthers for inoculation. The microspores cultural systems have improved in crop plants through embryogenesis rather than from callus sand thus reduces the extensive induced variability found in earlier reports on anther and microspore culture. Haploids thus produced can be doubled through colchicines treatment. Doubled haploid plants are obtained with high frequency of chromosome doubling occurring on the early phase of microspore embryogenesis in rapeseed, tobacco, wheat, barley and rice (kasha and Maluszynski, 2003) Spontaneous or induced chromosome doubling permits the regeneration of doubled haploid (DH) homozygous material, with restored fertility that can be used in different breeding strategies. Because all the alleles of DH lines are fixed, selection for quantitative characters is often more reliable than in conventional populations.

Gynogenesis

Culture of unfertilized ovaries to obtain haploid plants from egg cells or other haploid cells of the embryo sac is called ovary culture and this process of haploid production is termed *gynogenesis*. The first report of gynogenesis was by San Noem in 1976 in case of barley. Subsequently, success has been obtained with many species, *e.g.*, wheat, rice, maize, tobacco, petunia, Gerbera, sunflower, sugarbeet, rubber, onion, potato, cotton, etc. A bout 0.2-6 per cent of the cultured ovaries show gynogenesis and one or two, rarely upto 8, plantlets originate from each ovary. The rate of success varies considerably with species and is markedly influenced by the genotype so that some cultivars do not respond at all. In rice, japonica genotypes are far more responsive than *indica* cultivars (Singh, 2006).

Bulbosum Technique

Bulbosum technique was first developed by Kasha and Kao, in 1970 through interspecific hybridization of cultivated barley (*Hordeum vulgare L.*) with the wilds species *H. bulbosum*. The embryo was rescued under in vitro after pollination and the chromosomes of H. bulbosum were gradually eliminated. The haploids were doubled with colchicines treatment. This techniques has also been successful in wheat with maize, maize with oat.

Gametoclonal Variation

There is considerable evidence that haploid plants regenerated from callus cultures show genetic variation that is *gametoclonal variation*. For example, gametoclonal variation for heading date, plant height, etc., has been reported in rice. Such a variation may be subjected to selection at the haploid level and the chromosome number of the selected plants may be doubled to obtain homozygous plants (1) the mutant characteristic is expressed in the R_0 plants, *i.e.*, plants regenerated from cells in vitro and (2) cells having detrimental mutations may be expected to regenerate much less frequently in the case of haploid than in diploid cells. However, regeneration of haploid plants is feasible in fewer plant species than regeneration from somatic cells.

Applications of in vitro Haploid Techniques

The rapid attainment of homzygosity at any generation is probably the most valuable feature of doubled haploidy for plant breeding. Other general benefits include the development of large numbers of homozygous lines, efficient genetical analysis and the development of markers for trait selection (particularly valuable tor recessive traits). More specific benefits include the possibility of seed propagation as an alternative to vegetative multiplication in ornamentals and in species such as: trees in which long life cycles and inbreeding depression preclude traditional breeding methods, doubled haploidy provides new alternatives. The application of doubled haploidy, even in the most responsive species is restricted by genotype dependency and there is a challenge to develop more genotype specific independent methods.

The DH lines themselves cane be released directly as cultivars, they may be used as parents in hybrid cultivar production or more indirectly in the creation of breeders lines. The barley cultivar 'Mingo' was the first major DH crop cultivars. It was produced and grown in Canada in the late 1970s Doubled haploidy now features in the production of many crops. Barley has over 100 direct FH cultivars and a similar number of rice cultivars have involved doubled haploidy in their breeding. Over 150 named DdH cultivars are listed (Thomas *et al.* 2003) which is updated on the Website *http;//www.scri.sari.ac.uk/assoc/cost851/Default.htm.* According to the published information, there are currently around 300 DH derived cultivars in 12 species worldwide.

Problems Concerned with Haploid Production

Although haploids have been raised mainly from anther culture of a large number of species, this technique has not proved successful in respect of all genotypes of crop species. A number of problems are encountered with the induction of haploids.

1. Anthers often fail to grow in vitro or the initial growth is followed by abortion of the embryos.
2. The tissue or callus developing from the anther generally comprises a chimera of diploid, tetraploid and haploid cells.
3. Selective cell division must take place in the haploid microspores, concomitantly restricting proliferation of unwanted diploid and polyploidy tissues. Selective cell division is often impossible.
4. Formation of albinos in anther cultures, especially with cereals can neither be avoided nor the loss of plants due to albinism.
5. It is difficult to isolate to isolate a haploid from a mixture of haploids and higher ploidy levels since the polyploids outgrow the haploids.
6. Doubling of haploids is time consuming and may not always result in the production of a homozygote. Double haploids sometimes exhibit segregation in their progeny.
7. The anther culture technique works well on plants belonging to only a few families, of which *Solanaceae* is one.
8. The frequency of embryoids obtained is often very low.

Micro Propagation

The most widely used tissue culture technology is the micro propagation as an alternate for the vegetative propagation of plants. It has been used with all classes of plants although some problems still need to be resolved (*e.g.*, hyperhydricity, aberrant plants). There are three ways by which micro propagation can be achieved. These are enhancing auxiliary bud breading production of adventitious buds directly or indirectly via callus, and somatic embryogenesis directly or indirectly on explants. Auxiliary bud breaking produces the smallest number of plantlets, but they are generally genetically true-to-type; whereas somatic embryogenesis has the potential to produce the greatest number of plantlets, but is induced in the lowest number of plant species. Commercially, numerous ornamentals are produced, mainly via auxiliary bud breaking. As well, there are many lab-scale protocols for other classes of plants, including field and vegetable crops, fruit, plantation and forest trees, but production is often a limiting factor in their use commercially due to the availability of less facilities.

Shoot tip Culture

Micro propagation through proliferation of axillary buds of the shoot tip cultures is the most popular approach because the organized growth and multi-polication minimizes the risk of chromosomal aberrations and somaclonal variation (Suprasanna, 2009). But this does not mean that these resks are zero; many fruit varieties are bud mutants (mutant branches arising from axillary buds) and a sweet potato variety 'Scarlet' is a somaclonal variant recovered from plants derived via axillary branching. In additions, this method preservers chimaeras, and is ideal for the propagation of chimaeric varieties. But sometimes plants may exhibit epigenetic morphological changes, *e.g.*, bsuhiness in the case of Gerbera jamesonii, reduced or lack of root regeneration, excessive flowering, abnormal fruits in Fragaria, etc.. These anomalies are thought to be the consequence of in vitro culture regimes like an excessive dose or a wrong choice of cytokinins (in the case of Gerbera) unlimited subculture conditions/procedures. The apical meristem excised from the shoot tip has been used in micro propaganton to generate virus free plants. In sugarcane inverted and splitted shoot tip cultures hastened the growth and reduced the phenolic exudations from the explants.

Somatic embryos and Synthetic Seeds

Somatic embryos have been for micropropagation of several plant species, and in some species they are the only route available for this purpose, *e.g.*, oil palm, date palm, etc. This method is the only way amenable to scaling up to the bioreactor level and in continuous cultures. In case of those species, for which protocols for regeneration have been refined *e.g.*, for species like: alfalfa carrot, yellow-poplar, Norway spruce, etc.. SEs offer very high rate of multiplication; one liter of suspension culture may contain 1.35×10^6 carrot SEs. An automated large scale micropropagation system based on SEs, bulblets, microtubers, etc., has been devised. This system integrates a bioreactor with a bio processor gor separation, isolation (mainly based on size) and subculturing of the propagules.

Artificial seeds prepared from shoot buds can also be used for plant propagation. This technology would be feasible and even competitive economically with the seed methods. Synthetic or artificial seeds are the living seed like structure derived from somatic embryoids in vitro culture after encapsulation by a hydrogel, the preserved embryoids are termed as synthetic seeds. Automated encapsulation process is the recent and quick method of artificial seed production. An encapsulation machine can be used successfully to encapsulate somatic embryos, *e.g.*, for alfalfa. Blank alginate capsules were planted in seedling trays using a vacuum seeder. However, because for the rapid drying and the thickness of the alginate capsules, a hydrophobic coating is required for mechanical handling.

An additional concept that has greatly aided the improvement of artificial seed performance is *mass balance,* Mass balance considers the amount of tissue at the beginning of the experiment (or production run) and the number of high quality plants produced at the end of it .In fact, treatments that lead to higher numbers of embryos may actually produce fewer superior quality of embryos than another protocol.

Co Cultivation with Microbes

Inoculation of plantlets with a suitable bacterial culture (co cultivation) *e.g.*, Pseudomonas sp., Rhizobium, etc., is called bacterization. Bacterization of potato plantlets with Pseudomonas significantly increased their root number, root dry weight, stem length and leaf area. In addition bacterized plantlets showed a higher total plant lignin content, and improved stomatal function that increased their tolerance to dehydrating conditions. In sugarcane, Methylobacterium and Aospirillum improved in vitro multiplication, Similarly, root colonization by endomycorrhizal fungi is reported to enhance plantlet survival in strawberry. Coculture with Piriformospora indica which is similar to mycorrhiza fungi, promoted survival of tobacco plantlets from 62 per cent (untreated control) to>70 per cent.

Photoautotrophic Micro Propagation

The conventional in vitro environment used for micro propagation has high relative humidity (RH) constant temperature, low photosynthetic photon flux density (PPFD), large difference in light and dark period CO_2 concentration, high sugar concentration and growth regulators. These factors lead to low rates of transpiration, photosynthesis, and water, nutrient and Co_2 uptake and a high rate of dark respiration which resulted in poor growth. In order to overcome these problems, several types for sugar-free, been developed. These systems use a sugar-free medium, a relatively high RPFD (100-200mol $M^{-2}S^{-1}$) and a suitable strategy to maintain a relatively high Co_2 concentration (340 mol^{1-1} or high) within the culture vessels during the light period. These culture systems offer the following advantages: *(i)* more uniform and faster growth and development of the plantlets; *(ii)* reduced physiological and morphological abnormalities in the plantlets *(iii)* reduced contamination risk, *(iv)* increased survival during hardening and field transfer *(v)* reduced production costs due to enhanced survival *(iv)* reduced contamination *(vii)* use of simpler media and *(viii)* use of larger culture vessels due to the lower contamination risk.

The most popular Application of micropropagation is the mass clonal propagation of desired genotypes, It is being used for commercial propagation of large number of horticultural plantation and forest species. Since micropropagation achieves very high rates of multiplication it cane be used to reduce the time between development/release of cultivar and its use by the growers. It can be used for rapid multiplication of superior introduced genotypes following the release of their propagules from quarantine. It provides a reliable and economic method for maintenance of pathogen-free plantlets in a state that allows rapid clonal propagation. In case of dioecious species, plants of one sex may be more desirable than the other *e.g.*, male plants of asparagus ,female plants of papaya etc. In such cases, plants of the desired sex cane be multiplied in vitro, Plantlets produced by micropropagation are usually pathogen-Free Therefore, they are well-suited for germplasm exchange of such species, where seed exchange is not desirable/possible.

In vitro Conservation of Germplasm

The conservation of biodiversity is widely recognized as a high priority area of attention in the ongoing debate linking environment and development. In particular the conservation of plant genetic resources for food and agriculture, one sector of biodiversity, is considered to be a major element of any strategy to achieve sustainable agricultural development, along with the conservation of other natural resources (Kumar and Sharma , 2008). The slow growth cultures and the cryopreservation are the two methods being adapted for the conservation of vagetatively propagated plants, orchids, endangered species and species with recalcitrant seeds.

Slow Growth Cultures

Slow-growth of shoots in vitro provides an attractive alternative to freeze preservation of germplasm as it is simpler, cheaper and very effective. Shoot cultures are used for storage since there is minimal risk of somaclonal variation during the storage> Slow growth may be achieved by maintaining the plantlets either at a low temperature (4-9°C or 15-20°C) or on a medium having high osmotic concentration (*e.g.* 20% sorbitol or sucrose) or both. In addition the nutritional status of the emeium may be lowered to further restrict the growth of plantlets. Under the conditions of slow growth, cultures may be attended to only once in several months and subculture may be necessary only after very long periods once in every 13-36 months. Frequent Subcultures would increase the cost and the risk of contamination. But a much longer interval would reduce culture viability. Therefore, the protocol of slow growth should be such that it ensures a high percentage of plant recovery. For example, grape plants stored at 9°C need to be transferred after every 12 months; they have been thus maintained for more than 15 years. It has been estimated that 6 replicates of 800 grape varieties can be maintained in only 2 m2 laboratory space while et would require one ha in the field, In sugarcane some clones of S. spontaneum could be maintained under medium term storage for 3 years.

Cryopreservation

Cryopreservation is an economical space saving method for long-term storage (Withers and Street, 1977) In cryopreservation, plant cells tissues or organs are stored in liquid nitrogen (LN) at-176°C. Since at this temperature all metabolic processes and growth are suppressed and the occurrence of genetic, karyotypic, morphological and biochemical changes are also prevented Cryopreservation has proved to be the most reliable method for long-term preservation of cell cultures. Calli, cell suspensions. Protoplasts, pollen anthers shoot-tips and embryos have all been successfully preserved. Survival tends to decline with storage period in most of the cases, most likely due to injuries sustained by cells during the freezing step.

Despite the genetic stability inherent in organized plant structures such as: meristem, there are risk to DNA structure, integrated metabolism and viability under slow growth due to the oxidative activity of free radicals.

The early work on the cryopreservation of in vitro plant cultures focused on a two method based on chemical cryoprotection and dehydrative cooling. The transition of extra-and intracellular water into ice causes damage to the physical or biochemical nature of the explants. It can be prevented by the new vitrification-based procedures which offer practical advantages in comparison with classic freezing techniques. Vitrification is more appropriate for complex organs (shoot tips or embryos) which contain a variety of cell types each with unique requirements under conditions of freeze-induced dehydration. By precluding ice formation in the system, vitrification based procedures are operationally less complex than classic ones (*e.g.*, they do not require the use of controlled freezers) and have Greater potential for broad applicability requiring only minor modifications for different cell types.

Applications of Molecular Markers in Tissue Culture

Various molecular markers (Isozymes, RFLP and PCR-based markers such as: RAPDs, AFLP, SSR) have been used to investigate mechanisms that underline somaclonal variations in the nuclear, mitochondrial and chloroplast genomes. It represents powerful tools to determine precisely the origin of plants drrived from microspore, anthers protoplast fusion and other tissue culture induced variability (Cloutier and landry, 1994). These markers could detect changes in the somaclonal and gametoclonal variants in many crops *viz;* sugarcanes sugar beet rice, wheat, cotton, barley etc.

The RAPD markers did not exhibit polymorphism in the regenerants derived from somatic embryos and micropropagated clones in many species

It shows that RAPD is insufficiently sensitive to detect small genetic changes unless many primers are used. Alternately the RFLP markers exhibited altered banding pattern in Lathyrus, banana, picea, carrot, Solanum. And bamboo (Veilleux and Johnson, 1998). For restriction fragment length polymorphism (RFLPs) differences in the sequences recognized by restriction endonucleases insertions or deletions are required to visualize somaclonal variants Restriction enzymes that specifically recognize methylated bases are especially useful for detecting somaclonal variation due to DNA methylation. Development of new marker systems on modification of existing ones, *e g.*, the CRED – RA procedure of Cai *et al.* (1996) to particular RAPD fragments offer promise for tagging somaclonal variation more directly. With improvements in tissue culture technique, populations of DH lines have been produced in several major crop species Doubled haploids have proven useful in the production of molecular maps and in tagging important agronomic traits.

The success of using molecular markers to identify somaclonal variants has been erratic. In some cases, phenotypically obvious variants have gone undetected by markers and in others phenotypically normal regenerants have exhibited polymorphism for molecular markers. These facts exemplify the enormity of the plant genome and the limited windows that current marker systems provide us to view it. The probability of finding a marker that corresponds directly with an obvious phenotypic change, although occasionally reported, is small Given that so much of the higher plant genome occurs as noncoding sequences, the probability of observing marker polymorphism that has no phenotypic effects is also high. However, marker technology has been and will continue to be useful for analyzing somaclonal variation, especially as additional technical advances are made in its application and our understanding of the plant genome increases.

Nanotechnology and Tissue Culture

Biologists made a breakthrough in introducing nanotechnology to penetrate cell wall and to simultaneously deliver a gene and a chemical that triggers its expression with controlled precision. By using mesoporous silica nanoparticles, genes of two or more biogenic species could be introduced through the process of endocytosis in the protoplasts. In Arabidopsis, tobacco and corn DNA and chemicals were successfully introduced (Wang *et al.* 2007).

The successful tissue culture of all plants depends on the removal of exogenous and endogenous microorganisms. Use of antibiotic causes variation and toxicity to the cultures. Recently, use of nanosilver (NS) particles in the removal of bacterial contamination in valerian was reported by Abdi *et al.* (2008). Further investigations on other plant species are needed to clarify the effectiveness of NS for the removal of bacterial contamination in tissue culture of other crops.

Table 7.2: Various Tissue Culture Techniques used for Crop Improvement

Sl. No.	Method	Explant	Purpose
1.	Embryo rescue in vitro pollination In vitro fertilization Somatic hybridization	Hybrid embryo Pollen Ovules, ovary Protoplast	Distant hybrids " "
2.	Callus culture	Young leaf bits, stem, root, Cotyledons or any part.	Creation of variation and mutants
3.	Anther and microspore culture Ovule culture Bulbosum method	Anther and microspore Ovule Hybrid embryo	Haploid and doubled haploids "
4.	Micro propagation	Shoot tips, somatic embryo	Rapid multiplication
5.	Cryopreservation	Shoot tips, embryos. Calli, pollen	Long-term storage of germplasm
6.	Somatic embryogenesis	Leaf bits, coteledonary leaf Bits, ovules	Multiplication and Conservation

Commonly used Terms in Tissue Culture

- *Adventitious:* Development of organs such as: buds, leaves, roots, shoots and somatic embryos from shoot and root tissues and callus.
- *Agar:* Natural gelling agent made from algae.
- *Aseptic Technique:* Procedures used to prevent the introduction of microorganisms such as: fungi, bacteria, viruses and phytoplasmas into cell, tissue and organ cultures, and cross contamination of cultures.
- *Autoclave:* A machine capable of sterilizing by steam under pressure.
- *Axenic Culture:* A culture without foreign or undesired life forms but may include the deliberate co-culture with different types of cells, tissues or organisms.
- *Callus:* An unorganized mass of differentiated plant cells.
- *Cell Culture:* Culture of cells or their maintenance in vitro including the culture of single cells.
- *Chemically defined Medium:* A nutritive solution or substrate for culturing cells in which each component is specified.
- *Clonal Propagation:* Asexual multiplication of plants from a single individual or explant.
- *Clones:* A group of plants propagated from vegetative parts, which have been derived by repeated propagation from a single individual. Clones are considered to be genetically uniform.
- *Contamination:* Infected by unwanted microorganisms in controlled environment.
- *Cryopreservation:* Ultra-low temperature storage of cells, tissues, embryos and seeds.

- *Culture:* A plant growing in vitro in a sterile environment.
- *Differentiated:* Cultured cells that maintain all or much of the specialized structure and function typical of the cell type in vivo.
- *Embryo Culture:* In vitro culture of isolated mature or immature embryos.
- *Explant:* An excised piece or part of a plant used to initiate a tissue culture.
- *Ex vitro:* Organisms removed from tissue culture and transplanted; generally plants to soil or potting mixture.
- *Hormone:* Generally naturally occurring chemicals that strongly affect plant growth.
- *In Vitro:* To be grown in glass.
- *In Vivo:* To be grown naturally.
- *Laminar Flow Hood:* An enclosed work area where the air is cleaned using HEPA filters.
- *Medium:* A solid or liquid nutritive solution used for culturing cells.
- *Meristem:* A group of undifferentiated cells situated at the tips of shoots, buds and roots, which divide actively and give rise to tissue and organs.
- *Micro propagation:* Multiplication of plants from vegetative parts by using tissue culture nutrient medium.
- *Propagule:* A portion of an organism (shoot, leaf, callus, etc.,) used for propagation.
- *Somatic embryos:* Non-zygotic bipolar embryo-like structures obtained from somatic cells.
- *Subculture:* The aseptic division and transfer of a culture or portion of that culture to a fresh synthetic media.
- *Tissue Culture:* In vitro culture of cells, tissues, organs and plants under aseptic conditions on synthetic media.
- *Totipotency:* Capacity of plant cells to regenerate whole plants when cultured on appropriate media.
- *Transgenic:* Plants that have a piece of foreign DNA.
- *Undifferentiated:* Cells that have not transformed into specialized tissues.

Conclusion

The applications of various tissue culture techniques for crop improvement are summarized in the Table 7.1. Among the various tissue culture techniques, micro propagation and somaclonal variations are popularly used in majority of the crops. Other techniques especially the haploid production and distant crosses are not successful in many species as they species as they are largely influenced by the exogenous and endogenous factors. These techniques are to be further strengthened to increase the scope of In vitro techniques to other species for further improvement. However, the tissue culture techniques have been proved as an efficient tool for crop improvement and revolutionized the agricultural research through several remarkable achievements which could not be attained through conventional methods.

REFERENCES

Abdi, G., Salehi, H. and Khosh-Khui. (2008). Nano Silver: A Novel Nanomaterial for Removal of Bacterial Contaminants in Valerian (*Valeriana officinalis L.)* Tissue Culture.

Brown, D.C.W. and Thorpe T.A. (1995). Crop Improvement through Tissue Culture. *World Journal of Microbiology and Bio-tecgbikigt*, 2, 408-415.

Cai, Q., C.L. Guy and G.A. Moore. (1996). Detection of Cytosine methylation and Mapping of a Gene Influencing cytosine Methylation in the Genome of citrus Genome, 39 :235-242.

Chase S.S. (1952). Analytical Breeding of Solanum mberosum L. Can *J. gene. cyto.* 15:359-363.

Cloutier S. and Landry B.S. (1994). Molecular Markers Applied to Plant Tissue Culture. In *Vitro Cellular and Developmental Biology*, 30 (1), 32-39.

Evans, D.A. (1989). Somaclonal Variation Genetic Basis and Breeding Application. Trends Genet, 5(2): 46-50.

Forster, B.P. and Thomas T.B. (2005). Doubled Haploids in Genetics and Plant Breeding. *Plant Breeding Reviews*, 25,57-81.

Guha C. and S.C. Maheshwari. (1964). In vitro Production of Embryos from anthers of Datura Nature. 204:497.

Holder, P.R. (1995). Somaclonal Variation and Crop Improvement. *New Phytologist*, 106 (4),786-787.

Kranz, E and Lorz, H. (1990). Micro manipulation and in vitro Fertilization with Single Pollengrains of Maize. *Sexual Plant Reproduction* 3:160-169.

Kumar, U and A.K. Sharma. (2008). *Plant Biotechnology and Biodiversity Conservation*. Eds. Agrobios. 2008.

Larkin, l.J. and Scowcroft, W.R. (1981). Somaclonal Variation - A Novel Source of Variability from Cell Cultures for Crop Improvement. *Theor. Appl. Genet.* 75:841-846.

Monnier, M. (1990). Zygotic Embryo Culture. In: Plant Tissue Culture: Applications and Limitations. SS. Bhojwani (ed.) Elsevier, Amsterdam. pp. 366-393.

Mortison, R.A., Evans D.A. and Fan, Z. (1991). Haploid Plants from Tissue Culture Application in Crop Improvement. *Subcell Biochem,*. 17:53-72.

Singh, B.D. (2006). Plant Biotechnology Kalyani Publishers.

Suprasanna, P., V.Y. Patade and U.A. Bapat. (2008). Sugarcane Biotechnology: A Perspective on Recent Developments and Emerging Opportunities. In: Advances in Plant Biotechnology, Eds: Rao, G.P., Zhao, Y., Radchuk ,V.V. and S.K. Bhatnagar, pp. 313:342 Maluszynski, M., Kasha, K.J., Forster, B.P. And Szarejko, I. 2003. Doubled haploid Production in Crop Plants A Manual, pp. 337-351.

Veilleux, R.E. and Johnson, A.A. (1998). Somaclonal Variation: Molecular Analysis, Transformation Interaction and Utilization. *Plant Breeding Reviews*, 16:229-265.

Wang, K., Lin, V., Trewyn, B. and Torney F. (2007). Mesoporous Silica Nano Particles Deliver DNA and Chemicals into Plants. *Nature Nanotechnology*, pp. 11.

Warra, S. and Glimelius, K. (1995). The Potential of Somatic hybridization in Croop Breeding. *Euphytica* 85: 217-233.

Witners, L.A. and Street. H.E. (1977). Freeze Preservation of Cultured Plant Cells *Physiol. Plant*. 39:171-178.

Page 162-175

FARMING TECHNIQUES AND CROP PRODUCTION
Edited by : **Dr. Alka Chauhan; Dr. Anubhuti Sharma & Jaswant Ray**
Edition : **2017**
ISBN : 978-93-5056-855-2
Published by : **Discovery Publishing House Pvt. Ltd., New Delhi (India)**

8 Weather and Crop Pests

Alok Kumar Patra

ABSTRACT

Weather plays a major role in determining the survival and growth rates of insect populations because of its direct impact on them and on their food supply. Similarly, weather plays a vital role in plant disease development, affecting both the dispersal and infection processes. Thus, the local weather patterns have a significant impact on the abundance of diseases and insect pests in the crops. The severity of disease and pest development depends on the combination of weather conditions during the growing season and is variable from season to season. The weather conditions include: the maximum and the minimum temperature, light, rain, humidity, dew, cloudiness, sunshine, wind, air currents, evaporation, snow and atmospheric pressure. However, among these weather parameters, temperature, rainfull and relative humidity play the major roles in infection of crops due to insect pests and diseases. So, a thorough understanding of these interactions is useful in developing forewarning models. Pest weather calendars are also prepared by using these parameters, which can act as reference tool. In this paper, an attempt has been made to establish the relationship of major insect pests and diseases of various field and garden crops with weather parameters.

INTRODUCTION

Weather refers to the state of atmosphere at any given time denoting the short-term variations of atmosphere in terms of temperature, pressure, wind, moisture, cloudiness, precipitation, etc. It is highly variable, constantly changing, sometimes from hour to hour and at other times from day-to-day. These weather elements are closely related with each other. Climate on the

Professor (Agronomy), All India Co-ordinated Research Project on Integrated Farming Systems, Orissa University of Agriculture and Technology, Bhubaneswar - 751 003, Odisha, India.

other hand, can be defined as the state of the atmosphere expressed over a longer period of time (generally 30 years) and includes a statistical description in terms of mean and variability of relevant weather elements. It really represents a kind of frequency distribution of weather types in a given region and over a period of time. Until mid-twentieth century, climate was considered to be sufficiently constant and the average weather of 30 years at any location usually represented the climate of that location. However, the variation of climate averaged over time is now widely acknowledged. The distinction between weather and climate can be appreciated with the popular quotations *'Climate lasts all the time, weather only for few days'* (Mark Twain) or *'Climate is what you expect, weather is what you get'* (Robert Heinlein).

Many diseases, nematodes, insects and weeds affect crop production, causing severe yield loss. Weather is the most important factor that determines the geographical distribution of these crop pests. The local weather patterns have a significant impact on the abundance of diseases and insect pests in the crops (Patra, 2016). The severity of disease and pest development depends on the combination of weather conditions during the growing season and is variable from season to season. The weather conditions include temperature (both the maximum and the minimum), light, rain, humidity, dew, cloudiness, sunshine, wind, air currents, evaporation, snow and atmospheric pressure. However, among these weather parameters, temperature and humidity play the major roles in infection of crops due to insect pests and diseases.

Effect of Weather Parameters on the Crop Pests and Diseases

Temperature

Temperature is the driving force behind insect development, growth and behaviour. Usually insects are cold blooded and they are unable to regulate their body temperature. Their internal temperature varies along with that of the ambient environmental temperature. Each species of insects has a range of temperature within which it can survive and this range is referred as the tolerable zone (Atkins, 1978). Most insects have a lower temperature tolerance of one degree Celsius and an upper temperature tolerance up to 50°C (Campbell *et al.* 1974). Some insects can adapt physiologically to survive several months of severe hot in summer while some others can adapt to severe cold in winter in a dormant state and such adaptation is referred as summer or winter diapause. But their activity and development begin again as soon as the temperature becomes favourable. The movement, mating behaviour and reproduction of insects are influenced by temperature. A temperature range of 15 to 35°C is optimum for the development and multiplication of most of the insects. Aphids cannot fly at a temperature less than 13°C. If temperature is not suitable for mating for several days, some adults may die without leaving offspring and others may become less fertile due to age (Mavi and Tupper, 2004).

Infection and spread of crop diseases occur under certain temperature conditions. Under favourable temperature, the development of disease continues so long as the healthy plant tissue is available. The development of fungal disease stops under extremely low and high temperature conditions since the growth and multiplication of fungi is highly influenced by temperature fluctuations. Sometimes, especially with viral and mycoplasmal diseases, the vectors such as: aphid, leafhopper, thrips, mite, nematode, etc., play the major role in spread of diseases. These organisms may be highly sensitive to weather conditions, and thus may have an influence on the incidence or severity of the disease. Mosaics are viral diseases that attack many crops. The great majority of mosaics are transmitted from plant to plant by the feeding of various species of aphids. If the weather remains warm and dry, large aphid populations build up, causing the spread of mosaics.

Moisture and Humidity

Moisture plays a critical role in the incidence of crop pests and diseases. The atmospheric humidity, rain, snow, dew, soil moisture and surface water influence the water balance of insects. The moisture content in the habitat of an insect directly determines their survival rate. Moisture also has indirect effects on insect populations through its influence on plant growth (Mavi and Tupper, 2004). In fact, many crop insect pests do not require free moisture to survive. They obtain water through their food supply. Rainfall can be quite deleterious to insects. Aphid activity remains low in stormy and wet weather. Rainy weather is conducive to high aphid mortality; hence, there is little spread of mosaic viruses. Insect eggs and larvae may be washed away from their host plants by heavy rain. Heavy downpours also wash off aphids from their host plants. Soil moisture content also has an influence on the severity of soil borne diseases and survival of insect pests living in soil.

Relative humidity plays an important role in the infection process. It can influence insect growth and behaviour by affecting the insect's ability to regulate water loss. Low humidity is often detrimental to insect development, but most insects found in desert crops have adapted physiological and behavioural mechanisms to prevent dehydration. Relative humidity directly influences sporulation by many fungi. The high relative humidity of 50 to 90 per cent is favourable for development and multiplication of most of the insects. On the other hand, high atmospheric moisture may have some indirect effect on the insect population by facilitating the spread of some insect pathogens and thus the insect population remains in check.

Wind

Wind has both direct and indirect effects on the crop insect pests and diseases. Locust, a pest of the desert moves from one place to another in the same direction in which wind blows. Wind acts as a carrier of insects from place to place and also transport many diseases causing organisms through the insects. High wind velocity may carry spores of pathogens and insects from a favourable site to an unfavourable site, and *vice versa*. Thus, wind influences the insect and pathogen population of a place.

Light

Light intensity and photoperiodism greatly influence the insect behaviour. Some insects are more active during day time and some others prefer feeding on crop plants during night time. Even some insects are active during the faint light of dawn and dusk. Similarly, plant pathogens are sensitive to intensity and quality of light to which they are exposed. Some pathogens enter their hosts at night. However, many fungi germinate better in light of moderate intensity than in complete darkness. The germination of several powdery mildew is much greater in light than in darkness but ecologically powdery mildew are more common in shade than in full day. On the other hand, the germination of certain rusts may be much greater in darkness than in light (Mahi and Kingra, 2007).

Weather Requirements of Insect Pests

There is no doubt that weather plays a major role in determining the survival and growth rates of insect populations because of its direct impact on them and on their food supply. Weather factors, especially temperature, rainfall and relative humidity play a dominant role in the population dynamics of many insect pests. So, a thorough understanding of these interactions is useful in developing forewarning models. Pest weather calendars are also prepared by using these parameters, which can act as reference tool.

Insect Pests of Rice

Table 8.1: Insect Pests of Rice and their Relationship with Weather

Insect Pest	Effect of Weather Parameters on Pest and its Infection
Gall midge (*Orseolia oryzae*)	Continuous cloudy weather or rainfall with high relative humidity (RH) above 90 per cent favours infestation; minimum and maximum temperatures of 19.8 and 35.2°C, respectively are favourable for infestation.
Stem borer (*Scirpophaga incertulas*)	Minimum and maximum temperatures of 14-27 and 28-30°C, respectively are ideal for maximum moth emergence; moths are active at 19-33°C and maximum number of eggs are laid at 29-30°C with 90 per cent RH.
Brown plant hopper (*Nilparwata lugens*)	Large scale occurrence is favoured by mild winters followed by hot summer with little rain; heavy rain of more than 30 mm per week for at least two weeks during September with minimum temperature of 21-23°C are conducive for attack.
Gundhi bug (*Leptocorisa varicornis*)	Continuous cloudy weather or intermittent rainfall with high temperature is conducive for attack; threshold temperatures of development of the eggs and nymphs are 13 and 8-15°C, respectively.
Swarming caterpillar (*Spodoptera mauritia*)	Active at temperature 22-32°C and RH 65-70 per cent; outbreaks occur after a period of prolonged drought followed by heavy rain; wind and rain storm helps in migration of moths to long distances; heavy rainfall leads to high mortality of larval population.
Grass hopper (*Hieroglyphus banian*)	Quick multiplication of pest with dry and warm weather during hatching and moulting phases.
Rice hispa (*Dicladispa armigera*)	Heavy rains, especially in premonsoon or early monsoon periods, followed by abnormally low precipitation, minimum day-night temperature differential for a number of days, and high RH are favourable for the insect's abundance.
Leaf folder (*Cnaphalocrosis medinalis*)	High humidity and shade favour the development of the pest.

Insect Pests of Sorghum

Table 8.2: Insect Pests of Sorghum and their Relationship with Weather

Insect pest	Effect of Weather Parameters on Pest and its Infection
Sorghum shoot fly (*Atherigona soccata*)	High maximum temperature of 30-40°C and low RH of 40-75 per cent are conducive for egg laying and larval activity; very high RH of 86-90 per cent or heavy rains are not favourable for infestation.
Sorghum mite (*Oligonychus indicus*)	One or two showers in April-May favours pest population; maximum and minimum temperatures of 34.5-38.8 and 24.4-25.5°C, respectively are favourable for infestation.
Stem borer (*Chilo partellus* and *Sesamia inferens*)	Pest incidence positively correlated with RH; rainfall determines the time of adult emergence and the relationship is positive.
Sorghum midge (*Contarinia sorghicola*)	Average temperature, high rainfall and high humidity favour increase in pest population.

Insect Pests of Pulses

Table 8.3: Insect Pests of Pulses and their Relationship with Weather

Insect Pest	Effect of Weather Parameters on Pest and its Infection
Pod borer (*Helicoverpa armigera*)	Larval population build up is positively correlated with minimum and maximum temperatures; negatively correlated with relative humidity.
Blue butterfly (*Lampides boeticus*) in pigeon pea	Pest population has a positive correlation with rainfall and negative correlation with temperature, RH and wind velocity.
Plume moth (*Exelastis atomosa*) in pigeon pea	Pest population has a positive correlation with maximum and minimum temperatures, bright sunshine hour and afternoon RH; negative correlation with rainfall, morning RH and wind velocity.
Termite in chick pea	Periods of drought and dry spells attract the infestation.
Red legged earth mite (*Halotydeus destructor*)	Active only during winter months; mites hatch once the temperature drops below 20° C for six days and adequate moisture (about 15 mm) is available.

Weather Factors for Crop Disease Outbreaks

Weather influences all stages of host and pathogen life cycles. It plays a vital role in plant disease development, affecting both the dispersal and infection processes. Each disease has its own specific weather requirements. The severity of disease fluctuates annually depending on seasonal changes in weather. To infect, pathogens have to gain entry to their host. When the spores of airborne pathogens land on a leaf surface, they germinate only under optimum conditions of temperature and humidity and then the infection process starts.

Insect Pests of Oilseed Crops

Table 8.4: Insect Pests of Oilseeds and their Relationship with Weather

Insect Pest	Effect of Weather Parameters on Pest and its Infection
Sucking pests (jassids, thrips and aphids) in groundnut	Temperature and rainfall play a dominant role in the population dynamics of aphids; temperatures below 20°C and above 25°C limit the build up; high rainfall reduces the population of these sucking pests.
Tobacco caterpillar in groundnut (*Spodoptera litura*)	Maximum temperature, RH, rainy days, sunshine hours and wind speed have a negative correlation with pest population.
Red hairy caterpillar in groundnut (*Amsaecta albistriga*)	Pest population increases after 3rd or 4th day of heavy rainfall.
Mustard aphid (*Lipaphis erysami* and *Myzus persicae*)	Rainfall, high humidity and cloudy weather invite aphids and the crop gets spoiled completely; mean daily temperature of 10-14°C and RH of 67-85 per cent favour aphid infestation.
Sesame capsule borer (*Antigastra catalaunalis*)	Larval population is maximum at maximum temperature of 31-36°C, mean temperature around 27°C with low rainfall of below 55 mm.
Grass hopper and jassids in sunflower	Dry spells favour increase in pest population and cause severe infestation.
Safflower aphid (*Uroleucon compositae*)	High temperature, low humidity and low rainfall adversely affect pest population.
Castor semilooper (*Achoea janata*)	Minimum temperature has a positive correlation with egg population.

Insect Pests of Cotton

Table 8.5: Insect Pests of Cotton and their Relationship with Weather

Insect Pest	Effect of Weather Parameters on Pest and its Infection
Spotted bollworm (*Earias vitella*)	Morning RH 95-100 per cent and weekly rainfall of 17-210 mm favours infestation in July and August; larval activity is more in October and November when maximum and minimum temperatures are 30-32 and 19-20°C, respectively; no eggs are hatched at temperatures less than 10° or more than 37.5°C.
Cotton boll worm (*Helicoverpa armigera*)	Maximum temperature of 30-40°C, morning and afternoon RH of 70-96 and 40-85 per cent, respectively favour pest population build up.
White fly (*Bemisia tabaci*)	Low rainfall, high temperature, moderate RH and high sunshine hours favours fast growth and development of the pest.
Cotton aphids (*Aphis gossypii*)	A mean temperature of less than 25°C favours increase in the aphid population; increases in minimum temperature and evening humidity and an appreciable decrease in sunshine hours with occasional rain favour aphid infestation during elongation stage of cotton; rainfall is the predominant variable controlling the aphid population in the boll formation stages.

Insect Pests of Sugarcane

Table 8.6: Insect Pests of Sugarcane and their Relationship with Weather

Insect Pest	Effect of Weather Parameters on Pest and its Infection
Shoot borer (*Chiloinfuscatellus snellen*)	Maximum and minimum temperatures of 37.8-41.4 and 24.4-31.1°C, respectively and morning and afternoon RH of 23-73 and 16-61 per cent, respectively favour infestation.
Pyrilla (*Pyrilla purpusilla*)	Heavy rainfall followed by 75-80 per cent RH, intermittent drought periods, high temperature of 26-30°C and wind movement favour rapid build up of pest.
Whitefly (*Aleurolobus barodensis*)	Incidence is high in summer when the air temperatures are very high; summer droughts and dry spells during monsoon season also favour build up of this pest; incidence is more with low diurnal temperature.
Mites	Moderate temperature and moderate to high RH favour multiplication of pest.
Scale insect (*Melanaspis glomerata*)	Waterlogging, high temperature and humidity favour build up of scale insect population; rainwater and high wind velocity facilitate dispersal of the pest.

Insect Pests of Vegetables

Table 8.7: Insect Pests of Vegetables and their Relationship with Weather

Insect pest	Effect of Weather Parameters on Pest and its Infection
Colorado potato beetle (*Epilachna philippinensis*)	Very active at temperature of 16-27°C; egg laying is maximum at 25°C; incubation period is 5 days at 30°C and 19 days at 12°C and a temperature of 38°C is lethal for larva; beetles go hibernation when temperature falls below 12°C; annual rainfall of 600-1500 mm is favourable for its development.
White fruit fly in tomato	High temperature and RH favour increase in the pest population.
Shoot and fruit borer in brinjal (*Leucinodes orbonalis)*	Larvae is active throughout the year but more during monsoon period.
Midge in brinjal (*Asphondylia* sp.)	Infestation is severe during cooler months.
Stem fly in beans (*Ophiomya phaseoli)*	Severe incidences observed during dry period of monsoon.

Weather parameters therefore play a major role in the initiation of disease, and each pathogen has its own optimum requirements for infection. Pathogens are generally spread by wind and rain. Some pathogens are also transmitted by vectors and this will be dependent on weather conditions suitable for the vectors. Some spores are released under drying conditions or in films of water arising from rain or dew on the leaf surface. High humidity, or the presence of free water on a leaf surface, is required for initiating the infection process. Temperature will speed or slow the infection process and disease development (Hardwick, 2002).

Diseases of Rice

Table 8.8: Diseases of Rice and their Relationship with Weather

Diseases	Weather Parameters Affecting the Pathogen and its Infection
Blast (*Pyricularia oryzae*)	A temperature range of 24-28° with RH of 86-98 per cent and heavy dew is the most conducive for the disease spread; favourable years of blast are usually associated with more number of days of minimum temperature of 24°C and high RH of 85-90 per cent and large differences between day and night temperatures.
Brown leaf spot (*Pyricularia oryzae*)	Conidia germinate at a temperature of 25-30°C and infection occurs when RH is more than 90 per cent; heavy late rains and cloudy weather favour the spread of the disease.
Stem rot (*Helminthosporium sigmoideum* var. *irregular*)	High RH, high temperature and waterlogging conditions favour spread of disease.
Bacterial leaf blight (*Xanthomonas oryzae*)	Cloudy weather, dull windy days and a mean temperature of 21-33°C are conducive for lesion development; minimum temperature below 17°C and maximum temperature above 37°C adversely affect lesion development.
Sheath blight (*Rhizoctonia solani*)	Temperature of 28-32°C with RH of more than 95 per cent is very conducive for spread of disease.
Sheath rot (*Sarocladium oryzae*)	Occurs in areas with high RH and temperatures (20-28°C) at heading to mature crop stages.
False Smut (*Ustilaginoidea virens*)	The incidence of the disease is more in those years when spells of wet weather coincide with the heading stage; the disease is favoured by the prevalence of relatively low temperature and high RH with moderate rainfall well distributed during the period of flowering.

Diseases of Wheat

Table 8.9: Diseases of Wheat and their Relationship with Weather

Diseases	Weather Parameters Affecting the Pathogen and its Infection
Brown or leaf rust (*Puccinia recondita*)	Disease develops rapidly when free moisture is available and temperatures are near 20°C; high humidity associated with dew, fog or rainfall favours spread of disease.
Black or stem rust (*Puccinia graminis* var. *tritici*)	Disease develops rapidly when free moisture (rain or dew) and moderate temperatures prevail; if mean temperatures remains 20°C or more, the first generation of urediospores will be produced in 10-15 days.
Yellow or stripe rust (*Puccinia striiformis*)	Disease develops rapidly when free moisture (rain or dew) occurs and temperatures range between 10 and 20°C; at temperatures above 25°C, the production of urediospores is reduced or ceases.
Karnal bunt (*Neovossia indica*)	Maximum and minimum temperatures of 19-23 and 8-10°C, respectively with RH of 85-90 per cent during flowering stage favour quick spread of the disease; the degree of disease establishment and development depends on environmental conditions from spike emergence through grain filling.
Loose smut (*Ustilago tritici*)	Infection and disease development are favoured by cool and humid conditions; fungus germinates at a temperature of 18-20°C.
Flag smut (*Urocystis agropyri*)	Infection is favoured by low soil moisture and cool soil temperatures.
Powdery mildew (*Erysiphe graminis* var. *tritici*)	Development of powdery mildew is favoured by cool temperature of 15-22°C, RH of 75-100 per cent and cloudy conditions.
Alternaria leaf blight (*Alternaria triticina*)	High humidity or irrigation and warmer temperatures of 20-25°C favour infection and disease development.

Diseases of Maize and Millets

Table 8.10: Diseases of Maize and Millets and their Relationship with Weather

Diseases	Weather Parameters Affecting the Pathogen and its Infection
Downy mildew of maize (*Sclerophthora rayssiae*)	Optimum temperature for production and germination of conidia is 25°C; conidia production ceases below 13°C and above 31°C temperature but can germinate at 10-34°C temperature, if free water is available.
Maize leaf blight (*Setosphaeria turcica*)	Cool and wet conditions with temperature of 18-27°C and RH of above 80 per cent favour the development of disease.
Maize grey leaf spot (*Cercospora zeae-maydis*)	Disease development is favoured by wet, cloudy and warm weather with a temperature of 22-30°C and RH of above 80 per cent.
Downy mildew of sorghum (*Peronosclerospora sorghi*)	Rapid growth of fungal pathogen is favoured by cool, wet and intermittent rains.
Ergot or sugary disease of sorghum (*Claviceps purpurea*)	Relative humidity greater than 80 per cent and temperatures between 20 and 30°C favour the development of the disease.
Head smut of sorghum (*Sporisorium reilianum*)	Relative humidity greater than 80 per cent and temperatures between 20 to 30°C favour development of the disease.
Downy mildew or Green ear disease of pearl millet (*Sclerospora graminicola*)	Warm, wet and humid weather with intermittent rains favour incidence of the disease; temperatures between 25 and 30°C and RH above 85 per cent favour high level of secondary infection.
Grain mould of millets caused by *Alternaria, Fusarium, Aspergillus, Pencillium*, etc.	Untimely rain and high RH during crop maturity and harvest favour the disease spread.

Diseases of Pulses

Table 8.11: Diseases of Pulses and their Relationship with Weather

Diseases	Weather Parameters Affecting the Pathogen and its Infection
Collar rot of chickpea (*Sclerotium rolfsii*)	Disease is common in areas where soil moisture is high and temperature is around 30°C.
Ascochyta blight of chickpea (*Ascochyta rabiei*)	High humidity and cool temperature favour disease development; rainfall during October and November favours the build up and subsequent spread of disease.
Grey mould of chickpea (*Botrytis cinerea*)	Optimum temperature for growth is 18-30°C; day temperature of 25°C favours development of disease.
Stemphylium blight of chickpea and lentil (*Stemphylium sarciniforme*)	Day temperature of 20-22°C and night temperature of 4-6°C with morning RH of 90-96 per cent favour spread of the disease; cloudy and foggy weather is suitable for disease development.
Stem rot of chickpea and pigeon pea (*Sclerotinia sclerotiorum*)	Disease becomes very severe where high humidity is built up during January.
Powdery mildew of pea (*Erysiphe polygoni*)	Cool and dry weather is favourable for disease development; morning RH more than 90 per cent with temperature more than 28°C is ideal for quick spread of the disease.
Downy mildew (*Peronospora* spp.)	Conidia cause infection at a temperature of 10-20°C; disease is favoured by a temperature of 15°C and heavy dew.
Stem blight of pigeon pea (*Phytophthora drechsleri* var. *cajani*)	High humidity with a temperature of 20-25°C is favourable for the initiation of the disease; a temperature of 27°C with 92 per cent RH and cloudy weather causes severe of disease incidence.
Cercospora leaf spot of greengram and blackgram	Mean temperature of 22.5-23.5°C with RH 77-86 per cent and intermittent rains are favourable for disease development.

Diseases of Oilseed Crops

Table 8.12: Diseases of Oilseed Crops and their Relationship with Weather

Diseases	Weather Parameters Affecting the Pathogen and its Infection
Early and late leaf spot (Tikka disease) of groundnut (*Cercospora arachidicola* and *C. personata*)	Average maximum and minimum temperatures of 33 and 20°C, respectively and monthly rainfall of 88 mm is favourable for outbreak of the disease; RH more than 90 per cent with temperature 25-35°C and continuous leaf wetness due to rain, fog or dew favour quick spread of the disease.
Rust of groundnut (*Puccinia arachidis*)	Infection is influenced by temperature, leaf wetness and humidity; temperature around 24°C, RH 87 per cent with intermittent rainfall favours quick spread of the disease.
Blight of mustard (*Alternaria brassicae*)	Maximum and minimum temperatures of 16-26° and 1.5-9.5°C, respectively with morning RH 75-95 per cent favours quick development of the disease.
Downy mildew of mustard (*Peronospora brassicae*)	Conidia cause infection at a temperature of 10-20°C; disease is favoured by a temperature of 15°C and heavy dew or fog.
Blight of sunflower (*Alternaria helianthi*)	Warm humid environments favour spread of the disease; a temperature of 24-27°C and frequent rain (free water or dew present for a few hours) alternating with periods of dryness is favourable for the sporulation of the fungus.
Leaf spot of safflower (*Alternaria carthami*)	Warm weather with frequent showers or cloudy conditions favour spread of the disease.

Diseases of Cotton

Table 8.13: Diseases of Cotton and their Relationship with Weather

Diseases	Weather Parameters Affecting the Pathogen and its Infection
Fusarium wilt (*Fusarium oxysporum*)	Hot and dry periods with soil temperature at 20-30°C followed by rains are favourable for spread of the disease.
Verticillium wilt (*Verticillium dahliae*)	Low temperature of 15 to 20°C is favourable for spread of the disease.
Leaf spot (*Alternaria macrospora* and *Cercospora gossypina*)	High humidity, intermittent rains, moderate temperature of 25 to 28°C and rains followed by bright sunshine are favourable for spread of the disease.
Bacterial blight (*Xanthomonas citri* sub sp. *malvacearum*)	High atmospheric temperature of 30 to 40°C with RH of 85 per cent is favourable for spread of the disease.
Boll rot (*Asochyta gossypii*)	Heavy rainfall at boll formation stage is favourable for spread of the disease.
Root rot of cotton (*Rhizoctonia bataticola* and *Rhizoctonia solani*)	Dry weather followed by rains and high soil temperature of 35 to 39°C is favourable for the disease.

Diseases of Sugarcane

Table 8.14: Diseases of Sugarcane and their Relationship with Weather

Diseases	Weather Parameters Affecting the Pathogen and its Infection
Red rot (*Colletotrichum falcatum*)	Disease spreads at a high temperature of 37-40ºC.
Smut (*Ustilago scitaminea*)	Smut initiation and spread is high at ambient temperatures of 25-30ºC.
Wilt (*Cephalosporium sacchari*)	Moisture stress coupled with high temperature and low humidity reduces plant resistance to wilt.
Yellow leaf spot (*Cercospora koepkei*)	Prolonged rain with intermittent sunshine, waterlogged conditions are congenial for disease development; warm humid weather favours rapid and abundant production of conidia by the pathogen and spread of the disease.
Eye spot (*Helminthosporium sacchari*)	Cloudy weather, high humidity with drizzle coupled with low night temperatures, wetting of leaves either through precipitation or dew greatly enhance disease development.

Diseases of Vegetables

Table 8.15: Diseases of Vegetables and their Relationship with Weather

Diseases	Weather Parameters Affecting the Pathogen and its Infection
1	2
Late blight of potato and tomato (*Phytophthora infestans*)	Sporangia develop on the leaves, spreading through the crop when temperatures are above 10°C and humidity is 75-90 per cent for 2 days or more; rain can wash spores into the soil where they infect young tubers; sporulation can occur at 3-26°C, but the optimum range is 18-22°C; Cool nights, warm days, and extended wet conditions from rain and fog can result in late blight epidemics in which entire potato fields are destroyed in less than two weeks.
Early blight of potato and tomato (*Alternaria solani*)	Warm, humid (24-29°C) environmental conditions are conducive for infection; conidia germinate in the presence of free moisture at an optimum temperature of 28-30°C; wet conditions at harvest provide a favourable environment for spore germination; lesions appear quickly under warm, moist conditions on older foliage.
Seedling damping off (*Pythium* and *Rhizoctonia* species)	Cool, cloudy weather, high humidity, wet soils favour development of damping-off.
Powdery mildew of okra (*Erysiphe cichoracearum*)	Increased humidity can increase the severity of the disease, and infection is enhanced during periods of heavy dew.
Club-root disease of cabbage, broccoli, cauliflower (*Plasmodiophora brassicae*)	Infection and disease development are promoted by acidic or neutral, cool, wet soil; can also occur in alkaline soils when inoculums levels are high, soil moisture is greater than 70 per cent of field capacity, and temperature is 17-23°C.
Downy mildew (*Peronospora parasitica*)	Abundant sporulation and rapid disease development occur when RH is greater than 98 per cent, temperature is 8-16°C and leaves are wet.
Alternaria blight of cucurbits (*Alternaria cucumerena*)	Spore germination requires RH above 85 per cent and optimum temperature is 25-28°C; a minimum period of 48 hours of very high RH is required for infection; prolonged cloudy weather and rains favour quick spread of the disease.

Contd...

1	2
Anthracnose of beans (*Colletotrichum lindemuthianum*)	Cool temperature below 16°C and wet condition favour spread of the disease.
Leaf and pod spot of beans (*Ascochyte boltshauseri*)	Moderate temperature 16-24°C with high RH favours spread of the disease; pathogens become inactive at above 30°C; rainy and overcast weather encourage development of the disease.
Angular leaf spot of beans (*Isariopsis griseola*)	Humid conditions favour disease development; optimum temperature for symptom development is 24°C, however, develops over a wide range of temperature, 16-28°C.

Diseases of Fruit Crops

Table 8.16: Diseases of Fruit Crops and their Relationship with Weather

Diseases	Weather Parameters Affecting the Pathogen and its Infection
Powdery mildew of mango (*Oidium mangiferae*)	Rains or mists accompanied by cooler nights during flowering are congenial for the disease spread.
Anthracnose of mango (*Colletotrichum gloeosporioides*)	The disease causes serious losses to young shoots, flowers and fruits under favourable climatic conditions of high humidity, frequent rains and a temperature of 24-32°C.
Leaf spot or leaf streak of banana (*Mycosphaerella musicola* and *M. fijiensis*)	Rainfall, dew and temperature determine the spread of the disease; conditions favouring mass infection are most common during the rainy season with temperature above 21°C.
Powdery mildew of ber (*Oidium ziziphi*)	High RH of 85-90 per cent and maximum and minimum temperatures of 33-34° and 23-25°C, respectively favour conditions for the initiation of disease infestation; maximum and minimum temperatures of below 27 and 10°C, respectively check spread of the disease.
Downy mildew of grapes (*Plasmopara viticola*)	Optimum temperature for germination of sporangia is 10-16°C; below 5°C germination fails.

Physiological Disorders of Vegetables

Both abiotic and biotic factors influence growth and development of plants. Abiotic factors include the physical environmental conditions and biotic factors include animals, insects, and diseases. Each plant has certain environmental requirements. To attain the highest potential yields a crop must be grown in an environment that meets these requirements. A crop can be grown with minimal adjustments if it is well matched with its climate or growing condition. Unfavourable environmental conditions can produce a stress on plants resulting in physiological disorders of the economic produce. These disorders are more pronounced in vegetables. The quality of the produce is deteriorated to a great extent and sometimes may not fetch a good market value.

Table 8.17: Physiological Disorders of Vegetables and their Weather Factors

Physiological Disorders	Weather Factors
Buttoning of cauliflower and broccoli	Hot and dry weather is unfavourable for vegetative growth of plants but favourable for inducing curd formation and inhibits further enlargement; curds remains very small in size like buttons.
Lack of heads in cauliflower and broccoli	During periods of extremely warm weather (days over 30°C and nights 27°C) broccoli and cauliflower can remain vegetative since they do not receive enough cold for head formation.
Development of curd bracts in cauliflower	Curd bracts or small green leaves between the segments of the curd in cauliflower is caused by too high of temperature or drought; high temperatures cause a reversion to vegetative growth with production of bracts on the head.
Leafiness in cauliflower	Prevalence of high temperature during curding phase aggravates leafiness.
Cracking in tomato	Cracking is common during the rainy season when the rain follow a long dry spell.
Sunscald in tomato	A high temperature along with a high light intensity may result in 100 per cent sunscald in tomato.
Ripening disorders in tomato	The hot weather after a period of cloudy, rainy weather may be a contributing factor to the onset of tomato fruit ripening disorders.
Carrot splitting	When there is a heavy rainfall after a period of drought, the inner flesh of the carrot expands faster than the toughened skin leading to splitting.
Cupping and rolling	High temperatures may cause leaf cupping and rolling in vegetables like: tomato, potato, watermelon, bean, etc.

Conclusion

Many diseases, nematodes, insects and weeds affect crop production, causing severe yield loss. Weather is the most important factor that determines the geographical distribution of these crop pests. The severity of disease and pest development depends on the combination of weather conditions during the growing season and is variable from season to season. Weather plays a major role in determining the survival and growth rates of insect populations because of its direct impact on them and on their food supply. Each disease has its own specific weather requirements. To infect, pathogens have to gain entry to their host. When the spores of airborne pathogens land on a leaf surface, they germinate only under optimum conditions of temperature and humidity and then the infection process starts.

Each species of insects has a range of temperature within which it can survive. Most insects have a lower temperature tolerance of one degree Celsius and an upper temperature tolerance up to 50°C. The movement, mating behaviour and reproduction of insects are influenced by temperature. A temperature range of 15 to 35°C is optimum for the development and multiplication of most of the insects. The development of fungal disease stops under extremely low and high temperature conditions since the growth and multiplication of fungi is highly influenced by temperature fluctuations.

The atmospheric humidity, rain, snow, dew, soil moisture and surface water influence the water balance of insects. Rainy weather is conducive to high aphid mortality; hence, there is little spread of mosaic viruses. Soil moisture content also has an influence on the severity of soil borne diseases and survival of insect pests living in soil. Relative humidity can influence insect growth and behaviour by affecting the insect's ability to regulate water loss. Relative humidity directly influences sporulation by many fungi. The high relative humidity of 50 to 90 per cent is favourable for development and multiplication of most of the insects.

REFERENCES

Atkins, M.D. (1978). Insects in Perspective. Macmillan Publishing Company, New York.

Campbell, A., Franzer, B.D., Gilbert, N., Gutierrez, A.P. and Mackauer, M. (1974). Temperature Requirements of some Aphids and their Parasites. *Journal of Applied Ecology* 11: 431-438.

Hardwick, N.V. (2002). Weather and Plant Diseases. *Weather* 57: 184-190.

http://agropedia.iitk.ac.in/content/climatic-requirements

http://en.wikipedia.org

http://www.imdagrimet.gov.in

http://www.indiaweather.gov.in

http://www.krishiworld.com/html/crop_pat

Mahi, G.S. and Kingra, P.K. (2007). Fundamentals of Agrometeorology. Kalyani Publishers, Ludhiana, 392 pp.

Mavi, H.S. and Tupper, G.J. (2004). Agrometeorology: Principles and Applications of Climate Studies in Agriculture. Food products Press, Binghamton, New York.

Patra, A.K. (2016). Principles and Applications of Agricultural Meteorology. New India Publishing Agency, New Delhi. pp. 434.

Page 176-195

FARMING TECHNIQUES AND CROP PRODUCTION
Edited by : **Dr. Alka Chauhan; Dr. Anubhuti Sharma & Jaswant Ray**
Edition : **2017**
ISBN : 978-93-5056-855-2
Published by : **Discovery Publishing House Pvt. Ltd., New Delhi (India)**

9 Postharvest Handling of Fruit and Vegetable Crops

Chandan Singh Ahirwar[1]; Ankit Kumar[2] & Dr. D.K. Singh[3]

INTRODUCTION

Farmers grow Horticultural crops to make money. To be successful they must deliver products to buyers who are so pleased with the quality and value of that product that they will purchase them again and again. Growers must therefore continuously satisfy consumer needs and desires for fresh green house-grown products by using all the available technology and knowledge to produce, harvest. While crops may be sold in the local village or on a nearby market, most crops are sold far from the production sites, in major cities or at far away markets.

Asia and the Pacific region have witnessed rapid growth in horticultural development. Changes in dietary habits owing to increasing incomes continue to accelerate demand for horticultural produce in the region. This increased demand must be met in an environment of shrinking land and water resources. At the same time, developments in science and technology could provide an opportunity for intensifying the production of horticultural produce. Poor infrastructure for storage, processing and marketing in many countries of the region contributes to a high proportion of waste, which average between 10 and 40 per cent. Major infrastructural limitations also continue to impose severe constraints to domestic distribution as well as to the export of

1. Ph.D. Scholar, Department of Vegetable Science, College of Agriculture, Govind Ballabh Pant University of Agriculture and Technology, Pantnagar, Uttarakhand - 263 145, India.
2. M.Sc. Scholar, Department of Horticulture, College of Agriculture, Govind Ballabh Pant University of Agriculture and Technology, Pantnagar, Uttarakhand - 263 145, India.
3. Professor, Department of Vegetable Science, College of Agriculture, Govind Ballabh Pant University of Agriculture and Technology, Pantnagar, Uttarakhand - 263 145, India.

horticultural produce. Considerable waste occurs owing to the fact that small farmers lack resources and are unable to market their produce and implement suitable postharvest handling practices. Spoilage of fresh produce is also accelerated by the hot and humid climate of the region. Postharvest management and processing of horticultural produce has assumed considerable significance in light of increasing demand for fruits and vegetables in the region.

For the most part, fruits and vegetables are not considered to be primary sources of carbohydrate, protein and fat. However, those with storage roots and tubers are rich in carbohydrate, particularly starch, in amounts comparable to the cereal crops, and can be used as staple foods. Leguminous vegetables supply as much as 14 per cent protein, while dry seeds supply even more. The lipid content of most vegetables is less than 0.1 per cent. Most fruits, vegetables and root crops are rich in minerals, carotene (Pro-vitamin A) and vitamin C, and are reasonably good sources of trace elements such as: copper, manganese and zinc, which act as enzyme cofactors. The nutrient content of fruits and vegetables varies in accordance with the fruit or vegetable variety, cultural practices, stage of maturity, Postharvest handling and storage conditions. Natural physiological and biochemical activity in fruits and vegetables results in compositional changes following harvest.

Due to progress in science and technology and the growing globalization of production and trade of food and the increasingly stringent national and international legislation that has resulted – today's agri-foodstuffs sector must respect ever stricter standards and increasingly rigorous quality control and monitoring procedures. Product quality is a prime criterion in gaining access to competitive markets. Most marketers will agree that, apart from everything else, commercial markets require a stable supply and consistent quality.

This means that produce has to be harvested, sorted, packed, stored and transported to storage facilities or markets, with sales often taking place several days or sometimes weeks after harvesting.

Food safety and quality assurance in fresh produce should be ongoing processes that incorporate activities from the selection and preparation of the soil in agricultural operations through the final preparation and consumption of the food. Both food safety and quality assurance (QA) should focus on the prevention of problems, since once safety or quality has been reduced it is difficult or impossible to restore. Also, implementing QA programmes should help ensure that problems experienced in the past do not affect the future product the same way.

Therefore growers, agents, wholesalers and retailers will always be concerned about maintaining quality and minimizing Postharvest losses that may occur in the chain from grower to consumer. Quality of the end product can only occur when there is a realistic, integrated and co-ordinated linkage between the stages in the supply chain.

Defects and improper food quality may result in consumer rejection and lower sales, while food safety hazards may be hidden and go undetected until the product has been consumed. If detected, serious food safety hazards may result in market access exclusion and major economic loss and costs. Since food safety hazards directly affect public health and economies, achieving proper food safety must always take precedence over achieving high levels of other quality attributes.

What is Quality?

We all think we know what a quality product is when we see it. In practice, quality always lies in the eyes of the beholder. A quality product for a farmer will different from a quality product for a retailer, a rich sophisticated housewife or a poor malnourished child. Each has their own perception of quality. Quality is sometimes defined as fitness for purpose. Have defined quality as 'the degree of excellence or superiority comprising a combination of attributes, properties or characteristics that give each product value in relation to its intended use'. Herein, quality is defined according to particular market or country grade standards. Thus, external attributes such as: size, weight, colour, shape and freedom from physical, physiological and pathological defects are key factors, as are internal attributes, such as: texture, taste, aroma and chemical composition (nutritional and health-conferring compounds) that are very difficult to measure objectively and non-destructively. The extent to which these dominate depends on the nature of the market. However, it is the end-user who ultimately decides on quality; if they purchase a product, then it's perceived (often external) quality satisfies them at the time. If the internal quality of the product is unsatisfactory when consumed, then it will not be purchased again on the next visit to the retailer. The challenge faced by producers is to provide consistent quality such that the consumer is entirely satisfied and makes repeat purchases of that farmer's product or brand.

Quality is a measure of how much the end-user values a product. Product quality is very important to growers because it determines marketable yield and can affect price. Because quality can be subjective, objective market standards have been developed for many commodities that define what is 'marketable' and establishes 'grades' of marketable produce and other commodities. These grades vary with commodity but are generally based on physical attributes. In fruits and vegetables these characteristics include maturity, size, shape, color and the absence of damage and other defects.

In general, consumers judge quality and choose to buy on the basis of the appearance of the product, while subsequent purchases are based on their satisfaction with the internal attributes of the product, such as: flavour and texture. In other words, they buy using their eyes and their memory. Market grades are not the only measure of quality. Flavor is generally the most important quality attribute for consumers, which is why markets frequently have fresh cut or prepared samples of their products out to share with shoppers. The most important quality attributes influencing consumer choices include:

- *External features* – Appearance, size, shape, colour, gloss, firmness, freshness.
- *Internal features* – Texture, crispness, juiciness, mealiness, toughness, composition, nutritional and health value.
- *Flavour* – Sweetness, sourness (acidity), aroma, taste, astringency, bitterness, off-flavours.
- *Nutritional value* – Vitamins (C, A, B, thiamine, niacin), minerals, dietary fibre, antioxidants and phytonutrients (*e.g.*, carotenoids, flavonoids, isoflavones and phytosterols).
- *Freedom from defects* – Physical damage (cuts, bruises, scars, scabs, russetting), rotting, insect and disease damage.
- *Safe food* – Freedom from toxins and contaminants, human pathogens.

Other things growers can do to improve produce quality include:

1. Know your crop and your market.
2. Manage your crop to avoid stress (pest, water, nutrient, heat etc).
3. Follow good agricultural practices (GAP) for food safety.
4. Store, package and ship your products appropriately.

Nutritional Value

Fruits and vegetables are a major source of both 'macro' nutrients such as: fiber and carbohydrates, and 'micro' nutrients such as: Vitamin C, B complex (thiamin, riboflavin, B6, niacin, folate), A, E, minerals, and the lesser-studied polyphenolics, carotenoids, and glucosinolates. Nutrients may be classified as either water or lipid soluble – meaning they dissolve in water or a lipid medium. Water soluble nutrients include Vitamin C, B complex, polyphenolics, and glucosinolates. Fat soluble nutrients include Vitamin A, E, and other carotenoids such as: lycopene and β-carotene. Vitamin C is one of the most sensitive vitamins, being degraded relatively quickly by exposure to heat, light, and oxygen. For this reason it is often used as an index of nutrient Department of Health and Human Services and the degradation.

Consumers expect fresh fruits and vegetables to be good sources of dietary fiber and many vitamins and minerals. Unfortunately they have no way of distinguishing between individual products that have high versus low concentrations of phytonutrients. Many factors contribute to the nutrient content of a fruit or vegetable available for sale including genetics, growing conditions (light, temperature, etc.,) and production practices (fertilization, irrigation, etc.), maturity at harvest, and Postharvest handling conditions. During storage little change occurs in dietary fiber and mineral content, but the vitamins are lost. Cutting stimulates ethylene production which in turn increases respiration and senescence leading to even more rapid loss of certain vitamins. Vitamin C is the vitamin that usually degrades most rapidly and can be used as an index of freshness.

Pre-harvest Factors affecting Product Quality

Quality at harvest is influenced by a range of pre-harvest factors, including: original planting material, growing conditions, substrate type, nutrient and pest and disease management, and temperature, water and light intensity experienced during plant growth and development. For example, vitamin C is an essential nutrient for humans and comes from fruit and vegetables; its concentration can increase with high light intensity and slight water stress during leaf growth, but decrease with high nitrogen levels in the growing media. Pre-harvest factors can affect product quality during postharvest storage. If quality at harvest is not optimum, postharvest quality and shelf-life are compromised. A problem with tomatoes and sweet peppers is the physiological disorder, blossom end rot, caused by an interaction of low calcium, high nitrogen and fluctuating water availability during growth. A judicious programme is required to optimize calcium and nitrogen nutrition while applying a management system for consistent water availability and good relative humidity control in greenhouses. Foliar applications of appropriate Ca2+ salts may help reduce the disorder as part of a programme to obtain optimum Ca2+: N ratios in susceptible plants.

Harvesting and Postharvest Handling of Seed

The germination of seed is of vital importance and the threshers, combine harvesters etc., must be properly set up to thresh the seed without inflicting damage to the seed. The crop should be harvested at proper moisture so as to minimize the damage to the seed. In hybrid seed production, where two parents are involved, the male parent rows are harvested first and moved to a distant place. The whole field is then inspected and broken or lodged male parent plants are removed from the female parent rows. The hybrid seed on the female parent rows is then harvested. All our efforts in rouging and care during earlier stages may go waste if proper care is not taken during harvesting, threshing, processing, seed treatment, packaging etc., to avoid mechanical mixing. Correct labelling is very important. The threshers, combine harvesters, trailers, threshing floors, processing machinery etc., should be thoroughly cleaned in between handling of different varieties.

Harvesting

Consumers always prefer fresh, properly matured, insect and disease free vegetables of attractive appearance. Vegetables should be harvested as and when they attain the maximum size and yet are tender. Over maturity in root crops such as: carrot, radish etc., causes sponginess and pithiness and therefore, their harvesting should not be delayed. The delayed harvesting of onion and garlic reduces their storage quality. Almost all the crops are badly affected due to delayed harvesting. Ripe Cucurbits vegetables are not preferred by the consumers. In case of ripening in trees is seldom preferred. Most of the fruits are harvested at proper maturity stage but quite earlier than the ripening stage. They are ripened artificially later on as per the market demands.

Washing and Grading

Almost all the vegetables require special preparation before they are packed. Vegetables such as: root and tuber crops are often washed to remove the soils adhering over them. Washing of fruits before packing is also very important, especially of those which have been treated with poisonous chemicals. Besides cleanliness, water used for washing improves the appearance of vegetables and prevents their wilting.

Grading is an important practice for successful marketing of vegetables. The produce is generally sorted out into different grades and attractive forms to fetch a good price from them. Fruits and vegetables are graded according to shape, size and colour. Some vegetables are graded according to their maturity (okra, cucumber, ridge gourd etc.), ripeness (tomato) and general appearance as well. In sorting the vegetables, all the characters that influence their appearance and quality should be considered.

Pre-cooling

It is desirable to remove field heat of the harvested vegetables, particularly when harvested during hot weather. This prevents the ripening and ageing of the produce. Prompt cooling conserves weight which gives an added advantage during the extended period of storage in tomato, for *e.g.* Physiological loss in weight during storage can be reduced from 6 to 2.9 per cent. Vegetables such as: artichokes and okra which deteriorate fast need prompt cooling and their storage losses can be reduced by pre-cooling. Cooling is equally useful in case of fruits. It reduces their respiration rate especially, climatic vegetable such as: tomato, chilli and capsicum, thereby preventing over-ripening. Sometimes, stages of ripening and the level of field heat also determine the need of pre-cooling. For *e.g.*, unless tomato fruits are kept above 26.7°C and ripening is to be delayed, there is no need for pre-cooling.

Pre-cooling can be accomplished by *(i)* placing the produce in refrigerated trucks with forced humidified air circulation; *(ii)* placing ice in packages; *(iii)* placing ice in water and passing through a spray of cool water, and *(iv)* through vacuum cooling. Hydro-cooling, accomplished by flooding, spraying or immersing, is a rapid and affective method since water is an excellent material to transfer the heat from the produce to the cooling medium a minute amount of an effective fungicide can also be added in hydro cooling water to control the fungal growth. However, the usefulness of hydro cooling is often questioned for large fruits or vegetables such as: brinjal. Risk of water spotting is also evident.

Highly perishable leafy vegetables and salad crops are often cooled by reducing the atmospheric pressure in hermetically sealed chamber until the reduced vaporizing point of water produced at low pressure in the cooling chamber cool the produce. The technique is termed as vacuum cooling and its outstanding advantages are speed and uniformity in cooling of the commodity. Leafy vegetables and some fruits like grapes are especially difficult to cool with water or air, but they can be field packed and cooled rapidly and uniformly by vacuum cooling.

Waxing

The outer surface of fruits and vegetables (excluding under-ground ones) have a natural waxy layer, which is partly removed during handling and washing an extra discontinuous layer of wax applied artificially, provides the necessary protection against the entry of decay organisms. The practical benefit from wax coating is usually a reduction in evaporation and respiration. It has been reported that where refrigerated storage facilities are not available, protective skin coating with wax is one of the methods developed for increasing the storage life of vegetables.

Postharvest studies have shown that reducing transpiration provides a means of extending the shelf-life of fresh produce.

Water loss during transpiration leads to shrinkage, drying and softening and triggers senescence, leading to accelerated deterioration of produce. Waxing is commercially used to reduce the transpiration rate of fruits and vegetables. While it is, adequate for reducing transpiration rates, it is effective in restricting oxygen and carbon dioxide exchange, with the consequent development of alcohols, aldehydes and off flavors. Vegetables passed through the water emulsified with mustard oil increase the storage life of many vegetables like: tomato, okra, parwal, leafy vegetables, etc. Sealing of fruits in plastic films of high-density polyethylene, results in marked resistance to water vapor loss. Individual seal packaging has been demonstrated to be practical for treating fruits and vegetables in a water-saturated environment Films appear to be more effective than waxes for reducing transpiration and to not appear to have any deleterious effect on internal quality.

Chemical Treatment

There are certain chemicals other than fungicides which increase the storage life vegetables by delaying the ripening and senescence process. Postharvest treatment with gibberellic acid markedly delayed the ripening of banana. Potassium per magnate is used as an ethylene absorbent to keep the ethylene below the threshold level a commercial preparation of this absorbent called 'purafil' is available. The effect of maleic hydrazide on the ripening process varies with different fruits. Maleic hydrazide at 1000-2000 ppm (parts per i million) delays the ripening of mangoes while, it may hasten ripening in sapota. Foliar sprays of ipc (isopropyl-n- phenyl carbonate) reduce the rate of respiration, ripening and spoilage of fruits during storage.

Postharvest applications of plant hormones have been found to prolong the storage life of vegetables too. The effect of cytokinin is more conspicuous, especially in leafy vegetables. Postharvest application of gibberelins markedly retards the ripening of tomatoes. To maintain the green colour of pods of different vegetables, they can be treated with indole acetic acid (1aa) solution. Application of 2,4-d if combined with ba (m6-benzyladenine), will retard the yellowing of cauliflower and some other green vegetables. Pre-harvest sprays of maleic hydrazide (mh) is used to inhibit onion and potato sprouting in storage. Inhibition of the synthesis of solanine in potato by alar (m, m-dimethyl amino-succinamic acid) and prolonged storage life of leaf lettuce, have also been reported.

Use of In-package Desiccants

Recently, to maintain the succulent nature and tenderness of vegetables, partial dehydration is done and then in-package desiccants are used to limit the moisture availability to the micro-organisms the use of in package desiccants such as: calcium oxide or fumed silicas, to bring the moisture content of the storage environment to i per cent or lower, permits the storage of dehydrated fruits and vegetables for a longer period.

Packaging

Packaging is an integral element in the marketing of fresh horticultural produce. It provides an essential link between the producer and the consumer. Owing to its favorable properties, wood has remained the main packaging material for fruits and vegetables. Timber conservation is, however, critical in order to maintain an ecological balance, and there is an urgency to identify substitutes for the use of timber in an effort to protect forest resources in many developing countries. Packaging has been identified as one of the most important areas where substitution of wood is not only possible but also obviously desirable. Considerable work has been done by different agencies in introducing alternative types of packaging. Corrugated fibre board (CFB) containers consume one third of the wood required for producing timber boxes of the same size. CFB boxes can also be fabricated from kraft paper produced from bamboo, long grasses and many other types of agricultural residues like: bagasse, paddy, cotton stalk, jute stick, wheat straw and recycled paper and cardboard. Packaging produced from timber is often used as a source of firewood, owing to the severe shortage of fuel wood in India. CFB cartons on the other hand are recycled as pulp or paper. Thus switching over from wood to CFB boxes for the packaging of horticultural produce is a very practicable and environmentally friendly option.

Packaging of fresh vegetables has a great significance in reducing the wastage. Packaging also provides protection from mechanical damage, undesirable physiological changes and pathological deterioration during storage, transportation and marketing. Through proper packaging, freshness, succulence and flavour of fruits and vegetables can be maintained for a longer period.

A wide variety of containers such as: wooden boxes, bamboo baskets, jute bags, earthen pots and corrugated fiber board boxes are the important packaging materials used in most of the developing countries including India. Cheap packaging technique and materials such as: polythene films, paper board boxes lined with polyethylene and other materials can effectively prolong the storage-life of vegetables. Vegetables can be protected from the influence of dry air by packing in various types of plastic films. Polyethylene packaging provides a modified atmosphere and can consequently reduces decay, softening and loss of solids as observed in tomato, cauliflower, brinjal and okra.

All the packages must be provided with some amount of ventilation in order to prevent the physiological breakdown of the produce if there is impermeability to carbon dioxide (co~, oxygen (02) and water vapour inside the package, there may be the development of off-flavour.

While packing for transportation, care should also be taken to avoid bruising and damage of fruits for this purpose dry grasses or paddy straw can be successfully used between the layers of vegetables. In india, corrugated fibre boxes for the packaging of fruits are getting popular they have many advantages:

1. They are light in weight.
2. They cause much less damage to fruits.
3. They are easy to handle and print.
4. They improve the image of the product.
5. They reduce the freight cost.
6. They can be made from cheaper wood and other plant cellulose waste.

However, packaging is a highly innovative technology and newer techniques and material are being added every year, both for fresh vegetables and also for processed products. Packages can be flexible or rigid, each group having distinct advantages and limitations. An important application of flexible film is in wrapping the produce for low temperature. A mixture of gases can be inserted in film packs that delay postharvest changes tetraking r, a d-shaped cylinder formed from two webs of polystryene and expanded polystyrene material has been recently introduced along with thermo formed pots for aseptic filling. Sterilization is carried out by either using liquid or vapour of hydrogen peroxide or using ultra violet or gamma radiation.

Transportation System

Railways and roads are two important transportation systems for the movement of goods in India. The use of railways for the transportation of fruits and vegetables in India could be greatly enhanced by: making provisions for cooling and ventilation, providing improved handling facilities at platforms and providing storage space to accommodate the goods upon arrival at their destinations. Similarly road services could be considerably improved by widening roads, upgrading surfaces and through the introduction of one way traffic. Long waits at level crossings should be avoided by introducing flyovers at intersections in order to increase the speed and movement of goods by road. Facilities such as: sheds, for temporary cool storage should be available on highways and major roads.

Transportation and distribution of the fruits and vegetables are the most important areas of postharvest loss. In India, the transportation of perishable commodities is in the most precarious stage. For local market, the produce is brought either by bullock cart or tractor trollies. The long distance transportation is mainly by rails and trucks, which is very costly. The basic reason for preference to road transportation is because it takes short transit period.

Quick transport of vegetable in order to maintain the quality with minimum damage during transportation is very important for successful marketing of the produce the losses in transportation occur due to physical and mechanical injury and uncontrolled conditions, mainly temperature and humidity. To ensure fewer losses, adequate long distance facilities especially by rails should be developed. The produce should be properly packed and stacked in well ventilated carriages. Refrigeration and relative humidity control in carriages is of vital significance. This can be achieved without using high cost mechanical refrigeration, simply, by adopting the technique of evaporation cooling with a slight modification in the existing road trucks and railway wagons. The surface of roads and their maintenance, need improvement in order to have smooth transportation without severe jerks and vibration. The road transport can even become faster if all national highways are made one way and unnecessary delay caused by the closure of the level crossing is prevented. Hence, efficient transport system can go a long way, not only in reducing the postharvest loss of horticultural produce but also in stabilizing the price fluctuations of the same commodity available in different markets of the country.

Reducing Moisture Loss

Prevention of weight loss from vegetables is a major advantage of consumer packaging when moisture retentive films are used, particularly for leafy green vegetables and root crops as a result, storage life of packaged produce may be lengthened over non-wrapped produce, particularly when marketing from refrigerated display cases. It has been reported that moisture proof cellulose film, reduced the weight loss of tomatoes to one fourth the amount lost by non-wrapped tomatoes. Lettuce packed in polythene or polystyrene, loses fewer weights and may have a longer storage life than non-packaged lettuce.

Regulation of accumulating humidity is far more essential for packaged vegetables. Humidity attaining saturation is detrimental to onion, potatoes and sweet potatoes as ventilation with holes of one fourth to half inch sizes are a way of regulating package humidity to improve the keeping of onions and other produce.

Marketing

The Asia-Pacific Region accounts for approximately 30 per cent of the world's land area. Three countries of that region: China, India and Indonesia are among the four most populous nations globally. The Region is characterized by a gradient of developmental levels which bears a strong correlation to achievements in Postharvest management and capacity for agro-industrial development in its member countries. The fruit and vegetable sector across region is increasingly shifting toward the adoption of a market-oriented focus. This shift in focus within the sector must be facilitated and supported by enabling technologies and infrastructure, Postharvest handling skills, proper logistics and organization, as well as proper marketing and management skills and a supportive policy and regulatory environment. This paper will review recent trends across the region, issues and challenges which impact upon horticultural chain management and marketing and will discuss the role of governments in facilitating horticultural chain management and marketing in the region.

It is very important that horticultural produce reaches the market as soon as it is possible and at a time when the market needs it the most. A perfect and efficient marketing system is essential to avoid the losses of vegetables, and also to get a good return from the same. Marketing of perishable horticultural products presents more problems compared to other durable agricultural products. It is not efficiently managed in most of the developing countries the interests of producers as well as consumers are poorly served, the grower gets less return and the consumer pays more than what is necessary.

Rising incomes, consumer demand for safety, quality and convenience, increasing levels of fruit and vegetable imports, increasing rates of urbanization, scientific and technological developments, and the growth of fast food chains and supermarkets necessitate that countries across the region put in place appropriate policies, regulatory frameworks and infrastructure, and build capacity in Postharvest management and marketing, if their fruit and vegetable sectors are to remain competitive.

Sometimes, the market is in glut with a particular vegetable or fruit and a lot of wastage or loss is experienced. Also, prices are considerably reduced and farmers get dejected. Therefore, glutting should be avoided and the market should be so facilitated as to reduce the loss to the minimum.

Storage

Storage is one of the most important aspects of postharvest handling of vegetables. The main objective of storage is to extend the storage life of vegetables and increase their period of availability a substantial quantity of fruits go waste in our country due to lack of proper storage facilities. It should be known vegetables are living entities and they carry out all the vital physiological activities even after harvest. The primary purpose of storage is to control the rate of respiration, transpiration, ripening and also any un-desirable bio-chemical changes and disease infection. The loss of many fruits and vegetables can be prevented to a great extent by controlling the postharvest environmental conditions of temperature, relative humidity and atmospheric concentration of certain gases. There are various techniques and methods to store fruits and vegetables safely and are discussed below.

Modified atmosphere packaging, also known as 'maintain and preserve' technology is employed to maintain and preserve the quality of fruit for shipping and packing. Modifying the environment around fresh produce, can alter its rate of respiration and metabolism, and increase its commercial storage life. Modified atmospheres can be generated by either active or passive systems. In the passive system, respiring fruit, over time, self-generate an atmosphere of elevated carbon dioxide and reduced oxygen, while in the active system, desired end-point concentrations of oxygen and carbon dioxide are established by flushing the fruit with a desired mix of gases.

Development of a MAP system must integrated consideration for the type, thickness and method of fabrication of the film, package size, temperature, and relative humidity, duration of storage, type, quantity and physiological stage of fruit and tolerance of fruit to the various gases.

Refrigeration

The principle of refrigeration is to take out heat in mechanical refrigeration, the refrigerated gas (*e.g.*, ammonia, freon, etc.,) takes out the heat from the chamber or store as it expands. The expanded gas is then compressed, and the heat is removed from the compressed air over the tubes containing the hot gases. The gas is liquefied and the cycle is then repeated. With such a system accurate temperature control is possible.. Vegetables can be safely kept for a long period through refrigeration. However, many vegetables are of low unit value to bear the cost and are also susceptible to low temperature injury.

Cold Storage

In cold store, the temperature control is very important. An ideal environment condition for fresh vegetables in storage is the lowest temperature, which does not cause chilling injury to the produce. Any variation from the desired condition is detrimental. Relative humidity of the store rooms also has a considerable bearing on the keeping quality of the horticultural produce. It is very difficult to control the moisture in air. A small temperature difference between the cooling coil and the stored products is required to maintain an adequate control of RH in storage room. In order to increase the RH, water may be sprayed into the controlled storage chamber.

The rate of respiration has direct correlation with temperature. Higher the temperature more is the rate of respiration and multiplication of decay organisms. The temperature and relative humidity requirements are specific for each fruits and vegetables. The optimum cold storage conditions for fruits and vegetables are given separately in Table 9.1. Most of the vegetables require a storage temperature of few degrees above the freezing points excepting okra, cucumber, brinjal, green beans, sweet potatoes, squash and tomato. Low but non-freezing temperatures may lead to chilling injury as in tomato, brinjal etc., and becomes noticeable only after the vegetables are transferred to room temperature *i.e.* 22°C. A low cost cooling chamber in which a drop in temperature up to 15°C can be produced by evaporative cooling was developed at Indian agricultural research institute (jari), new delhi. The technique requires bricks, riverbed sand, bamboo, khas-khas or any other similar plant material and gunny bags it consists of a brick-wall of two layers with a layer of sand in between. Careful sprinkling of water on the wall twice a day can bring down the temperature and increase the storage life of different vegetables and fruits from 3 to 15 days. This technology is useful in places where transportation is problem, to reach the market place daily.

Table 9.1: Recommended Storage Temperature and Relative Humidity for different Vegetables

Sl. No.	Name of Vegetable	Temperature (°C)	Relative Humidity (%)	Storage Life (Weeks)
1.	Asparagus	0-0	95	3-5
2.	Beet (Topped)	0.0-1.7	90-95	8-14
3.	Beet (Bunched)	0.0	90	1.5
4.	Cabbage (Early)	0.0-1.7	92-95	4-6
5.	Cabbage (late)	0.0-1.7	92-95	12
6.	Carrot (Topped)	0.0	95	20-24
7.	Cauliflower	0.0-1.7	85-95	7
8.	Celery	0.6-0.0	92-95	8
9.	Garlic	0.0	65	28-36
10.	Ginger	7.2-10.0	75	16-24
12.	Lettuce (Head)	0.0	90-95	3
13.	Lettuce (Leaf)	0.0	95	1
14.	Onion (Leaf)	0.0	90-95	2
15.	Onion (bulbs)	0.0	70-75	20-24
16.	Pea (green)	0.0	88-92	2-3
17.	Potato (Irish)	3.0-4.4	85	34
18.	Radish (Topped)	0.0	88-92	3-5
19.	Turnip	0.0	90-95	8-16

Controlled Atmosphere Storage

The controlled atmosphere (ca) storage, in which high level of carbon dioxide (co2) and low level of oxygen (02) are maintained, is one of the most significant contributions to the storage technology. When combined with refrigeration, it markedly retards the respiratory activity and may delay softening, yellowing, quality changes, and other deteriorative processes. However, important factor in ca storage is the tolerance or susceptibility of the vegetables to the injury caused by decreased o2 and increased co2 concentration. The relative tolerance of individual vegetables varies considerably and is largely dependent on temperature, age, morphology and the anatomy of the horticultural products.

In this system, the produce is held under the atmospheric conditions modified by package, over wrap, box liner or pallet cover. The first requirement of the controlled atmosphere is a gas-tight envelope around the produce and the second requirement is some means of maintaining the concentration of co_2 and o_2 at a desired level.

The vegetable that has derived the most benefit from ca storage is apple. Among the tropical vegetables, the best atmosphere for storage of mangoes is 5 per cent co_2 and 5 per cent o_2 at 13°C.

The beneficial effect of ca storage are *(i)* prolonged storage life of perishables by arresting the respiration and senescence process; *(ii)* reduction in sensitivity to ethylene and *(iii)* decrease in the incidence and severity of disease causing organisms such as: fungi, bacteria, insects and pests, in selected commodities. theca storage proves beneficial for fruits and vegetables that deteriorate rapidly or those that complete ripening after harvest.

Although ca storage is beneficial for extending the storage life of vegetables, it can also cause adverse effects such as: *(i)* aggravation of physiological disorders; *(ii)* irregular ripening; *(iii)* development of off-flavour and *(iv)* accumulation of organic acids. Injury to the tissue or unfavorable changes due to the accumulation of high co2 and low o2 concentrations no gas mixture is suitable under all circumstances because the temperature, duration of storage and the commodity are interdependent factors, each influencing the use of gas mixture in the ca storage. Althoughca storage is a practical method, the probable effects of its use still need critical studies to determine the limits of co2 and o2 - the response of citrus fruits to ca storage has been disappointing ca storage of florida citrus is not recommended. Vegetable decay from stem end rot is a limiting factor and in many cases it seems to be increased by high level co2, there is also a hazard of ethylene accumulation, therefore, commercial ca storage recommendation cannot be given to citrus fruits.

To enhance efficiency, a packhouse must be well designed to facilitate flowfrom the harvested product at one end through to coolstores and loading outletsat the other. There must be adequate space to contain packing line(s) (withroom for future expansion) for washing, sizing, sorting, segregating, sanitizing, waxing, packing and accumulation of produce. Space must be made available for (temporary) storage of excess products out of the sun, as well as conveyors, packing materials, labels and pallets. In addition, a centralized computer control room should be in a central and elevated position so that operators can view all aspects of the system easily. A separate space is required for the quality assurance team, an integral part of any modern packing and marketing operation. In some large operations it may be desirable to have a laboratory where physical and chemical analyses can be undertaken. Good agricultural practice management should ensure that the speed of produce movement is appropriate for the quality level of any line: the more variable the product quality, the slower the line. Adjustment of the bin dump rate is an efficient way of ensuring optimum efficiency and accuracy of sorting at a rate consistent with the overall quality of each product line. Sorting and segregating staff must be well trained, and consistency of quality for minimum acceptability and criteria for rejection agreed and implemented by all team members. Staff should have specific responsibilities, with experienced workers located downstream of less experienced workers. Staff rotation is important to avoid tiredness and reduced worker efficiency. Computer-controlled sorting systems can segregate for weight, colour, blemish, diameter, shape, density and internal taste.

Ionizing Radiation

Irradiation of food is one of the useful methods developed with the last three decades. One of the significant advantages of the ionizing radiation is that it can destroy the pathogenic organisms without appreciably raising the temperature of the produce. Though it involves high initial capital involvement. The randomization (pasteurization with ionizing radiations) is being well accepted due to its easy application it leaves no potential residue and needs minimal energy expenditure. Ionizing radiation extends the storage life of perishables through its action as surface pasteurization, sprout inhibition and retardation of senescence process.

Ripening of mangoes can be delayed by the application of ionizing radiation. Irradiation with 25-35 krads is also useful to delay the initiation of natural ripening of banana without interfering with ethylene induced ripening or affecting the quality of the fruit. Ionizing radiation also inhibits the sprouting of potatoes, onions and other bulbs most effectively at. 10-15 krads.

Postharvest Pathogens and Decay

All fresh vegetables are very perishable and susceptible to infection by a number of postharvest pathogens. Although most products are resistant to most pathogens, certain specialized pathogens cause substantial financial losses. Infection occurs when the spores of fungi or bacteria grow on and penetrate wounded or stressed tissue. Most losses are caused by organisms infecting produce that:

- Has been under stress during the growing season.
- Has suffered physical damage during harvest and handling.
- Has been stored too long after harvest or
- Has sustained chilling injury.

It is very important to ensure that any chemicals applied pre-or postharvest to eradicate or prevent infection, are applied according to the manufacturer's instructions in order to prevent buildup of residues above the accepted minimum threshold levels. Such chemicals must be registered for use in both the country of production and the country where the product is to be marketed. Physical damage creates avenues through which it is possible for fungal and bacterial pathogens to enter the fruit and cause infection resulting in serious economic. In some cases physiological disorders (*e.g.*, blossom end rot) can lead to infection.

Minimizing Postharvest Decay

1. Maintain good sanitation in the growing area, at harvest and throughout the supply chain.
2. Ensure that all equipment is kept clean and sanitized regularly.
3. Prevent physical damage from occurring throughout the chain from harvest to retailer.
4. Ensure removal from packing house and cool store of senescing and decaying products and vegetation.
5. Use appropriate and permissible chemicals to eradicate or suppress growth of pathogens.
6. Remove field heat and achieve recommended storage temperature as soon as possible after harvest; store and transport products at lowest recommended temperatures, but above critical threshold temperatures that can induce chilling injury.
7. Avoid storing wet produce and wetting product surfaces; create RH conditions to minimize water loss.
8. Use CA or MA storage where applicable and economically viable to do so.

Use of Fungicides

The control of micro-organisms is of prime importance. Pre-harvest spraying of fungicides can result in significant reduction of the pathogens in the harvested produce. The best method of application of fungicides and antibiotics is to mix them in wax emulsions. Fumigation of stored materials with sulphur dioxide (so2) can prevent the spread of fungi like botrytis. Other fumigants like: ethylene oxide, propylene oxide, bi-phenyl, acetaldehyde, nitrogen trichloride can also be used. Biphenyl impregnated tissue wrappers control the growth of penicilium fungi. benomyl is also good in preventing the growth of most of the damaging fungi of tomatoes. Bacterial soft rot of packed spinach and lettuce could be prevented by dipping in 1000 ppm streptomycin (50-500 ppm). It has also shown marked inhibitory activity towards a number of micro-organisms, prolong shelf life and added nutritive value to foods.

As far as possible, postharvest treatment of vegetables with poisonous chemicals should be avoided in case, it is absolutely imperative, the consumption of fruits and vegetables should be withheld at least for one or two weeks as they may create different respiratory and digestive disorders in consumers.

In India, the uses of these chemicals have been mainly limited towards checking the spoilage in more important economic crops such as: onion, tomato and potatoes.

Conclusion

Postharvest loss of vegetables occurs due to improper harvesting, transportation, storage and distribution. Postharvest life of vegetables is governed by water content, respiratory rate, ethylene production, endogenous plant hormones, and exogenous factors such as: microbial growth, temperature, relative humidity and atmospheric compositions. Postharvest loss of vegetables can be considerably minimized and there: storage life can be greatly increased by careful manipulation of these factors. The loss can be minimized by adopting necessary cultural operations, careful handling and packaging.

A number of deficiencies currently exist in the postharvest management and processing of fruits and vegetables in India. Action must be taken in order to upgrade systems, in order to reduce the levels of postharvest losses in India. In a civilized world, when millions go hungry, it would be a crime to allow postharvest losses to continue. It is unfortunate that in India, policy-makers and planners set targets for increased production without making any effort to reduce postharvest losses. The use of appropriate chemicals at pre and postharvest stage, may extend the availability of fruits and vegetables over a long period by protecting them from microbial as well as environmental agencies of damage. The vegetables can also be stored under controlled atmosphere, modified atmosphere, redurization at low temperature with appropriate chemical treatment to delay senescence and inhibit microbial decay. Therefore, steps as already mentioned should be adopted, according to the suitability, and postharvest loss of vegetables should be kept at minimum.

REFERENCES

Brecht, J., Ritenour, M. and Sargent, S. (2007). *Keeping Cool: Mobile Cooling Unitsand Cooling Tunnels may be Viable Temperature Management Approaches for Small Vegetable Operations* (available at http://www.growingproduce.com/americanvegetablegrower/?storyid=719).

Cantwell, M. and Suslow, T. (2006). Cabbages (Round and Chinese types): Recommendations Formaintaining Postharvest Quality. UC Davis Postharvest Technology Research Information Center.

Chanthasombath, T. (2007). Problems and Needs of Leafy Vegetable Value Chains in Selected Upland Areas in Lao PDR and Available Country Interventions. Paper Presented during the RETA 6376 Workshop on Best Practices in Postharvest Management of Leafy Vegetables in GMS Countries, 25-27.

Chen, Q. (2007). Postharvest Technologies for Fresh Leafy Vegetables in Yunnan, China. Paper Presented during the RETA 6376 Workshop on Best Practices in Postharvest Management of Leafy Vegetables in GMS Countries, 25-27 October 2007, Hanoi, Vietnam.

Fraser, H. (1998). Tunnel Forced Air Coolers for Fresh Fruits and Vegetables. Ministry of Agriculture, Food and Rural Affairs, Canada (available at *http://www.omafra.gov. on.ca/english/engineer/facts/98-031.htm#components).*

Gross, K., Wang, C.Y. andSaltveit, M.E. (eds). (2002). *The Commercial Storage of Fruits, Vegetables, and Florist and Nursery Stocks.* USDA Agric. Handbook 66 (draftavailable at *http://www.ba.ars.usda.gov/hb66/index.html).*

Heenan, S.P., Dufour, J.P., Hamid, N., Harvey, W., and Delahunty, C.M., (2009). Characterisation Offresh Bread Flavour: Relationships between Sensory Characteristics and Volatile Composition. *Food Chem.* 116, 249-257.

Hertog, M.L.A.T., Boerrigter, H.A.M., van den Boogaard, G.J.P.M., Tijskens, L.M.M., and van Schaik, A.C.R., (1999). Predicting Keeping Quality of Strawberries (cv. 'Elsanta') Packed under Modified Atmospheres: An Integrated Model Approach. *Postharvest Biol. Technol.* 15, 1-12.

Hertog, M.L.A.T., Lammertyn, J., Scheerlinck, N., and Nicolai, B.M., (2007). The Impact of Biological Variation on Postharvest Behaviour: The Case of Dynamic Temperature Conditions. Postharvest *Biol. Technol.* 43, 183-192.

Hörtensteiner, S., (2006). Chlorophyll Degradation during Senescence. *Annu. Rev. Plant Biol.* 57, 55-77.

Hörtensteiner, S. and Kräutler, B., (2011). Chlorophyll Breakdown in Higher Plants. *BBA Bioenergetics* 1807, 977-988.

Hotelling, H., (1933). Analysis of a Complex of Statistical Variables into Principal Components. *J. Educ. Psycol.* 24, 417-441.

Hutchings, J.B., (1999). Food Color and Appearance, Second ed. Aspen Publishers, Gaithersburg.

Iqbal, T., Rodrigues, F.A.S., Mahajan, P.V., and Kery, J.P., (2009). Mathematical Modeling of the Influence of Temperature and Gas Composition on the Respiration Rate of Shredded Carrots. *J. Food Eng.* 91, 325-332.

Iqbal, Z. and Bjorklund, R.B., (2011). Assessment of a Mobile Phone for use as a Spectroscopic Analytical Tool for Foods and Beverages. *Int. J. Food Sci. Tech.* 46, 2428-2436.

Jayaraj, S. (2005). Use and Abuse of Chemical Pesticides: Need for Safer Pesticides for Sustainable Integrated Pest Management. (In): Sustainable Insect Pest Management (ed. Ignaciuthu, S. and Jayaraj, S.), Narosa Publishing House, New Delhi, 2005, 253-265 p.

Jayaraj, S. and Ignaciuthu, S. (2005). Progress and Perspectives of Sustainable Integrated Pest Management. (In) Sustainable Insect Pest Management (ed. Ignaciuthu, S. and Jayaraj, S.), Narosa Publishing House, New Delhi, 2005, 1-18 p.

Kader, A.A. (2006). *The Return on Investment in Postharvest Technology for Assuring Quality and Safety of Horticultural Crops* (available at http://www.aaaid.org/pdf/magazine4/Postharvest.PDF).

Kader, A. and Rolle, R. (2004). *The Role of Postharvest Management in Assuring the Quality and Safety of Horticultural Produce. FAO Agric. Services, Bulletin* 152, Rome.

Kitinoja, L. and Thompson, J.F. (2010). Precooling Systems for Small-scale Producers. *Stewart Postharvest Review*, 6(2): 1-14.

Larrigaudiere, C., Lentheric, I., Puy, J., and Pinto, E., (2004). Biochemical Characterisation of Corebrowning and Brown Heart Disorders in Pear by Multivariate Analysis. *Postharvest Biol. Technol.* 31,29-39.

Lawless, H.T. and Heymann, H., (2010). Sensory Evaluation of Food: *Principles and Practices, Seconded.* Springer, New York.

Leardi, R. and Nørgaard, L., (2004). Sequential Application of Backward Interval Partial Least Squares and Genetic of Relevant Spectral Regions. *J. Chemometr.* 18, 486-497.

Lee, D.S., Haggar, P.E., Lee, J., and Yam, K.L., (1991). Model for Fresh Produce Respiration in Modified Atmospheres Based on Principles of Enzyme-Kinetics. *J. Food Sci.* 56, 1580-1585.

Lee, E.J., Matsumura, Y., Soga, K., Hoson, T., and Koizumi, N., (2007). Glycosyl Hydrolases of Cell Wall are Induced by Sugar Starvation in Arabidopsis. *Plant Cell Physiol.* 48, 405-413.

Lee, S.K. and Kader, A.A. (2000). Pre-harvest and Postharvest Factors Influencing Vitamin C Content of Horticultural Crops. *Postharvest Biology and Technology*, 20: 207-220.

Lestremau, F., Andersson, F.A.T., and Desauziers, V., (2004). Investigation of Artefact Formation during Analysis of Volatile Sulphur Compounds using Solid Phase Micro-extraction (SPME). *Chromatographia* 59, 607-613.

Lindinger, C., Labbe, D., Pollien, P., Rytz, A., Juillerat, M.A., Yeretzian, C., and Blank, I., (2008). When Machine Tastes Coffee: Instrumental Approach to Predict the Sensory Profile of Espresso Coffee. *Anal. Chem.* 80, 1574-1581.

Lindinger, C., Yeretzian, C., and Blank, I., (2009). When Machine Tastes Coffee: Successful Prediction of Coffee Sensory Profiles by Instrumental Methods based on on-line PTR-MS. Chimia 63, 292.

Lleo, L., Barreiro, P., Ruiz-Altisent, M., and Herrero, A., (2009). Multispectral Images of Peach Related to Firmness and Maturity at Harvest. *J. Food Eng.* 93, 229-235.

Lonchamp, J., Barry-Ryan, C., and Devereux, M., (2009). Identification of Volatile Quality Markers of Ready-to-use Lettuce and Cabbage. *Food Res. Int.* 42, 1077-1086

Ludford, P.M., (2003). Hormonal Changes during Postharvest, in: Bartz, J.A. and Brecht, J.K. (Eds.), Postharvest Physiology and Pathology of Vegetables. *Second ed. Marcel Dekker*, New York, pp. 31-77.

Lunadei, L., Diezma, B., Lleo, L., Ruiz-Garcia, L., Cantalapiedra, S., and Ruiz-Altisent, M., (2012). Monitoring of Fresh-cut Spinach Leaves through a Multispectral Vision System. *Postharvest Biol. Technol.* 63, 74-84.

Luo, Y.G., Mcevoy, J.L., Wachtel, M.R., Kim, J.G., and Huang, Y., (2004). Package Atmosphere Affects Postharvest Biology and Quality of Fresh-cut Cilantro Leaves. Hortscience 39, 567-570.

Mahajan, P.V., Oliveira, F.A.R., Montanez, J.C., and Frias, J., (2007). Development of User-Friendly Software for Design of Modified Atmosphere Packaging for Fresh and Fresh-cut Produce. *Innov. Food Sci. Emerg.* 8, 84-92.

Mangaraj, S., Goswami, T., and Mahajan, P., (2009). Applications of Plastic Films for Modified Atmosphere Packaging of Fruits and Vegetables: *A Review. Food Eng. Rev.* 1, 133-158.

Ritenour, M.A., Sargent, S.A. and Bartz, J.A. (2008). *Chlorine use in Produce Packing lines.* University of Florida IFAS Extension, Publication HS761 (available at *http://edis.ifas.ufl.edu/ch160).*

Sargent, S., Ritenour, M., Brecht, J. and Bartz, J. (2007). *Handling, Cooling and Sanitation Techniques for Maintaining Postharvest Quality.* Florida Cooperative Extension Service, University of Florida, Publication Number HS719.

Tano, K., Oule, M.K., Doyon, G., Lencki, R.W., and Arul, J., (2007). Comparative Evaluation of The Effect of Storage Temperature Fluctuation on Modified Atmosphere Packages of Selected Fruit and Vegetables. *Postharvest Biol. Technol.* 46, 212-221.

Thomas, H., Ougham, H.J., Wagstaff, C., and Stead, A.D., (2003). Defining Senescence and Death. *J. Exp. Bot.* 54, 1127-1132.

Thompson, J.F., (2002). Psychrometrics and Perishable Commodities, in: Kader, A.A. (Ed.), Postharvest Technology of Horticultural Crops. Third ed. University of California, Agriculture and Natural Resources, Publication 3311, Oakland, CA, pp. 129-134.

Thygesen, L.G., Løkke, M.M., Micklander, E., and Engelsen, S.B., (2003). Vibrational Microspectroscopy of Food. Raman vs. FT-IR. *Trends Food Sci. Tech.* 14, 50-57.

Toivonen, P.M.A. and Brummell, D.A., (2008). Biochemical bases of Appearance and Texture Changes in Fresh-cut fruit and Vegetables. *Postharvest Biol. Technol.* 48, 1-14.

Torrieri, E., Perone, N., Cavella, S., and Masi, P., (2010). Modelling the Respiration Rate of Minimally Processed Broccoli (*Brassica rapa*var. *sylvestris*) for Modified Atmosphere Package Design. *Int. J. Food Sci. Tech.* 45, 2186-2193.

Tulio, A.Z., Yamanaka, H., Ueda, Y., Imahori, Y., and Chachin, K., (2003). Reversible and Irreversible Emission of Methanethiol and dimethyl disulfide from anaerobically Stored Broccoli. *J. Agric. Food Chem.* 51, 6774-6781.

Uchino, T., Nei, D., Hu, W.Z., and Sorour, H., (2004). Development of a Mathematical Model for Dependence of Respiration Rate of Fresh Produce on Temperature and Time. *Postharvest Biol. Technol.* 34, 285-293.

Wagstaff, C., Clarkson, G.J.J., Rothwell, S.D., Page, A., Taylor, G., and Dixon, M.S., (2007). Characterisation of Cell Death in Bagged Baby Salad Leaves. *Postharvest Biol. Technol.* 46, 150-159.

Wang, C.Y., (2003). Leafy, Floral, and Succulent Vegetables, in: Bartz, J.A. and Brecht, J.K. (Eds.), Postharvest Physiology and Pathology of Vegetables. Second ed. Marcel Dekker, New York, pp. 599-623.

Watada, A.E. and Qi, L., (1999). Quality of Fresh-cut Produce. *Postharvest Biol. Technol.* 15, 201-205.

Index

T